Wilbur & Orville Wright
Pictorial Materials

Wilbur & Orville Wright

Pictorial Materials

A Documentary Guide by
Arthur G. Renstrom

Library of Congress
Washington
1982

Library of Congress Cataloging in Publication Data

Renstrom, Arthur George, 1905–
    Wilbur & Orville Wright, pictorial materials.

    Includes index.
    Supt. of Docs. no.: LC 1.6/4:W93
    1. Wright, Wilbur, 1867–1912—Portraits, etc.—
Catalogs. 2. Wright, Orville, 1871–1948—Portraits,
etc.—Catalogs. 3. Aeronautics—United States—
History—Pictorial works—Catalogs. I. Title.
II. Title: Wilbur and Orville Wright, pictorial
materials.
TL540.W525R46 1982   016.62913'0092'2   82–600194
ISBN 0–8444–0399–7   AACR2

For sale by the Superintendent of Documents,
U.S. Government Printing Office, Washington, D.C. 20402

Contents

ix   **Preface**

xiii   **Abbreviations for Sources Cited**

3   **Wright Brothers**

11   **Wilbur Wright**
(April 16, 1867–May 30, 1912)

21   **Orville Wright**
(August 19, 1871–January 30, 1948)

38   **Bishop Milton Wright**
(November 17, 1828–April 3, 1917)

41   **Katharine Wright Haskell**
(August 19, 1874–March 3, 1929)

46   **Wright Brothers Gliding Experiments and Flights**

46   *1900, Kitty Hawk, North Carolina*

48   *1901, Kitty Hawk, North Carolina*

50   *1902, Kitty Hawk, North Carolina*

55   *1903, Kitty Hawk, North Carolina*

57   *1904, Huffman Prairie, Dayton, Ohio*

59   *1905, Huffman Prairie, Dayton, Ohio*

60   *1907, Miami River, Dayton, Ohio*

60   *1908, Kitty Hawk, North Carolina*

61   *1908, Hunaudières Race Course, Le Mans, France*

65   *1908, Camp d'Auvours, Le Mans, France*

73   *1908, Fort Myer, Virginia*

80   *1908, Fort Myer Accident, September 17*

82   *1909, Pont-Long, Pau, France*

91   *1909, Centocelle Field, Rome, Italy*

97   *1909, Fort Myer, Virginia*

104   *1909, Germany (Tempelhof Field, Berlin, and Bornstedt Field, Potsdam)*

107   *1909, Governors Island, New York*

113   *1909, College Park, Maryland*

113   *1911, Kitty Hawk, North Carolina*

118   **Wright Airplanes**

118   *Signal Corps Machine, 1909*

119   *Model B, 1910–1911*

124   *Model R, 1910 (also called the "Roadster" and the "Baby Grand")*

126   *Model EX, 1911*

126   *Model C, 1912*

127   *Model D, 1912*

127   *Model CH, Early Twin-pontoon Version, 1913*

129   *Model CH, with Single Pontoon, 1913*

129   *Model E, 1913*

130   *Model F, 1913*

130   *Model G, 1913*

132   *Model H, 1914*

132   *Model HS, 1915*

133   *Model K, 1915*

133   *Model L, 1916*

135   Bicycle Shop

137   Incidence Indicator

138   Motor

142   Orville Wright Experimental Devices

144   Propeller

146   Wind Tunnel Experiments

150   Wright Company

152   Home

156   Family, Friends, and Associates

162   Dayton Homecoming, 1909

165   Medals and Trophies

169   Monuments and Memorials

171   *Wilbur and Orville Wright Memorial, Dayton, Ohio*

172   *Wright Brothers National Memorial, Kitty Hawk, North Carolina*

174   Art

180   Caricatures and Cartoons

186   Appendix: Audiovisual Materials

191   Index

Preface

This guide is the fifth commemorative tribute to the Wright
brothers prepared by the Library of Congress since 1949, when
the Wright papers were given to the Library by the Orville
Wright estate, and is one of two publications originating in connection with the seventy-fifth anniversary of powered flight. Its
companion, entitled *Photographs by the Wright Brothers: Prints
from the Glass Negatives in the Library of Congress* (Washington: Library of Congress, 1978), includes all but two of 303 photographic glass-plate negatives taken by the Wright brothers in
highly reduced form as positive images on five microfiche. The
publication was prepared for the press by Leonard C. Bruno.

Twenty-five years earlier, to celebrate the fiftieth anniversary of powered flight, a two-volume edition of *The Papers of
Wilbur and Orville Wright, Including the Chanute-Wright Letters and Other Papers of Octave Chanute* (New York: McGraw-
McGraw-Hill Book Company, 1953) was published under the
sponsorship of Oberlin College. In that major initial tribute, the
Wrights' letters, diaries, notebooks, and other records of their
scientific and technical work in inventing and perfecting the airplane were edited by Marvin W. McFarland of what was then
the Library's Aeronautics Division.

As a contributor to that work, the present writer com-
piled several auxiliary files to supplement and help in organizing
the wealth of material in the Wright papers. Two of these, later
expanded, updated, and published to mark other anniversaries,
were *Wilbur & Orville Wright: A Bibliography Commemorating
the Hundredth Anniversary of the Birth of Wilbur Wright,
April 16, 1867* (Washington: Library of Congress, 1968) and
*Wilbur & Orville Wright: A Chronology Commemorating the
Hundredth Anniversary of the Birth of Orville Wright, August
19, 1871* (Washington: Library of Congress, 1975).

In 1953, in conjunction with the editing task, an extensive collection of photographs was assembled as a file from
which to select illustrations for the Wright papers volumes. At
the core were the glass negatives, which had been presented to
the Library in 1949 by the executors of the Orville Wright estate, Harold S. Miller and Harold W. Steeper. These were aug-
mented by approximately 750 photoprints from other sources.
The present writer also maintained a working card file that
identified photographs in the Wright collection and those acquired from other sources, including pictorial materials relating
to the Wright brothers' careers appearing in the world literature,

whether in books, periodicals, or other pertinent sources. That working card file formed the basis for the present guide, which is intended to make more generally available the information that was assembled. Its purpose is to serve as a ready informational reference that will provide a comprehensive guide and working tool for librarians, picture searchers, historians, and other serious students of science and technology. Judging from inquiries received by the Library, there is continuing interest in illustrative materials relating to the Wright brothers. Not surprisingly, this interest was heightened in 1978 with the many observances of the seventy-fifth anniversary of the first powered flight. It is hoped that this guide will facilitate the handling of requests made to the Library for such materials and assist others seeking such materials here and elsewhere as well.

Although the guide is based primarily on examination of the extensive aeronautical holdings of the Library of Congress, including the bequeathed Wright papers and photographic collection, extensive use was made also of the comprehensive Wright photographic collection in the documentary research files of the Smithsonian Institution's National Air and Space Museum Library. The museum's collection contains photographs of virtually all of the Wright aircraft. Also included are related Wright family photographs, photographs of their early flying experiments, and photographs of their later flight trials in the United States and Europe. It was not possible to list all items in the museum's collections, particularly the numerous photographs of the Wright 1903 airplane, some of which were taken before the return of the airplane to the United States from England in 1948, others at the presentation ceremonies on December 17, 1948, when the airplane was formally presented to the Smithsonian Institution, and still others before and after the airplane's installation in the museum. Likewise some photographs, such as those of the museum's William J. Hammer collection, which could not be readily identified by a catalog code number were not included. This was also true of some photographs in the Library of Congress. No examination was made of the outstanding Wright brothers collection of photographs at Wright State University in Dayton, Ohio. This collection of nearly three thousand photographs was acquired by Wright State University on December 19, 1975, by deed of gift from the surviving Wright heirs. The photographs are described and many illustrated in an excellent guide published under the title *The Wright Brothers Collection: A Guide to the Technical, Business and Legal, Genealogical, Photographic, and Other Archives at Wright State University,* by Patrick B. Nolan and John A. Zamonski (New York and London: Garland Publishing, 1977). Some additional, less extensive Wright brothers photographic collections are cited in an excellent recent study by Dominick A. Pisano, reference librarian at the National Air and Space Museum, appearing in *The Wright Brothers: Heirs to Prometheus,* edited by Richard P. Hallion (Washington: National Air and Space Museum, Smithsonian Institution, 1977), pp. 137–46.

Following this preface is a list of abbreviations of books, periodicals, and other sources cited in the guide. A total of 1,555 individual entries are then listed, some representing a series of photographs, bringing the total number of images described to more than 1,600. The inclusion of photographs is selective. Obviously no such list can be exhaustive and no claim is made for completeness. Illustrations from 104 monographs, primarily biographies of the Wright brothers and aeronautical histories and reference works, are listed. Numerous contemporary periodicals were examined for photographs, but only twenty-nine titles—because they were long or often cited—appear in the list of abbreviations, the remainder being cited in full in the main text. Special collections in the Prints and Photographs Division of the Library of Congress cited include: (1) the Wright brothers original glass-plate negative collection (LC W85 and W86); (2) the George Grantham Bain collection of news photos of aviation activities of Orville and Wilbur Wright, 1908–17 (LC-BAIN); (3) the Mabel Beck collection of Wright brothers photographs (LC-BECK); (4) the Alfred Hildebrandt collection of photographs of Orville Wright's flights in Germany, 1909 (LC-HILDEBRANDT); (5) the Ernest L. Jones collection of photographs concerning the history of aviation, particularly Army Signal Corps photographs relating to the flight trials of the Wright brothers at Fort Myer, Virginia, 1908 and 1909 (LC-JONES); and (6) a collection of copy negatives made from prints in the Prints and Photographs Division (LC-USZ62). Photographs in the Papers of Wilbur and Orville Wright in the Library's Manuscript Division are cited as LCPWOW. Other special collections often cited include the extensive photographic collections of the National Air and Space Museum, Smithsonian Institution (SMIN), the photographic collection of the U.S. Air Force (USAF), and the photographic collection of the Wright Air Development Center, Dayton, Ohio (WADC). The numerous photographs published in *The Papers of Wilbur and Orville Wright,* edited by Marvin W. McFarland, are designated MCFWP. Most of these photographs, particularly for the earlier years, are from the Library's Wilbur and Orville Wright photographic collection.

Although one sees many sources cited for the photographs of the Wright brothers' gliding and flight experiments taken during the period 1900 to 1905, all the photographs for this period, except for a few taken by Octave Chanute in 1902, are prints from the Wright brothers' original glass-plate negatives in the Library of Congress or from prints made from them. Most of the views on the glass-plate negatives were taken by the Wright brothers between 1898 and 1911, primarily to document their successes and failures in developing their airplane and to provide visual evidence of their spectacular achievements. Wilbur and Orville were aware of the important relationship of photography to their work, both scientifically and historically. They maintained a notebook in which they listed time of exposure, f-stop setting, date, place, type of plate used, and subject matter for each photograph. They occasionally used flashlight techniques for interior views. Their camera was big and bulky, had to be mounted on a tripod, and permitted only one exposure at a time. The Wrights purchased their first camera at about the same time they began their kite and gliding experiments. It cost $85 and was one of the finest and most expensive on the market in those days—a Korona-V manufactured by Ernst Gundlach, a

German craftsman who had emigrated to the United States from Berlin in 1873.

The date of publication of prints made from the glass negatives may be significant, because on March 25–27, 1913, a flood in Dayton did considerable damage to the Wright family home and property, including a wooden shed behind the home where the Wright brothers had a darkroom and kept their negatives and prints. Since the flood did affect the negatives in varying degree, a print made and published before that date may, in some instances, be in better condition than the existing negative.

The photographs listed here are grouped under twenty-two broad subject categories indicated in the table of contents, based on a combination of subject classifications used in the Library's earlier Wright brothers publications. The arrangement under each subject category is generally chronological, although this was not always feasible, particularly when no date could be determined for a photograph. The first five categories are devoted to the Wright family members: Wright brothers together, Wilbur, Orville, their father Bishop Milton Wright, and their sister Katharine Wright. The Wright brothers' gliding experiments and flights are listed in a following group of nineteen chronological categories covering the years 1900–1911, as used in the Wright brothers *Chronology* flight log. Photographs of specific Wright aircraft are next grouped in seventeen categories. A series of fourteen subject categories form the last main group. An appendix listing audiovisual materials is the concluding section. Materials cited in the appendix include audiotapes, microfiche, motion pictures, phonorecords, and slides.

Although the primary use of the guide is to assist those seeking photographs, it will serve also as a bibliography of materials relating to the Wright brothers, since the student or researcher seeking specific photographic sources will usually find accompanying text describing the individual, airplane, flight, or other event or subject depicted when the citation is to a book or periodical.

A comprehensive index of persons, institutions, and geographic names cited is provided to facilitate use of the guide.

Abbreviations for Sources Cited

Works cited in full in the text do not appear in this list.

ACANA   Aero Club of America. *Navigating the Air*. New York: Doubleday, Page & Company, 1907.

ACAWMB   Aero Club of America. *Wright Memorial Book*. New York, 1913.

ADAMSF   Adams, Heinrich. *Flug*. Leipzig: C. F. Amelangs Verlag, 1909.

Aerial Age W   *Aerial Age Weekly*.

Aero Club Am Bul   Aero Club of America. *Bulletin*.

Aero J   *Aeronautical Journal*.

Allg Auto Zeit   *Allgemeine Automobil-Zeitung*.

Allg Flug Zeit   *Allgemeine Flugmaschinen-Zeitung*.

Am Aeronaut   *American Aeronaut*.

Am Legion Mag   *American Legion Magazine*.

Am Mag   *American Magazine*.

Am R Rs   *American Review of Reviews*.

AMHHF   *The American Heritage History of Flight*. New York: Simon & Schuster, 1962.

ANGAEE   Angle, Glenn D. *Airplane Engine Encyclopedia*. Dayton: Otterbein Press, 1921.

ANDWF   Andrews, Alfred S. *The Wright Families*. Rev. ed. Fort Lauderdale, Fla., 1975.

ANGBW   Ångström, Tord. *Bröderna Wright och flygproblemets lösning*. Stockholm, Nordisk Rotogravyr, 1928.

ANMAD   André, Henri. *Moteurs d'aviation et de dirigeables*. Paris: Geisler, 1910.

APGAFM   Apple, Nick P., *and* Gene Gurney. *The Air Force Museum.* New York: Crown Publishers, Inc., 1975.

ASHWB   Ash, Russell. *The Wright Brothers.* London: Wayland Publishers, [1974].

ASMEJ   American Society of Mechanical Engineers. *Journal.*

Atlan   *Atlantic Monthly.*

Aviation W   *Aviation Week.*

BBAKH   Brown, Aycock. *The Birth of Aviation at Kitty Hawk, N.C.* Winston-Salem, N.C.: The Collins Company, 1953.

BERFF   Berger, Oscar. *Famous Faces: Caricaturist's Scrapbook.* New York and London: Hutchinson, [1950].

BIAFW   Bia, Georges. *Les Frères Wright et leur oeuvre.* [Saint-Mikiel]: Imprimerie du Journal La Meuse, [1909].

BLASF   Black, Archibald. *The Story of Flying.* New York and London: McGraw-Hill Book Company, 1943.

BRABSL   Braunbeck, Gustaf. *Braunbeck's Sport-Lexikon; Automobilismus, Motorbootswesen, Luftschiffahrt.* [Berlin: G. Braunbeck & Gutenberg-Druckerei, 1910].

BRFYF   Brewer, Griffith. *Fifty Years of Flying.* London: Air League of the British Empire, 1946.

BUFJM   Burda, Franz. *Fünfzig Jahre Motorflug.* Offenburg, Baden, 1953.

CAIAF   Caidin, Martin. *Air Force; a Pictorial History of American Air Power.* New York and Toronto: Rinehart & Company, [1957].

Cent   *Century Magazine.*

CHAHA   Chambe, René. *Histoire de l'aviation.* [Paris]: Flammarion, [1972].

CHBLWB   Charnley, Mitchell V. *The Boys' Life of the Wright Brothers.* New York and London: Harper & Brothers, [1928].

CLHAGW   Chandler, Charles D., *and* Frank P. Lahm. *How Our Army Grew Wings.* New York: Ronald Press, 1943.

COCKDH   Combs, Harry, *and* Martin Caidin. *Kill Devil Hill; Discovering the Secret of the Wright Brothers.* Foreword by Neil Armstrong. Boston: Houghton Mifflin Company, 1979.

CRWBDA Craig, Barbara. *The Wright Brothers and Their Development of the Airplane.* Raleigh, N.C.: State Department of Archives and History, 1960.

CWAUSC U.S. Architect of the Capitol. *Compilation of Works of Art and Other Objects in the United States Capitol,* Washington: U.S. Government Printing Office, 1965.

DAFFA Davidson, Jesse. *Famous Firsts in Aviation.* New York: G. P. Putnam's Sons, 1974.

DAIHF, 1937 Davy, Maurice J. B. *Interpretive History of Flight.* London: H. M. Stationery Office, 1937.

DAIHF, 1948 Davy, Maurice J. B. *Interpretive History of Flight.* London: H. M. Stationery Office, 1948.

D Zeit Luft *Deutsche Zeitschrift für Luftschiffahrt*

DHCUBC Drury, Augustus W. *History of the Church of the United Brethren in Christ.* Dayton, Ohio: Otterbein Press, 1924.

DOBOHA Dollfus, Charles, *and* Henri Bouché. *Histoire de l'aéronautique.* Paris: L'Illustration, 1942.

EIDWHS Edison Institute. *Dedication of Wright Brothers Home and Shop in Greenfield Village.* Dearborn, Mich., 1938.

EWBNM East, Omega G. *Wright Brothers National Memorial.* Washington: National Park Service, 1961.

EWWLM *Essais de Wilbur Wright, Le Mans—1908. Wilbur Wright's Trial.* [Le Mans] Usines Léon Bollée [1929?].

FAHAMUSM Failor, Kenneth M., *and* Eleonora Hayden. *Medals of the United States Mint.* Washington: U.S. Government Printing Office, 1969.

FRFH Freudenthal, Elsbeth. *Flight into History; the Wright Brothers and the Air Age.* Norman, Okla.: University of Oklahoma Press, 1949.

FRMNI Franklin Mint. *Numismatic Issues of the Franklin Mint.* 1970 ed. Covering the years 1965–70. [Yeadon, Pa., 1970].

FWGMBH *Flugmaschine Wright G.m.b.H.* Berlin, [1909].

FWGWA Flugmaschine Wright-Gesellschaft, G.m.b.H. *Wright-Aeroplan.* [Berlin, 1910].

GANAC Garber, Paul E. *The National Aeronautical Collections.* Washington: Smithsonian Institution, 1965.

GAOMFF *Golden Anniversary Observance of Man's First Successful Powered Flight.* Proceedings . . . December 14–17, 1953. Washington: U.S. Government Printing Office, 1954.

GCDCA Grand-Carteret, John, *and* Léo Delteil. *La Conquête de l'air.* Paris: Librairie des Annales, 1910.

GHUSAF Goldberg, Alfred, ed. *A History of the United States Air Force.* New York: D. Van Nostrand, 1957.

GLWB Glines, Carroll V. *The Wright Brothers; Pioneers of Powered Flight.* New York: Franklin Watts, [1968].

GSAHS Gibbs-Smith, Charles H. *Aviation; an Historical Survey from Its Origins to the End of World War II.* London: H. M. S. O., 1970.

GSBHF Gibbs-Smith, Charles H. *A Brief History of Flying from Myth to Space Travel.* London: H. M. S. O., 1967.

GSEFM Gibbs-Smith, Charles H. *Early Flying Machines, 1799–1909.* London: Eyre Methuen, 1975.

GSIA Gibbs-Smith, Charles H. *The Invention of the Aeroplane (1799–1909).* London: Faber and Faber, [1966].

GSPA Gibbs-Smith, Charles H. *Pioneers of the Aeroplane.* London: Usborne Publishing, 1976.

GSREA Gibbs-Smith, Charles H. *The Rebirth of European Aviation, 1902–1908.* London: H. M. S. O., 1974.

GSWB Gibbs-Smith, Charles H. *The Wright Brothers.* London: H. M. S. O., 1963.

GSWFAF Gibbs-Smith, Charles H. *The World's First Aeroplane Flights (1903–1908) and Earlier Attempts to Fly.* London: H. M. S. O., 1965.

HAHFC Hall, Edward H. *The Hudson-Fulton Celebration, 1909.* 2 vols. Albany, N.Y., 1910.

HARFF Harris, Sherwood. *The First to Fly, Aviation's Pioneer Days.* New York: Simon and Schuster, 1972.

HATFYF Harper, Harry. *Twenty-five Years of Flying: Impressions, Recollections, and Descriptions.* London: Hutchison & Co., [1929].

HAWBHP Hallion, Richard P., ed. *The Wright Brothers; Heirs of Prometheus.* Washington: Smithsonian Institution Press, 1978.

HAYPA Hayward, Charles B. *Practical Aeronautics.* Chicago: American School of Correspondence, 1912.

HEGOV   Hegener, Henri. *Overwinning op vleugels; Wilbur en Orville Wright leerden ons vliegen.* Haarlem: N. V. Drukkerij de Spaarnestad, [1953].

HFGAUBT   Hall of Fame for Great Americans. *Unveiling of Busts and Tablets for Wilbur and Orville Wright, May 7, 1967.* New York, 1967.

HGCA   Howard, Frank, *and* Bill Gunston. *The Conquest of the Air.* New York: Random House, [1972].

HILBV   Hildebrandt, Alfred. *Die Brüder Wright; eine Studie über die Entwicklung der Flugmaschine von Lilienthal bis Wright.* Berlin: Otto Elsner, 1909.

HMSHSA   Hodgins, Eric, *and* F. Alexander Magoun. *Sky High; the Story of Aviation.* Boston: Little, Brown, and Company, 1935.

HSAFPHA   Haggerty, James J., *and* Warren R. Smith. *The U.S. Air Force; a Pictorial History in Art.* New York: Books, Inc., [1966].

HWBETD   Hobbs, Leonard S. *The Wright Brothers' Engines and Their Design.* Washington: Smithsonian Institution Press, 1971.

HWMHD   *A Handbook of the Wright Memorial; Historical, Descriptive.* n.p., 1935.

Ill Aero Mitteil   *Illustrierte Aeronautische Mitteilungen.*

J Franklin In   *Journal of the Franklin Institute.*

J U.S. Artillery   *Journal of United States Artillery.*

JOHHU   Johnston, S. Paul. *Horizons Unlimited; a Graphic History of Aviation.* New York, Duell, Sloan and Pearce, 1941.

JUDAE   Judge, Arthur W. *Aircraft Engines.* Vol. 2. London: Chapman & Hall, 1941.

KELMKH   Kelly, Fred C. *Miracle at Kitty Hawk; the Letters of Wilbur and Orville Wright.* New York: Farrar, Straus and Young, 1951.

KELWB   Kelly, Fred C. *The Wright Brothers.* New York: Harcourt, Brace & Co., 1943.

KRBCUBC   Koontz, Paul D., *and* Walter E. Roush. *The Bishops, Church of the United Brethren in Christ.* Dayton, Ohio: Otterbein Press, 1950.

LANFL   Lane, Peter. *Flight.* London: B. T. Batsford, 1974.

LECNA Lecornu, Joseph. *La Navigation aérienne; histoire documentaire et anecdotique.* Paris: Vuibert & Nony, 1910.

LC-W85 and LC-W86 Library of Congress. Wright brothers original glass negative collection. Prints and Photographs Division (lot 11512).

LC-BAIN Library of Congress. George Grantham Bain collection of news photos of aviation activities of Orville and Wilbur Wright, 1908–1917. Prints and Photographs Division (lot 10965).

LC-BECK Library of Congress. Mabel Beck collection of Wright brothers photographs. Prints and Photographs Division (lot 11512-A).

LC-HILDEBRANDT Library of Congress. Alfred Hildebrandt collection of photographs of Orville Wright's flights in Germany, 1909. Prints and Photographs Division (lot 8131).

LC-JONES Library of Congress. Ernest L. Jones collection. Prints and Photographs Division (lot 6131).

LC-USZ62 Library of Congress. A collection of copy negatives in the Prints and Photographs Division.

LCPWOW Library of Congress. The Papers of Wilbur and Orville Wright. Manuscript Division.

LOCA *Livre d'or de la conquête de l'air.* Paris: Pierre LaFitte & Cie, 1909.

LOOWGF Loening, Grover C. *Our Wings Grow Faster.* Garden City, N.Y.: Doubleday, Doran & Co., 1935.

LOUVA Loughheed, Victor. *Vehicles of the Air.* Chicago: Reilly and Britton Co., 1910.

LVTDAO La Vaulx, Henri de. *L'Aéronautique des origines à 1922.* Paris: H. Floury, 1922.

LVTNA La Vaulx, Henri de. *Le Triomphe de la navigation aérienne.* Paris: Librairie Illustrée Jules Tallandier, 1911.

MAIKA Maitland, Lester J. *Knights of the Air.* Garden City, N.Y.: Doubleday, Doran & Co., 1929.

MARCD Marcosson, Isac F. *Colonel Deeds, Industrial Builder.* New York: Dodd, Mead & Co., 1947.

MARWBC Marshall, Fred F. *The Wright Brothers chronology from 1903 to 1909.* [Xenia, Ohio, 1971].

MCFWP   McFarland, Marvin W., ed. *The Papers of Wilbur and Orville Wright.* New York: McGraw-Hill Book Co., 1953. Reprint. New York: Arno Press, 1972. (Note: references are to plate numbers.)

MCMWB   McMahon, John R. *The Wright Brothers; Fathers of Flight.* Boston: Little, Brown, and Co., 1930.

MEFMF   Meynell, Laurence. *First Men to Fly.* London: Werner Laurie, 1955.

MILWA   Miller, Francis T. *The World in the Air; the Story of Flying in Pictures.* 2 vols. New York and London: G. P. Putnam's Sons, 1930.

MOORKH   Moolman, Valerie. *The Road to Kitty Hawk.* Alexandria, Va.: Time-Life Books, [1980].

MOPBA   Moedebeck, Hermann W. L. *Pocket-book of Aeronautics.* London: Whittaker, & Co., 1907.

MTWWDA   Musée de Tessé. *Wilbur Wright et les débuts de l'aviation.* Le Mans, 1958.

Nat Aero Assn Rev   *National Aeronautic Association Review.*

Nat Geog Mag   *National Geographic Magazine.*

NOZWBC   Nolan, Patrick B., *and* John A. Zamonski. *The Wright Brothers Collection; a Guide to Technical, Business and Legal, Genealogical, Photographic, and Other Archives at Wright State University.* New York and London: Garland Publishing, 1977.

NPG   National Portrait Gallery. Catalog of American Portraits.

PEOA   Peyrey, François. *Les Oiseaux artificiels.* Paris: H. Dunod et E. Pinat, 1909.

PEPHO   Peyrey, François. *Les Premiers Hommes-oiseaux; Wilbur et Orville Wright.* Paris: H. Guiton, 1908.

Pop Sci   *Popular Science.*

R Aero Soc J   Royal Aeronautical Society. *Journal.*

REPAT   Repossi, Girodano. *Ala tricolore.* Rome: Giunti-Nardini Editore, 1975.

RGSPA   *Revue générale des sciences pures et appliqués.*

RIESW   Riedel, Peter. *Start in den Wind.* Stuttgart: Motorbuch Verlag, [1977].

ROSF Rosenthal, Felix. *Flight.* Zurich: L'Art Ancien, S.A., 1980 (L'Art Ancien S.A. Catalogue 70).

SAE Q Trans Society of Automotive Engineers. *Quarterly Transactions.*

Sat Eve Post *Saturday Evening Post.*

SBNA Savorgnan di Brazza, Francesco. *La navigazione aerea.* Milan: Fratelli Treves, 1910.

SC U.S. Signal Corps photograph.

Sci Am *Scientific American.*

SMIN Smithsonian Institution. National Air and Space Museum. Photographic collections of the National Air and Space Museum.

SMINAR 1902 Smithsonian Institution. *Annual report . . . 1902.* Washington: Government Printing Office, 1903.

SMINAR 1908 Smithsonian Institution. *Annual report . . . 1908.* Washington: Government Printing Office, 1909.

SMINAR 1910 Smithsonian Institution. *Annual report . . . 1910.* Washington: Government Printing Office, 1911.

STAERO *The Story of the Aeroplane.* New York: Wright-Martin Aircraft Corporation, [1917].

SUBDF Supf, Peter. *Das Buch der deutschen Fluggeschichte.* 2 vols. Berlin-Grunewald: Hermann Klemm, AG, [1935].

TAPHF Taylor, John W. R. *A Picture History of Flight.* New York: Pitman Publishing Corporation, 1958.

TAYAP Taylor, C. Fayette. *Aircraft Propulsion; a Review of the Evolution of Aircraft Piston Engines.* Washington: Smithsonian Institution Press, 1971.

THOOB Thompson, Henry A. *Our Bishops.* Chicago: Elder Publishing Co., 1889.

TILLMU Tillman, Stephen F. *Man Unafraid.* Washington, Army Times Publishing Co., [1958].

TMHA Taylor, John W. R., *and* Kenneth Munson. *History of Aviation.* London: New English Library, 1972.

USAF U.S. Air Force. Photographic collections.

VCAAF *Vingt cinq ans d'aéronautique française, 1907–1932.* Paris: Chambre syndicale des industries aéronautiques, 1934.

Vie grand air *La Vie au grand air.*

VOMLF Vorreiter, Ansbert. *Motoren für Luftschiffe und Flugapparate.* Berlin: Richard Carl Schmidt & Co., 1910.

WADC U.S. Wright Air Development Center. Photographic collections.

WCWAM Wright Company. *Wright Airplane Motor: Type "6–60."* Dayton, Ohio, [1913].

WIGLIG Wissman, Gerhard. *Geschichte der Luftfahrt von Ikarus zur Gegenwart.* Berlin: VEB Verlag Technik, 1970.

WIWRM *Wilbur Wright Memorial.* [New Castle, Ind.]: Circle Printing Service, [1923].

WODKH Walsh, John E. *One Day at Kitty Hawk; the Untold Story of the Wright Brothers and the Airplane.* New York: Thomas Y. Crowell Co., [1975].

WRAMG *The Wright Aeroboat Model "G."* Dayton, Ohio: The Wright Co., [1913].

WRBR *The Wright Brothers.* Dayton, Ohio: Carillon Park, [1949].

W Soc Eng J Western Society of Engineers. *Journal.*

YPHA Year. *A Pictorial History of Aviation.* Chicago: Year, Inc., 1953.

Wilbur & Orville Wright
Pictorial Materials

Wilbur and Orville Wright walking on the Boulevard des Pyrénées, Pau, France, in January 1909.

Wright Brothers

Photographs of the Wright brothers taken when they were conducting their early flight experiments, 1900–1905, are included under the chronological list of flight photographs, pp. 46–117.

Orville and Wilbur, head and shoulders, group portrait with Courtlandt F. Bishop, Alan R. Hawley, and James C. McCoy, one of the earliest published photographs of the Wright brothers together, taken about 1907.
> **ACANA facing 4**

Orville, Katharine Wright, and Wilbur en route to Pau, where they stayed January–March 1909, Saint-Lazare railway station, Paris.
> **Vie grand air, v. 15, Jan 23, 1909: 57**

Wilbur assisting Orville as he leaves taxi on arrival at flying field, Pau.
> **Vie grand air, v. 15, Jan. 30, 1909: 72**

Orville and Wilbur with workmen, Wilbur giving directions for construction of hanger, Pau.
> **Vie grand air, v. 15, Jan. 30, 1909: 72**

Orville and Wilbur walking on the Boulevard des Pyrénées, Pau.
> **L'Aérophile, v. 17, Mar. 1, 1909: 107. Similar:**
> **LC-BECK**

Orville, Katharine, and Wilbur promenading on the Boulevard des Pyrenées, Pau.
> **L'Aviation illustrée, v. 1, Jan. 30, 1909: 4; Flight, v. 1,**
> **Mar. 20, 1909: 11; Fly, v. 1, June 1909: 10; Vie grand**
> **air, v. 15, Jan. 30, 1909: 72. Similar: LC-BECK**

Orville and Wilbur promenading with Katharine and the Countess Charles de Lambert, Boulevard des Pyrenées, Pau.
> **Vie grand air, v. 15, Feb. 27, 1909: 134**

Orville and Wilbur, full length, facing camera, Pau.
> **DOBOHA 171**

Wilbur and Orville, pointing his cane toward Wright airplane, Pau.

Fachzeitung für Automobilismus, v. 3, Feb. 21, 1909: 22

Wilbur, back to camera, and Orville, side view, at Pau.

Automotor, v. 14, Mar. 13, 1909: 302; Flight, v. 1, Mar. 13, 1909: 141

Orville and Wilbur with Wilbur's pupils, Capt. Paul N. Lucas-Girardville, Count Charles de Lambert, and Paul Tissandier, Pau, early 1909.

LC-BECK; The Car, v. 28, Feb. 24, 1909: 65; KELWB b. 180–181

King Alfonso XIII of Spain greeting Wilbur and Orville on visit to Pau, February 20, with Hart O. Berg also in picture.

Ill Aero Mitteil, v. 13, Mar. 10, 1909: 192; Motor, v. 15, Feb. 23, 1909: 112; Revue aérienne, v. 5, June 10, 1912: 303. Similar, Wilbur and Orville, head and shoulders only: L'Illustration, v. 139, June 8, 1912: 493

Orville and Wilbur conversing with King Alfonso near Wright airplane hangar.

L'Aérophile, v. 17, Mar. 15, 1909: 133; LVTNA 292; World's Work, v. 20, Aug. 1910: 13304

Hart O. Berg, King Alfonso's equerry with back to camera, Wilbur, King Alfonso with back to camera, Orville with back to camera, Pau, February 20.

LC-BECK

King Alfonso, Orville, Wilbur, and king's equerry at Pau, February 20, Orville and Wilbur explaining the mechanism of the Wright airplane.

LC-BECK

Wilbur in pilot's seat of Wright airplane, King Alfonso, and Orville, Pau, February 20.

Vie grand air, v. 15, Feb. 27, 1909: 133

King Edward VII of England walking with Wilbur and Orville to Wright airplane hangar, Pau, March 17.

ADAMSF 91; L'Aérophile, v. 17, Apr. 1, 1909: 157; Allg Auto Zeit, v. 10, Mar. 26, 1909: 39; ASHWB 73; Automotor, v. 14, Mar. 27, 1909: 375; Collier's, v. 80, Sept. 24, 1927: 19; Flight, v. 1, Mar. 27, 1909: 184

Orville and Wilbur with King Edward, Pau, March 17.

Collier's, v. 80, Sept. 24, 1909: 19; KELWB facing 276; Liberty, v. 5, Dec. 22, 1928: 20; MARWBC 42; MILWA v. 2: 170; NOZWBC facing 178; Vie grand air, v. 15, Mar. 27, 1909: 197; WRBK 19

Close-up of King Edward, Wilbur, and Orville, Pau,
March 17.
YPHA 30

Orville and Wilbur, full length, near outside stairway and ever-
green bush, probably Pau, 1909.
EWWLM 3; SMIN 76, 1281

Orville, Katharine (seated on bench), and Wilbur, probably at
Pau, 1909.
FWGWA 4; HILBW 55

King Victor Emmanuel III of Italy, Orville, and Wilbur, near
Wright airplane at Centocelle Field, about twelve miles south-
east of Rome, April 24, 1909.
LC-BECK

Orville and Wilbur walking with King Victor Emmanuel, Centocelle Field.
Pop Sci, v. 114, May 1929: 48

Wilbur and Orville in conversation with King Victor Emmanuel
and Hart O. Berg, Centocelle Field.
ADAMSF 1909: 106

Wilbur and Orville leaving the British War Office, London, May
3, 1909, following visit with War Secretary Richard B. Haldane.
Automotor, v. 14, May 8, 1909: 559; Collier's, v. 80,
Sept. 24, 1927: 19; Flight, v. 1, May 8, 1909: 255;
MILWA v. 2: 176; SMIN 32, 031-A

Orville and Wilbur seated in automobile with Griffith Brewer
about to leave British War Office.
Autocar, v. 22, May 8, 1909: 668

Wrights seated in rear of automobile on arrival at Carlton
Hotel, London, where they were luncheon guests of Frank
Hedges Butler, prominent British balloonist, May 3, 1909.
The Car, v. 28, May 12, 1909: 532

Group portrait at the Institution of Civil Engineers, London,
May 3, 1909, when Wilbur and Orville were presented with the
Aeronautical Society of Great Britain's gold medal.
Aero J, v. 13, July 1909: 78; Allg Auto Zeit, v. 10, May
16, 1909: 45; The Car, v. 28, May 12, 1909: 532;
R Aero Soc J, v. 57, Dec. 1953: 781

Wilbur and Orville with group of British aviation pioneers on
visit to Aero Club of the United Kingdom flight grounds, Shell-
beach, and Short Brothers' factory, Battersea, May 3, 1909.
Flight, v. 1, May 8, 1909: 257; R Aero Soc J, v. 52,
Mar. 1948: 143; R Aero Soc J, v. 57, Dec. 1953: 883;
TAPHF 42; TMHA 55; YPHA 35

Charles Rolls seated at the wheel of his Rolls-Royce, accompanied by Wilbur, Orville, and his chauffeur, at Shellbeach, England, in May 1909.

Orville and Wilbur with Griffith Brewer, Professor A. K. Huntingdon, and J. T. C. Moore-Brabazon at Shellbeach.
R Aero Soc J, v. 52, Mar. 1948: 145; R Aero Soc J, v. 57, Dec. 1953: 784

Wilbur and Orville at Short Brothers' factory to inspect six machines of their design being constructed there.
Flight, v. 1, May 8, 1909: 259

Orville and Wilbur departing Short Brothers' factory, Horace Short at their left, Oswald Short in background, Griffith Brewer at their right.
R Aero Soc J, v. 57, Dec. 1953: 785

Charles Rolls in his Rolls-Royce, accompanied by Wilbur, Orville, and Mr. Rolls's chauffeur, at Shellbeach.
LC-BECK; The Car, v. 28, May 12, 1909: cover; COCKDH following 168

Charles Rolls, Orville, Wilbur, and Griffith Brewer in Mr. Rolls's car, Shellbeach.

L'Aérophile, v. 17, May 15, 1909: 224; Flight, v. 1, May 8, 1909: 267, 268. Similar, on trip around the Aero Club's grounds at Shellbeach: Flight, v. 1, May 8, 1909: 267

Group portrait of guests at British Aero Club's luncheon honoring the Wrights at the Ritz Hotel, London, May 4, 1909.

R Aero Soc J, v. 52, Mar. 1948: 147; R Aero Soc J, v. 57, Dec. 1953: 783

Orville, Katharine, and Wilbur aboard ship arriving from Europe, May 11, 1909.

Am R Rs, v. 39, June 1909: 656; MILWA v. 2: 177; YPHA 36

Wilbur, Orville, and Katharine greeted on arrival in New York, May 11, 1909, by A. Holland Forbes, acting president, Aero Club of America.

Dayton Journal, May 13, 1909

Group photo taken at Aero Club of America luncheon for the Wright brothers, at the Lawyers' Club, New York, May 12, 1909.

Fly, v. 1, June 1909: 9; New York American, May 18, 1909

Group portrait, including Lorin Wright, Wilbur, Bishop Wright, Orville, and Charles Taylor, taken on return of Wright brothers to Dayton from their European trip.

Dayton Journal, May 14, 1909

Governor Judson Harmon of Ohio presenting Ohio Medal to Wilbur and Orville, Dayton, June 18, 1909.

Collier's, v. 43, July 3, 1909: 4

Orville and Wilbur, full-length view, Union Station, Washington, June 10, 1909.

Washington Star, June 10, 1909: 1; Washington Times, June 10, 1909

President William Howard Taft presenting Aero Club of America gold medals to the Wrights at the White House, June 10, 1909; Wilbur at the president's right, Orville and Katharine at his left.

MCFWP 181; ACAWMB; Aero Club Am Bul, v. 1, July 1912: 20-21; COCKDH following 168; MARWBC 49; Pop Sci, v. 114, June 1929: 53; Washington Herald, June 11, 1909: 1; World's Work, v. 20, Aug. 1910: 13304; WRBR 13; YPHA 36

Wright brothers seated on platform with Bishop Wright, Dayton Homecoming Celebration, June 18, 1909.

Collier's, v. 43, July 3, 1909: 4

Wilbur and Orville seated on the steps of the rear porch of their home in Dayton, located at 7 Hawthorn Street, following their return from Europe in June 1909.

Wilbur and Orville standing on platform at gold medal presentation ceremony, June 18, 1909.
Collier's, v. 43, July 3, 1909: 4; MILWA v. 2: 178; SMIN 31, 980–F

Orville and Wilbur with Bishop Wright in receiving line, Dayton Homecoming Celebration, June 1909.
Collier's, v. 80, Aug. 29, 1927: 9

Wilbur, Orville, and Bishop Wright, three-quarter length, conversing at Dayton Homecoming Celebration, June 1909.
World's Work, v. 20, Aug. 1910: 13307

Orville, front view, hands crossed, and Wilbur, side view, Dayton Homecoming Celebration, June 1909.
Bee-Hive, v. 28, Jan. 1953: 6; WRBR 22

Orville and Wilbur, three-quarter length, standing by porch railing, at their home, 7 Hawthorn Street, Dayton, 1909.
LC-USZ62–67331; LC-BECK

Wilbur and Orville seated on rear porch steps, 7 Hawtorn Street, Dayton, 1909.
LC-BECK; ANDWF 590; FAA World, v. 8, Jan. 1978: 7; HARFF 29; HAWBHP front; KELMKH b. 238-239; MARWBC cover; SMIN A43,268; WRBR cover

Wilbur, signal flag over shoulder, conversing with Orville, Fort Myer, Va., July 30, 1909.
LC-JONES; USAF 9690 A.S.

Orville and Wilbur and friends at party following Orville's successful flight to Alexandria, Va., July 30, 1909.
LC-JONES

Orville and Wilbur walking along starting rail, July 30, 1909, Fort Myer, Va.
LC-BAIN

Dr. Charles D. Walcott, Wilbur, Alexander Graham Bell, and Orville outside the Smithsonian Building just after the Wright brothers received the Langley Medal, February 10, 1910.
MCFWP 197; SMIN 31, 299

Wilbur, Orville, and Walter Brookins, Wright Company exhibition flier, at Indianapolis, Ind., air show, June 1910.
SMIN 42, 809

Orville and Wilbur walking together, Wilbur slightly in advance, Orville carrying topcoat over right arm, at the International Aviation Tournament, Belmont Park, N.Y., October 1910, one of the most frequently published Wright photographs.
LC-USZ62–5515; LC-JONES; MCFWP v. 2, front.; Airpost Journal, v. 50, Dec. 1978: cover; ASHWB 83; Bee-Hive, v. 28, Jan. 1953: cover; FRFH facing 227; MILWA 96; SMIN A3602; STAERO front.; USAF 1361A A.S.; U.S. Air Services, v. 13, Dec. 1928: cover; YPHA 74

Orville, Wilbur, and Katharine, Belmont Park, N.Y., October 1910.
Aero Blue Book, 1910: 28

Orville and Wilbur in front of one of their hangars, Belmont Park, N.Y., October 1910.
U.S. Air Services, v. 13, Dec. 1928: 30

Wilbur, Orville, and Ralph Johnstone, a Wright Company exhibition flier, in front of Wright airplane, Belmont Park, N.Y., October 1910.
U.S. Air Services, v. 13, Dec. 1928: 27

Orville and Wilbur discussing merits of the Wright "Roadster" with Charles Taylor and Wright Company exhibition fliers J. Clifford Turpin, Walter Brookins, and Ralph Johnstone, Belmont Park, N.Y., October 1910.
Aircraft, v. 1, Dec. 1910: 361

Wilbur and Orville, three-quarter length, conferring, Belmont Park, N.Y., October 1910.
LC-BAIN; YPHA 33

Wilbur and Orville conversing with Israel Ludlow, Belmont Park, N.Y., October 1910.
Aircraft, v. 1, Dec. 1910: 360

Orville and Wilbur seated near Wright airplane with pilots Walter Brookins and Frank T. Coffyn and manager, Wright Flying School, Roy Knabenshue, Dayton, 1911.
R Aero Soc J, v. 57, Dec. 1953: 792

Wilbur Wright

(April 16, 1867–May 30, 1912)

Wilbur, age five, posing for commercial photographer, half-length view.
> **Pop Sci, v. 114, Jan. 1929: 18**

Wilbur, age 13, head and shoulders, facing left, about 1880.
> **LC-USZ62–56248; LC-BECK; MCFWP 3; ASHWB 8; EWBNM 1; MCMWB 20; Pop Sci, v. 114, Feb. 1929: 42; SMIN A4441–A. Similar, facing forward: LC-W86–85; LC-BECK**

Wilbur, age 22, head and shoulders.
> **Pop Sci, v. 114, Mar. 1929: 44**

Wilbur, back to camera, at work in back room of Wright bicycle shop, 1897.
> **LC-USZ62–56241; LC-W85–81; COCKDH following 168; WRBR 3**

Wilbur, age 30, half-length side view, seated facing right, 1897.
> **LC–W85–78**

Wilbur, age 38, head and shoulders, about 1905; one of the earliest published photographs of him.
> **LC-USZ62–56246; LC–W86–91; LC–W86–92; L'Aérophile, v. 13, Dec. 1905; 265; L'Aérophile, v. 20, Dec. 1912: 205; Am Aeronaut, v. 1, Jan. 1908: 7; AN-GBW facing 8; PEPHO 7; SMIN 18,245–D; SMIN 42,545; Technical World, v. 5, June 1906: 335; U.S. Air Service, v. 8, Dec. 1923: 29**

Wilbur, head and shoulders, wearing bow tie, about 1906.
> **Wiener Luftschiffer-Zeitung, v. 5, July 1906: 140; Wiener Luftschiffer-Zeitung, v. 11, June 15, 1912: 215**

Wilbur, head and shoulders, facing right, about 1907.
> **LC-BAIN; Am Mag, v. 63, Apr. 1907: 620; Revue de l'aviation, v. 2, May 15, 1907: 4 (incorrectly named Orville)**

Wilbur, head and shoulders, similar to above, facing left; probably the single most widely used photograph of Wilbur.

LC-BECK; MCFWP v. 1, front.; Aero J., v. 4, June 8, 1912: 235; Aero Club Am Bul, v. 1, July 1912: 2; Air Force, v. 36, Dec. 1953: 32; Airway Age, v. 9, Dec. 1928: 16; Aviation, v. 15, Dec. 17, 1923: 753; BBAKH; Cent, v. 76, Sept. 1908: 643; EIDWHS facing 9; EWBNM 57; GANAC 37; HAWBHP 58; Sci Am, v. 106, June 8, 1912: 518; SMIN A32,497–A; SMIN 45,415; U.S. Air Services, v. 28, Dec. 1943: 23; WODKH facing 34

Wilbur, half length, from group photo taken about 1907.

Aeronautics, v. 2, June 1908: 5; Illustrated London News, v. 133, Aug. 15, 1908: 237; SMIN 10,794–A

Wilbur, half length, standing in gondola of balloon *Au Petit Bonheur* before ascension, Le Mans, July 26, 1908.

Graphic, v. 78, Aug. 15, 1908: 191

Wilbur Wright's flying activities in France: 30 photographs, eight postcards, and some ephemera, showing Wilbur, his French pupils, visiting celebrities, and Orville, Hunaudiéres Race Course and Camp d'Auvours, Le Mans, and Pont-Long, Pau, 1908-9.

ROSF no. 168

Wilbur and Léon Bollée, three-quarter length, Wilbur in business suit with straw hat, outside Bollée's factory, Le Mans, probably at the time Wilbur was flying at the Hunaudiéres Race Course, August 1908.

Automotor, v. 13, Aug. 22, 1908: 1120; COCKDH following 168; EWWLM 5

Wilbur, head and shoulders, in business suit with straw hat, August 1908.

BUFJM 13; Conquête de l'air, v. 5, Oct. 15, 1908: 5

Wilbur seated at controls of Wright airplane, Hunaudières Race Course flying field, August 1908.

L'Aérophile, v. 16, Aug. 15, 1908: 324; Avia, v. 2, June 15, 1912: 39; CHAHA 64; EWWLM 14; Flight, v. 64, Dec. 11, 1953: 796; MARWBC 21; NOZWBC facing 156; PEPHO facing 57; R Aero Soc J, v. 57, Dec. 1953: 786. Similar, Wilbur facing to right: GSPA 34

Wilbur engaged in repairing Wright airplane immediately following accident, August 13, 1908, Hunaudières Race Course, assisted by Fleury, Hart O. Berg's chauffeur, at his left.

LC-BECK; MCFWP 153; GSPA 32; MARWBC 47; SC–107933; SMIN A3415; WRBR 20

Wilbur, full length, conversing with Hart O. Berg and Léon Bollée on flying field, France, 1908.

Revue de l'aviation, v. 3, Sept. 15, 1908: 7

Wilbur seated in Wright airplane with Ernest Zens, his passenger, Camp d'Auvours, September 16, 1908.

> **L'Aérophile, v. 16, Dec. 1, 1908: 470; Allg Auto Zeit,
> v. 2, Oct. 19, 1908: 31; Flight, v. 1, Mar. 20, 1909: 11;
> Illustrated London News, v. 133, Oct. 3, 1908: 477;
> PEPHO facing 64; Revue de l'aviation, v. 3, Oct. 15,
> 1908: 14; SMIN 10,879–G; U.S. Air Services, v. 13,
> Dec. 1928: 32; VCAAF 57**

Mrs. Hart O. Berg seated in Wright airplane with Wilbur before the first real flight made anywhere in the world by a woman, October 7, 1908.

> **L'Aérophile, v. 16, Nov. 1, 1908: 428; Allg Auto Zeit,
> v. 2, Oct. 19, 1908: 31; ASHWB 71; Avia, v. 2, June
> 15, 1912: 39; Bee-Hive, v. 28, Fall 1953: 28; GSEFM;
> GSIA 148; GSPA 33; HILBW 38; Illustrated London
> News, v. 133, Oct. 24, 1908: 561; LECNA 417;
> PEPHO facing 76; SMIN A3405; SMIN A3416;
> SMIN 31,246–H**

Mrs. Hart O. Berg accompanied Wilbur on a flight on
October 7, 1908. National Air and Space Museum, Smithsonian
Institution, photo no. A3405.

Wilbur with Charles S. Rolls, his passenger, Camp d'Auvours, October 8, 1908.
> **Bee-Hive, v. 28, Fall 1953: 29; Illustrated London News, v. 133, Oct. 24, 1908: 561**

Wilbur seated in Wright airplane with Frank Hedges Butler, his passenger, Camp d'Auvours, October 8, 1908.
> **American Heritage, v. 11, Feb. 1960:62; Illustrated London News, v. 133, Oct. 24, 1908: 561**

Wilbur seated in Wright airplane with Griffith Brewer, his passenger, Camp d'Auvours, October 8, 1908.
> **Illustrated London News, v. 133, Oct. 24, 1908: 561**

Wilbur seated in Wright airplane with Hart O. Berg, his passenger, Camp d'Auvours, October 8, 1908.
> **Illustrated London News, v. 133, Oct. 24, 1908: 561**

Wilbur, half length, wearing cap, collar, tie, and gray business suit.
> **L'Aérophile, v. 17, Aug. 1, 1909: 356; Flugsport, v. 4, June 5, 1912: 455. Similar: Automotor, v. 14, Mar. 6, 1909: 279; LVTNA 43; Revue aérienne, v. 2, Mar. 10, 1909: 85**

Wilbur, full length, wearing cap, high collar, tie, and business suit, with dog named Flyer at his feet, Camp d'Auvours.
> **MCFWP 166; ADAMSF 1909: 70; YPHA 36. Head and shoulders only: AMHHF 114.**

Wilbur, full length, as above, standing beside wing tip of Wright airplane, two mounted horsemen at extreme left.
> **SMIN A43,434**

Wilbur, full length, examining his anemometer in preparation for a flight.
> **BIAFW facing 4**

Wilbur, three-quarter length, in conversation with Lazare Weiller, head of Lazare Weiller Syndicate, which purchased the Wrights' French patents.
> **Allg Auto Zeit, v. 9, Sept. 26, 1908: 46; Motor, v. 14, Jan. 5, 1909: 762**

Wilbur, full length, side view, conversing with Hart O. Berg, Wrights' business associate in Europe.
> **PEPHO facing 56**

Mrs. Lazare Weiller, Lazare Weiller, and Henri Deutsch de la Meurthe conversing with Wilbur near Wright airplane, Camp d'Auvours.
> **PEPHO facing 84; Revue aerienne, v. 1, Nov. 10, 1908: 39**

Hart O. Berg conversing with Wilbur, full length, facing camera.
>COCKDH following 168; Ill Aero Mitteil, v. 13, Jan. 13, 1909: 2

Wilbur in center of group of nine French aviation enthusiasts.
>SMIN 43,009–F

Wilbur near Wright airplane explaining its operation to two interested men at either side of him, another in rear.
>SMIN A3416; U.S. Air Services, v. 13, Dec. 1928: 29; YPHA 34

Wilbur standing on support at top of launching tower adjusting launching weight.
>Vie grand air, v. 15, June 8, 1912: 400. Similar: ADAMSF 53

Wilbur standing in front of Wright airplane making adjustments to motor.
>LC-BECK; Vie grand air, v. 15, June 8, 1912: 400

Wilbur, head and shoulders, wearing cap, high starched collar, and tie; his most characteristic photograph, taken in France, 1908, at the height of his fame.
>LC-BECK; Aero J, v. 16, July 1912: facing 148; Aero J, v. 20, July/Sept. 1916: facing 68; Aircraft, v. 1, June 1910: 141; Allg Auto Zeit, v. 13, June 9, 1912: 20; ASHWB 53; EWWLM 3; GSPA 22; GSWB 3; HGCA 44; KELMKH b. 238–239; MCMWB 274; Pegasus, v. 20, Apr. 1953: 8; PEPHO facing 65; Pop Sci, v. 114, May 1929: 48; SMIN 45,663: SMIN 76, 1280; U.S. Air Services, v. 40, Dec. 1955: 54; Vie grand air, v. 15, Mar. 20, 1909: 195; Vie grand air, v. 18, June 8, 1912: cover. Similar: London Magazine, v. 21, Feb. 1909: 622

Wilbur walking along edge of Camp d'Auvours before photographer who is posing him.
>LC-BECK; SMIN 43,063–F. Similar, Wilbur facing photographer: L'Aviation illustrée, v. 1, Feb. 6, 1909: 4; London Magazine, v. 21, Feb. 1909: 625; R Aero Soc J, v. 57, Dec. 1953: 787

Wilbur, full length, at edge of flying field, Camp d'Auvours, 1908.
>Avia, v. 2, June 13, 1912: cover; DOBOHA 169

Wilbur with Hart O. Berg, inspecting Léon Delagrange airplane.
>Revue aérienne, v. 1, Dec. 10, 1908: 119

Wilbur at dinner table with large group of Aéro-Club de France members attending banquet in his honor, Paris, November 5, 1908.
>L'Aérophile, v. 16, Nov. 15, 1908: 441; Motor, v. 14, Nov. 10, 1908: 436; Revue aérienne, v. 1, Nov. 25, 1908: facing 88

Group photo including Louis Blériot, Paul Tissandier, Capt. Paul N. Lucas-Girardville, Wilbur, Mrs. Hart O. Berg, Count Charles de Lambert, and Katharine, Pau, February 1909.
L'Aérophile, v. 17, Feb. 15, 1909: 85; Allg Auto Zeit, v. 10, Feb. 21, 1909: 39; CHAHA 66; Flight, v. 1, Mar. 20, 1909: 6; Graphic v. 79, Feb. 20, 1909: 224; HEGOV facing 97; Revue aérienne, v. 1, Feb. 25, 1909: facing 105; Vie grand air, v. 15, May 29, 1909: 356

Wilbur, three-quarter length, wearing gray business suit, in front of fireplace mantle.
SMIN A3418; SMIN 42,844; YPHA 36

Wilbur, three-quarter length, wearing cap and business suit, knee bent, right hand on knee.
CHAHA 52; Légion d'honneur, v. 1, Apr. 1933: 211; U.S. Air Services, v. 17, July 1932: 21; Zeitschrift für Flugtechnik und Motorluftschiffahrt, v. 3, June 15, 1912: 152

Wilbur, arm extended to right, testing wind direction, Pau.
Collier's, v. 43, May 15, 1909: 18; Vie grand air, v. 15, May 15, 1909: 324

Wilbur, half length, wearing derby hat and topcoat, seated on wicker chair.
Allg Auto Zeit, v. 10, Mar. 5, 1909: 35

Wilbur, three-quarter length, wearing derby hat and topcoat, conversing with Léon Delagrange, Port-Aviation, Juvisy, France, early 1909.
L'Aéronaute, v. 42, Mar. 15, 1909: 8

Wilbur, dressed in gray business suit, seated, leaning back, right finger touching chin.
HILBW 1909: 7; WIGLIG b. 548–549

Wilbur, full length, adjusting pulley on launching rail in preparation for flight, hangar and spectators behind fence in background at right.
MCFWP 172; SMIN 31, 991; Vie grand air, v. 15, May 15, 1909: 324

Wilbur conversing with Lord Northcliffe and Lord Balfour, who witnessed his flights, February 11, 1909, Pau.
LC-BECK; World's Work, v. 20, Aug. 1910: 13364

Wilbur seated in Wright airplane with Katharine, his passenger on her first flight, February 15, 1909.
LC-BECK; Collier's, v. 80, Aug. 20, 1927: 8; MCMWB facing 220; MEFMF facing 103; MILWA v. 2: 171; SMIN 42,783–L

Wilbur adjusts the pulley on a launching rail as he prepares for a flight at Pau, France, 1909.

Wilbur and Count de Lambert in front of Wright airplane, Countess de Lambert seated in it for flight with Wilbur, February 15, 1909, Pau.
L'Aérophile, v. 17, Nov. 1909: 483; Ill Aero Mitteil, v. 13, Feb. 24, 1909: 142; Vie grand air, v. 15, Feb. 27, 1909: 134

King Alfonso XIII of Spain greeting Wilbur on the flying field on visit to Pau, Orville and Hart O. Berg standing nearby, February 20, 1909.
Ill Aero Mitteil, v. 13, Mar. 10, 1909: 192; Revue aérienne, v. 2, Mar. 10, 1909: 155; SBNA 112

Wilbur greeting King Alfonso of Spain (back to camera), group gathered around and Lord Alfred Northcliffe (in derby) looking on behind Wilbur, Pau, February 20.
MCFWP 175; SMIN 31.246–G; WODKH b. 220–221. Similar, Wilbur only, head and shoulders: ADAMSF 1909: 77; World's Work, v. 20, Aug. 1910: 13314

Close-up view of Wilbur in Wright airplane explaining the mechanism to King Alfonso, seated facing him at his right, Pau, February 20.
LC-BAIN; ADAMSF 92; Allg Auto Zeit, v. 10, Feb. 28, 1909: 39; Autocar, v. 22, Feb. 27, 1909: 281; Automotor, v. 14, Feb. 27, 1909: 236; Fachzeitung für Automobilismus, v. 4, Mar. 7, 1909: 19; Flight, v. 1, Mar. 20, (suppl.) 6; Fly, v. 1, Apr. 1909: 12; GSEFM; HILBW 48; MARWBC 43; MCMWB 180: Pop Sci, v. 114, Feb. 1929: 43; Vie grand air, v. 15, Feb. 27, 1909: 136

Close-up view of Wilbur explaining the Wright airplane mechanism to King Alfonso, both men seated in the airplane, looking forward, the King to Wilbur's right, Pau, February 20.
LC-BAIN; LC-BECK; ASHWB 72; Collier's, v. 80, Sept. 24, 1927: 19; Ill Aero Mitteil, v. 13, Mar. 10, 1909: 193; MILWA v. 2: 146; Revue aérienne, v. 2, Mar. 10, 1909: 154; Sat Eve Post, v. 201, July 4, 1928: 19

Louis Barthou seated in Wright airplane while Wilbur, at front, makes adjustments before their flight, Pau, February 22, 1909.
LC-BECK

Wilbur, half length, facing left, wearing cap and leather jacket.
BRABSL 1910: 325; Deutsche Luftfahrer-Zeitschrift, v. 16, June 12, 1912; 289; Revue aérienne, v. 5, June 10, 1912: 302

Wilbur, head and shoulders, facing right, wearing gray business suit.
Automobile Topics, v. 19, Oct. 9, 1909: 10; MILWA v. 1: 4

Wilbur, wearing derby hat and topcoat, seated in automobile, side view, head and shoulders, England, May 1909.
Flight, v. 1, May 8, 1909: 262; Flight, v. 4, June 1, 1912: 488

Wilbur, head and shoulders, wearing derby hat and topcoat, smiling, England May 1909.
Flight, v. 1, May 8, 1909: 267

Katharine and Wilbur on arrival from Europe aboard *Kronprinzessin Cecilie,* New York, May 11, 1909.
SMIN 42,804–C

Wilbur, head and shoulders, facing left.
HATFYF facing 25

Wilbur and Guglielmo Marconi at left front of Wright airplane, as Wilbur is preparing for the Hudson-Fulton Celebration flights, Governors Island, N.Y., September 23, 1909.
U.S. Air Services, v. 17, Feb. 1932: 22

Wilbur, half length, side view, following his return from trip to Grant's Tomb, October 4, 1909.
LC-BAIN; LC-USZ62–5886 (copy negative)

Wilbur, head and shoulders, wearing cap, with half smile, Governors Island, October 1909.
Air-Scout, v. 1, Feb. 1911: 31 American R Rs, v. 40, Oct. 1909: 518

Wilbur, side view, head and shoulders, wearing business suit, white collar, and cap, facing to his left, soldier and woman nearby at his right, Governors Island, 1909.
NOZWBC facing 160

Wilbur, full length, wearing derby hat and business suit, carrying a large fuel can for use in Wright airplane, at International Aviation Tournament, Belmont Park, N.Y., October 22–30, 1910.
U.S. Air Services, v. 13, Dec. 1928: 64. Similar: American Petroleum Institute photo.

Wilbur at front of Wright airplane conversing with Ralph Johnstone, a Wright Exhibition Company flier, Belmont Park, N.Y., October 1910.
Collier's, v. 80, Sept. 24, 1927: 18; SMIN 43,062–B

Wilbur in conversation with Allan Ryan, Belmont Park, N.Y., October 1910.
LC-BAIN

Wilbur and Frank T. Coffyn, adjusting kite for Coffyn's young son, Crossland, Bayside, N.J., 1910.
MCFWP 195; MILWA v. 2: 248; SMIN 32,975–A. Similar: MCFWP 194; MCFWP 196; SMIN 38,681–B

Wilbur, head and shoulders, facing slightly right.
> **Aero Digest, v. 13, Dec. 1928: 1104; Aviation W, v. 49.**
> **Dec. 13, 1948: 17; SMIN 20,948**

Wilbur at speaker's table in group portrait, sixth annual dinner of the Aero Club of America at Sherry's, New York, January 27, 1912.
> **Aero Club Am Bul, v. 1, Feb./Mar. 1912: suppl.**

Wilbur, half length, wearing derby hat, overcoat, hands in pockets, and Frank T. Coffyn, Wright business associate, in cap and jacket, New York, February 1912.
> **MILWA v. 2: 245; SMIN 42,805–D; YPHA 72**

Orville Wright

(August 19, 1871–January 30, 1948)

Orville, age five, posing for commercial photographer, seated, half length.
> **Pop Sci, v. 114, Jan. 1929: 18**

Orville, age nine and a half, posing for commercial photographer, seated, half length, Cedar Rapids, Iowa, February 23, 1881.
> **LC-BECK; MCFWP 4; ASHWB 9; EWBNM 1; MCMWB 20; Pop Sci, v. 114, Feb. 1929: 42; SMIN A4441**

Orville (back row, center) and his friend the future poet Paul Lawrence Dunbar (back row, far left) with the Dayton Central High School class of 1891.
> **MOORKH 110**

Orville, side view facing right, half length, before he grew a mustache, 1897.
> **LC-USZ62–56240; LC–W85–77; KELMKH b. 238–239; Pop Sci, v. 114, Feb. 1929: 44**

Orville, age 34, head and shoulders, with mustache, 1905.
> **LC-USZ62–56249; LC–W86–88; LC–W86–89; LC–W86–90; ADAMSF 1909: 74; L'Aérophile, v. 13, Dec. 1905: 265; L'Aérophile, v. 16, Oct. 1, 1908: 384; Am Aeronaut, v. 1, Jan. 1908: 6; EWBNM 56; Lithopinion, v. 6, Winter 1971: 57; PEPHO 1908: 7; PEPHO 1909: facing 88; SMIN 10, 794–C; SMIN 42, 545–C; Technical World, v. 5, June 1906: 334; U.S. Air Service, v. 8, Dec. 1923: 29; Wiener Luftschiffer-Zeitung, v. 5, July 1906: 141. Similar: LC–W86–87**

Orville, head and shoulders, facing left, December 7, 1906.
> **LC-BAIN; Air Force, v. 36, Dec. 1953: 32; Am Mag, v. 63, Apr. 1907: 621; BBAKH; Cent, v. 76, Sept. 1908: 643; Fly, v. 1, Aug. 1909: 18; CHBLWB facing 198; GSPA 22; GSWB 3; Revue de l'aviation, v. 2, May 15, 1907: 5; SMIN 32,497; SMIN 42,844–A. In reverse: GANAC 37**

Orville, three-quarter length, arms folded, from group portrait taken about 1907.
Aeronautics, v. 2, June 1908: 5

Orville, full face, head and shoulders, 1908.
AMHHF 115; SMIN 34, 116–T; Vie grand air, v. 15, Jan. 2, 1909: 4; Vie grand air, v. 15, Mar. 20, 1909: 196

Orville on parade grounds walking toward his machine, Katharine walking slightly behind him to his left, Fort Myer, Va., 1908.
Everybody's Magazine, v. 20, Jan. 1909: 106

Orville, three-quarter length, wearing derby hat and overcoat, hands in pockets.
Revue de l'aviation, v. 3, Oct. 15, 1908: 10

Orville seated at the controls with passenger Lt. Thomas E. Selfridge in Wright airplane, September 17, 1908.
MCFWP 164; Aeronautics, v. 5, Apr. 1909: 145; Bee-Hive, v. 28, Jan. 1953: CLHAGW b. 168–169; SMIN 42,255–C; SMIN 42, 286–D; SMIN 42,869–E; USAF 48608; WODAKH b. 220–221; World's Work, v. 56, Sept. 1927: 518

Orville and Katharine aboard ship bound for Europe, January 1909.
WRBR 12

Orville, full length, aboard ship, wearing cap and overcoat, cane in right hand.
ADAMSF 82; Vie grand air, v. 15, May 15, 1909: 324

Orville seated in Wright airplane, instructing Count de Lambert and Paul Tissandier in its operation, Pau, 1909.
Vie grand air, v. 15, Mar. 13, 1909: 166. Orville alone: Vie grand air, v. 16, Aug. 21, 1909: 131

Orville and Count de Lambert seated in Wright airplane, Pau, 1909.
Vie grand air, v. 16, Aug. 21, 1909: 131

Orville demonstrating the use of anemometer to Katharine and the Countess de Lambert, Pau, 1909.
Ill Aero Mitteil, v. 13, Feb. 24, 1909: 141

Orville at skids of Wright airplane, in conversation with Hart O. Berg.
World's Work, v. 20, Aug. 1910: 13306

Orville standing in front of Wright airplane, Katharine and Wilbur seated in it, before flight at Pau, February 15, 1909.
Collier's, v. 80, Aug. 20, 1927: 8

Orville in conversation with King Alfonso XIII of Spain, Katharine and large group gathered around, Pau, February 20, 1909.
LC-BECK; Vie grand air, v. 15, Feb. 27, 1909: 136.
Similar: LC-BECK; World's Work, v. 20, Aug. 1910: 13307

Orville and Katharine in the gondola of the balloon *Icare* about to take off on a trip on February 25, 1909.
L'Aérophile, v. 17, Mar. 15, 1909: 139; HILBW 1909: 56

Orville conversing with King Edward VII, March 17, 1909, large group nearby at side and at rear.
LC-BECK; Revue de l'aviation, v. 4, Apr. 1, 1909: cover; TAPHF 34

Orville with King Edward in front of hangar awaiting takeoff of Wilbur on flight, March 17, 1909.
Allg Auto Zeit, v. 10, Mar. 26, 1909: 39

Orville, head and shoulders.
Die Woche, v. 11, Aug. 21, 1909: 1433

Orville, three-quarter length, conversing with five gentlemen gathered around him in front of his Berlin hotel, August 1909.
Die Woche, v. 11, Aug. 28, 1909: 1478

Group photograph of Orville with Gen. von Piessen, Prince Fürstenberg, Kaiser Wilhelm II, Prof. Hugo Hergesell, and Count Ferdinand Zeppelin at Tegel Field, Berlin, August 29, 1909.
Die Woche, v. 11, Sept. 4, 1909: 1523

Gen. Helmuth J. L. von Moltke congratulating Orville following his first public flight in Germany, September 4, 1909.
MILWA, v. 2: 200

Orville walking with Hart O. Berg and Capt. Paul Engelhard, German army, September 1909.
MILWA, v. 2: 200

Orville seated in Wright airplane with Capt. Paul Engelhard, September 1909.
U.S. Air Services, v. 13, Dec. 1928: 34

Orville in conversation with Crown Prince Friedrich Wilhelm, Hart O. Berg standing nearby, Germany, 1909.
Pop Sci, v. 114, Feb. 1929: 43

Orville with Prof. Hugo Hergesell, who flew with him as his passenger, near Wright airplane, Tempelhof Field, Berlin, September 13, 1909.
LC–USZ62–15798 (copy negative)

Orville with Count Zeppelin, before their trip in the dirigible LZ.6 from Frankfurt to Mannheim, September 15, 1909.
LC-BECK

Orville standing next to Hart O. Berg at Wright airplane, a guard stationed at right, Berlin, 1909.
L'Aérophile, v. 17, Sept. 15, 1909: 420

Orville conversing with Count de Lambert following the latter's flight over Paris, October 18, 1909.
FRFH facing 179; Vie grand air, v. 16, Oct. 23, 1909: 298

Orville, half length, seated, facing right.
HILBW 1909: 8; WIGLIG b. 548–549

Orville testing the wind with an anemometer.
Collier's, v. 45, July 2, 1910: 16

Probably Orville, active as instructor, in series of Wright flights, in May-July, just after opening of Wright Flying School, Simms Station, Dayton, 1910. LC–W86–127 shows large crowd of spectators at edge of field, trolley car visible in background.
LC–W86–122 through LC–W86–128

Group photo of flyers, including Duval La Chapelle, Arthur L. Welsh, Orville, James Davis, Ralph Johnstone, and Frank T. Coffyn, Simms Station, Dayton, 1910.
Dayton Herald, May 10, 1910

Orville seated in Wright airplane with Albert B. Lambert before takeoff, Simms Station, Dayton, May 18, 1910.
LC–W86–76; SMIN A43,062; TAPHF 34

Frank Coffyn, Ralph Johnstone, Wilbur, Orville, and Walter Brookins discussing upcoming air show, June 13–18, 1910, at Indianapolis, Ind., Motor Speedway.
Dayton Daily News, May 1910

Orville flying over Dayton in a flight that reached an altitude of 2,000 to 4,000 ft. from Simms Station, September 22, 1910. Balloon ready for ascension on Buck Island and Miami River visible below.
USAF 22444

Orville making the first flight over Dayton—the industrial area of the city visible below from a considerable altitude—Aviation Day, Exposition Week, Dayton, September 22, 1910.
USAF 22447

Orville, head and shoulders.
Aircraft, v. 1, June 1910: 140

Orville and Ralph Johnstone conversing at International Aviation Tournament, Belmont Park, N.Y., October 22–30, 1910.
SMIN 43,009–B; U.S. Air Services, v. 3, Dec. 1923: 19

Orville in front of Wright airplane talking to Ralph Johnstone seated in it just before taking off on record-breaking flight of 9,716 feet altitude, Belmont Park, N.Y., October 1910.
Air-Scout, v. 1, Dec. 1910; cover

Orville and Hubert Latham, Belmont Park, N.Y., October 1910.
LC–USZ62–46702

Orville, full length, wearing derby hat and topcoat, hands in pockets, walking on flying field, Belmont Park, N.Y., October 1910.
Air-Scout, v. 1, Dec. 1910; 14

Group portrait of Orville with German officers and officials of the Flugmaschine Wright company, Adlershof, Germany, November 1910.
Zeit Luft, v. 14, Dec. 14, 1910: 28

Orville, half length, seated, hands clasped together, Berlin, 1910.
LC-BECK; ASHWB 56; Aviation, v. 15, Dec. 17, 1923: 733; Encyclopedia Americana, 1977: 557; Encyclopaedia Britannica, 1976: 1032; HATFYF facing 25; Pegasus, v. 20, Apr. 1953: 8; U.S. Air Services, v. 1, Feb. 1919: 4; U.S. Air Services, v. 6, Dec. 1921: 8; U.S. Air Services, v. 7, Dec. 1922: 7; Who's Who in American Aeronautics, 1922: 167; WODKH facing 34

Orville with Thomas A. Edison when he was Edison's guest at his home at Llewellyn Park, Orange, N.J., December 18, 1913.
Flying, v. 1, Jan. 1914: 25; World's Work, v. 27, Feb. 1914: 365; WRBR 12

Orville in academic procession with Dean Herman Schneider, who presented him with honorary doctor of science degree, University of Cincinnati, June 16, 1917.
SMIN 43,009–E

Orville seated in chair in front of his home at Hawthorn Hill, Dayton, October 1917.
Aerial Age, v. 6, Oct. 15, 1917: 195

Orville with Lord Alfred Northcliffe, arriving in Dayton to present Orville with Albert Medal, October 27, 1917.
Dayton Herald, Oct. 27, 1917

Orville receiving Albert Medal of the Royal Society of Arts from Lord Northcliffe, Dayton, October 27, 1917.
Dayton Journal, Oct. 28, 1917: 1

Orville, half length, wearing derby hat and topcoat, with Katharine, as Lord Alfred Northcliffe presented him with Albert Medal, Dayton, October 27, 1917.
Aerial Age, v. 8, Oct. 21, 1918: 294

Orville, head and shoulders, full face, smiling, wearing derby hat.

Aerial Age, v. 6, Nov. 12, 1917: 373; Aerial Age, v. 13, Mar. 28, 1921: 61; Time, v. 4, Oct. 13, 1924: 22; Time, v. 5, May 11, 1925: 22; Time, v. 6, Oct. 26, 1925: 9

Orville with Howard M. Rinehart, standing beside recently completed Dayton-Wright Co. De Havilland 4 airplane, May 13, 1918. Orville made his last flight as pilot on this date in a Wright 1911 biplane, flying alongside the De Havilland 4 piloted by Howard M. Rinehart.

MCFWP 224; Aerial Age, v. 8, Oct. 21, 1918: 292; Aviation, v. 4, July 1, 1918: cover; GANAC 47; SMIN 30,950-C; SMIN 38,532-C

Orville, head and shoulders, wearing straw hat and bow tie, at Dayton annual meeting of Society of Automotive Engineers, June 17, 1918.

Aerial Age, v. 7, July 1, 1918: 770

Orville, head and shoulders, wearing fedora hat, broad smile, on day of annual meeting of Society of Automotive Engineers, Dayton, June 17, 1918.

Aviation, v. 4, July 1, 1918: 765

Orville, three-quarter length, with Col. Milton F. Davis, Col. Edward A. Deeds, and Lt. Harold H. Emmons, 1919.

SMIN 42,926

Orville, Capt. Eddie Rickenbacker, and Maj. Rudolph Schroeder when Orville met Rickenbacker for the first time, May 19, 1919.

SMIN A789

Lt. James H. Doolittle, Maj. Angel M. Zuloaga, Orville, and Juan G. Villasana outside the National Cash Register Company, Dayton, early 1920s.

SMIN 42,667–F

Orville feeding Scipio, a St. Bernard dog and family pet he acquired in March 1917, February 1921.

U.S. Air Services, v. 39, Dec. 1954: 10. Similar: Orville with Scipio: LC–W86–149; Scipio alone: LC–W86–145.

Group portrait of Orville with fellow members of the National Advisory Committee for Aeronautics following interview with President Warren G. Harding, in front of the White House, April 21, 1921.

Aerial Age, v. 13, May 2, 1921: 172; U.S. Air Services, v. 5, May 1921: 13

Orville with Katharine, Percy MacKaye, and Vilhjalmur Stefansson in new flying boat *Wilbur Wright,* just christened by Katharine, preparing for an initial flight over the Hudson River, September 26, 1922.

> **U.S. Air Services, v. 7, Dec. 1922: cover. Similar:**
> **ASHWB 78; Orville only: SMIN 43,061–C**

Orville, head and shoulders, seated in open Cadillac with Adm. William F. Fullam and William (Billy) Mitchell at Pulitzer Air Races, Detroit, October 7–14, 1922.

> **USAF 10672 A.S.**

Frederick B. Patterson, president, National Aeronautic Association, presenting National Aeronautic medal to Orville, part of the observance of the 20th anniversary of the Wright brothers' first flight at Kitty Hawk, N.C., 1903, on front steps of Orville's home, Dayton, December 17, 1923.

> **LOOWGF 36; Nat Aero Assn Rev, v. 2, Jan. 1, 1924: 1**

Orville, three-quarter length, and Elmer Sperry, 1924.

> **National Aeronautic Review, v. 2, Oct. 8, 1924: 5**

Orville, three-quarter length, as he appeared when he testified before the President's Aircraft Board, Washington, October 12, 1925.

> **U.S. Air Services, v. 10, Nov. 1925: 21**

Orville, full length, standing by the 1925 Collier Trophy, which, as chairman of the Contest Committee, National Aeronautic Association, he presented to S. Albert Reed, with Earl Findley at his left; George W. Lewis, Porter Adams, Gen. James E. Fechet, and Godfrey L. Cabot at Orville's right, March 19, 1926.

> **Nat Aero Assn Rev, v. 4, Apr. 1926: 57; SMIN 42,418**

Orville with Comdr. Richard E. Byrd, in Dayton to deliver a lecture, November 19, 1926.

> **Dayton Daily News, Nov. 19, 1926**

Orville, full length, with members of the National Aeronautic Association Contest Committee at association headquarters, Washington, January 20, 1927.

> **Nat Aero Assn Rev, v. 5, Feb. 1927: cover**

Orville and Dr. Michael I. Pupin, Orville's house guest when in Dayton to deliver a lecture, May 3, 1927.

> **Dayton News, May 4, 1927**

Orville, Maj. John F. Curry, and Col. Charles Lindbergh, who came to pay Orville a personal call, at Wright Field, Dayton, June 22, 1927.

> **LC–USZ62–56734; LC–W86–103; MCFWP 206. Similar: LC–W86–174**

Orville, Maj. John F. Curry, and Charles Lindbergh at Wright
Field, Dayton, June 22, 1927.

Orville on boardwalk approaching flag-raising ceremonies, where
he was the first to raise the flag at dedication of Wright Field,
Dayton, October 12, 1927.
USAF 33356

Orville, full length, holding fedora hat in right hand at side.
Aeronautic Review, v. 6, Aug. 1928: 114

Orville and Charles L. Lawrance, three-quarter length, when both were honored at luncheon and reception by the Philadelphia Chamber of Commerce, May 16, 1928.
Wright Engine Builder, v. 10, Dec. 1928: cover.

Orville, seated, wearing striped suit, with Lt. Albert Hegenberger, and Charles L. Lawrance, when Lawrance was presented with the Franklin Institute Cresson Medal, Franklin Institute, May 16, 1928.
SMIN 42,928–F

Porter Adams, president, National Aeronautic Association, Orville, three-quarter length, chairman, Contest Committee, and Maj. Charles A. Lutz, standing before the Curtiss Marine Trophy won by Lutz, Naval Air Station, Anacostia, Md., May 19, 1928.
Aeronautic Review, v. 6, June 1928: cover

Group photograph when Orville, a member, attended meeting of administrators of the Daniel Guggenheim Fund for the Promotion of Aeronautics, Inc., at home of Harry F. Guggenheim, Port Washington, Long Island, June 15, 1928.
HAWBHP 98; SMIN A3519

Orville, secretary, National Aeronautic Association's Committee of Awards, presenting second Gordon Bennett International Balloon Trophy to Assistant Secretary of War F. Trubee Davison, who accepts it on behalf of the Army Air Corps, November 8, 1928.
Aviation, v. 10, Nov. 17, 1928: 1570; SMIN A42,928

Orville, full length, standing beside Gordon Bennett International Balloon Trophy, Porter Adams at his left, Assistant Secretary of War F. Trubee Davison, Brig. Gen. Benjamin D. Foulois, and Ray Cooper at his right; at presentation ceremonies, November 8, 1928.
Aeronautic Review, v. 6, Nov. 1928: cover

Orville, three-quarter length, with Capt. John A. Macready and Lord Thomson, Dayton, December 10, 1928.
Dayton Daily News, Dec. 10, 1928

Group portrait including Orville and the many delegates to the International Civil Aeronautics Conference, held in Washington, D.C., December 12–14, who came to Dayton to honor him, taken on steps of Orville's home, December 10, 1928.
Dayton Journal, Dec. 11, 1928; USAF 35485

Orville and William F. Whiting, half length, standing, at opening session, International Civil Aeronautics Conference, Washington, D.C., December 12, 1928.
LC–USZ62–46704 (copy negative)

Orville, seated with Dr. William F. Durand at his left and
Daniel Guggenheim and John D. Ryan at his right, met with the
members and trustees of the Daniel Guggenheim Fund for the
Promotion of Aeronautics (which in 1930 established the
Division of Aeronautics in the Library of Congress) at Port
Washington, Long Island, on June 15, 1928. National Air and
Space Museum, Smithsonian Institution, photo no. A3519.

Orville standing behind Charles Lindbergh in the Chamber of
Commerce Building, when Lindbergh received the Harmon Trophy, Washington, D.C., December 13, 1928.
        U.S. Air Services, v. 14, Jan. 1929: 25

Orville, head and shoulders, wearing flying clothes with aviator's
helmet.
        **Liberty, v. 53, Dec. 22, 1918: 17; Pop Sci, v. 114, Apr.
        1929: 42; Time, v. 12, Dec. 3, 1928: cover**

Orville, head and shoulders, facing right, Dayton, 1928.
        **LC-BECK; Aerosphere, 1943: facing CV; Canadian Avi-
        ation, v. 16, Dec. 1943: 61; EIDWHS facing 8;
        Scientific Monthly, v. 42, June 1936: 569; SMIN
        42,731; U.S. Air Services, v. 28, Dec. 1943: 23. Similar,
        full face: LC-BECK; U.S. Air Services, v. 13, Mar.
        1928: 30**

Orville with aviation authorities who inspected the proposed markers for use on civil airways, displayed on the roof of the Commerce Building, Washington, December 14, 1928.
>**SMIN 43,037-A**

Orville, with Senators Simeon D. Fess and Theodore E. Burton of Ohio, Senators Furnifold M. Simmons and Lee S. Overman of North Carolina, and Senator Hiram Bingham of Connecticut, when Orville was honored on the floor of the Senate, December 15, 1928.
>**LC-USZ62–46710 (copy negative); SMIN 43,037**

Orville attending the unveiling by Senator Hiram Bingham of a granite boulder with memorial marker on the site of the Wrights' December 1903 flights, December 17, 1928.
>**MCMWB 306; MILWA, v. 2: 312; Pop Sci, v. 114, Apr. 1929: 44. Similar: U.S. Air Services, v. 14, Jan. 1929: 31**

Orville, head and shoulders, full face, turned to left.
>**Aeronautic Review, v. 6, Dec. 1928: cover; Airway Age, v. 9, Dec. 1928: 17; Pop Sci, v. 114, May 1929: 49; Schweizer Aero-Revue, v. 28, Dec. 1953: 417; SMIN 38,346; U.S. Air Services, v. 13, Dec. 1928: 24**

Orville, half length, full face, in formal dress with white tie, 1928.
>**LC-BECK; SMIN 42,928–E; Washington Post, Dec. 18, 1928**

Orville receiving the Distinguished Flying Cross from Secretary of War Dwight F. Davis, Assistant Secretary of War for Aeronautics F. Trubee Davison at Orville's right, February 27, 1929.
>**LC-USZ62–46703 (copy negative); Dayton Herald, Feb. 28, 1929; MILWA, v. 2: 313; Pop Sci, v. 114, June 1929: 53; Washington Evening Star, Feb. 27, 1929**

Orville talking to Harold F. Pitcairn at side of the Pitcairn autogiro, at the Fourth Annual Aircraft Engineering Research Conference of the National Advisory Committee for Aeronautics, Langley Field, Va., May 14, 1929.
>**Science News Letter, v. 15, May 25, 1929: cover**

Orville with Harold M. Harter, Brig. Gen. Benjamin D. Foulois, Clarence M. Young, and J. Muller at dinner in Orville's honor attended by high-ranking federal and state government officials, Dayton, February 25, 1930.
>**Dayton Journal, Feb. 26, 1930**

Orville receiving the Daniel Guggenheim Medal from Dr. William Durand, Chamber of Commerce Building, Washington, D.C., April 8, 1930.
>**LC-USZ62–46708 (copy negative); Dayton News, Apr. 10, 1930; National Aeronautic Review, v. 8, May 1930: 43**

Orville and visitor, Sir Capt. Hubert Wilkins, Dayton, May 20, 1930.
Dayton News, May 21, 1930; SMIN A3413

Dr. George W. Rightmire presenting Orville with honorary doctor of science degree from Ohio State University, Columbus, June 10, 1930.
Dayton News, June 11, 1930

Orville standing before portrait painting of Bishop Milton Wright which was presented to Wilbur Wright Junior High School, Dayton, April 16, 1931.
Dayton News, Apr. 17, 1931

Orville, three-quarter length, with Mrs. Amelia Earhart Putnam, Franklin Institute, December 16, 1933.
Today, v. 1, Mar. 31, 1934: 8

Orville at work on baggage lift at his summer home on Lambert Island, Georgian Bay, Canada, 1936.
ANDWF 587

In the office of Orville's laboratory in Dayton in 1937, Orville and Charles E. Taylor (center) show blueprints of the original Wright home and workshop to Henry Ford (right), who was working on their restoration.

Orville, head and shoulders, with a broad smile, wearing straw hat.
Time, v. 27, May 11, 1936: 44

Orville with Lorin Wright, Fred Black, Edward Cutter, and Henry Ford studying drawings for the planned restoration of the Wright bicycle shop, October 27, 1936.
Dayton Journal, October 28, 1936

Orville and Henry Ford on porch of former Wright home, 7 Hawthorn Street, (during negotiations for removal of home and Wright shop, 1127 West Third Street, to Dearborn, Mich.), Dayton, October 27, 1936.
LC-BECK; Dayton Journal, October 28, 1936

Lorin Wright, Edsel Ford, Orville, Henry Ford, Gov. James M. Cox, and friends outside the Wright home as they met for luncheon, Dayton, October 27, 1936.
Dayton Herald, October 27, 1936

Orville with Glenn L. Martin, when Orville visited and inspected the Glenn L. Martin factory, Baltimore, Md., November 12, 1936.
U.S. Air Services, v. 23, Jan. 1938: 19

Orville photographed in front of his home with fellow members of the Executive Committee, National Advisory Committee for Aeronautics, meeting there, December 17, 1936.
USAF 55537; USAF 55538

Group portrait of Orville with Gen. Augustine W. Robins, Col. Frederick W. Martin, Eugene Vidal, William P. McCracken, and Edward P. Warner, Wright Field, December 18, 1936.
USAF 55555

Orville and Col. Frederick W. Martin at Wright Field, December 18, 1936.
USAF 55553; USAF 55554; USAF 55556

Col. Edward A. Deeds, Orville, Henry Ford, and Charles F. Kettering, about 1937.
MARCD following 344

Orville, Charles E. Taylor, and Henry Ford poring over blueprints of Wright home and workshop in office of Orville's laboratory, Dayton, 1937.
MCFWP 207; Detroit News, Apr. 17, 1938; SMIN 38,496–E

Orville, three-quarter length, right hand raised to chin, looking right; photograph taken by Henry Ford, Greenfield Village, Dearborn, Mich., 1937.
U.S. Air Services, v. 41, Aug. 1956: 4

Orville, three-quarter length, hands clasped together, facing right, unidentified person with him with back to camera, Dearborn, Mich., 1937.
LC-BECK

Orville, Charles E. Taylor, and Henry Ford looking over drawings of the Wright shop engine, Greenfield Village, Dearborn, Mich., 1937.
LC-BECK

Charles E. Taylor and Orville at drafting table, Greenfield Village, Dearborn, Mich., 1937.
SMIN 21,020

Orville with Capt. William J. Tate, at time of meeting of National Advisory Committee for Aeronautics, Washington, D.C., 1937.
Washington Herald, Dec. 17, 1937

Orville, head and shoulders, leaving meeting of the Institute of the Aeronautical Sciences, Columbia University, New York, December 17, 1937.
New York Times, Dec. 18, 1937

Orville with A. D. Etheridge, Capt. William J. Tate, and John T. Daniels, at dedication of restored Wright home and workshop in Greenfield Village, Dearborn, Mich., April 16, 1938.
American Aviation, v. 1, May 1, 1938: 10; EIDWHS facing 26

Orville with members of the Wright family attending dedication of the restored Wright home and workshop in Greenfield Village, Dearborn, Mich., April 16.
Detroit News, Apr. 17, 1938

Henry Ford, Orville, and Charles F. Kettering seated at banquet table following dedication of the restored Wright home and workshop in Greenfield Village, Dearborn, Mich., April 16.
American Aviation, v. 1, May 1, 1938: 10; EIDWHS facing 45; U.S. Air Services, v. 23, May 1938: 12

Orville at speaker's table with many friends and associates at dinner honoring Wilbur and Orville, Dearborn, Mich., April 16.
EIDWHS facing 45; U.S. Air Services, v. 23, May 1938: 12

Orville, Charles E. Taylor, and four of the first military pupils of the Wright brothers, Col. Charles de F. Chandler, Maj. Gen. Benjamin D. Foulois, Col. Frank P. Lahm, and Col. Frederick E. Humphreys, at celebration, Dearborn, Mich., April 16.
EIDWHS facing 36; American Aviation, v. 1, May 1, 1938: 10

Franklin Delano Roosevelt, Orville, and former governor of Ohio
James M. Cox ride in the president's car to inspect Wright
Field, Dayton, on October 12, 1940.

Griffith Brewer, Orville, and Col. Frank P. Lahm conversing at
Greenfield Village, Dearborn, Mich., April 16.
American Aviation, v. 1, May 1, 1938: 10

Group portrait of Orville with laboratory staff of the National
Advisory Committee for Aeronautics, Langley Field, Va.,
April 17, 1939.
**Pegasus, v. 20, Apr. 1953: 11; U.S. Air Services, v. 24,
May 1939: 14**

Orville with Benny Howard, pilot, Maj. Carl A. Cover, and
William F. Mentzer, before a thirty-minute flight over Dayton
in a Douglas DC-4 aircraft, June 9, 1939.
Bee-Hive, v. 28, Jan. 1953: 15

Orville climbing aboard DC-4 transport aircraft as passenger on
a thirty-minute flight over Dayton, June 9, 1939.
Bee-Hive, v. 28, Jan. 1953: 14

Capt. Kenneth Whiting, U.S.N., Col. Edward A. Deeds, Orville, and Gen. Henry H. Arnold, 1940.
MARCD facing 252

Orville holding in his left hand Honorary U.S. Aircraft Pilot's Certificate No. 1, presented to him on August 19, 1940.
Airman, v. 6, Sept. 1962: 9

Orville seated on platform at dedication of Wilbur and Orville Wright Memorial, Dayton, August 19, 1940.
U.S. Air Services, v. 25, Sept. 1940: 11

President Franklin D. Roosevelt, Orville, and publisher and former Ohio governor James M. Cox in the president's automobile during an inspection tour of Wright Field, Dayton, October 12, 1940.
Dayton Daily News, October 12, 1940

Orville, half length, seated with hands resting on desk, holding reading glasses, Hawthorn Hill, Dayton, August 1943.
LC-BECK

Orville seated at work table in South Room, Orville's laboratory, 15 North Broadway, Dayton, November 17, 1943.
LC-BECK; SMIN 43,009–D

Orville and Gen. Franklin O. Carrol in Air Force Technical Data Museum, Dayton, December 23, 1943.
USAF 132389

Three photos of Orville with Gen. Franklin O. Carrol at Wright Field aviation exhibit and exercises, December 23, 1943.
USAF 142888; USAF 142894; USAF 142898

Orville at Wright Field boarding an Army C-69 Lockheed Constellation airplane for demonstration flight over Dayton, April 26, 1944.
New York Times, Apr. 28, 1944

Orville in the company of Maj. Gen. Benjamin W. Chidlaw, Col. Edward A. Deeds, and Maj. Gen. Lawrence C. Craigie viewing Air Force flying demonstration at the AAF Fair, Wright Field, Dayton, October 12, 1945.
MARCD facing 352

Col. Edward A. Deeds, Lt. Gen. George C. Kenney, and Orville, half length, about 1945.
MARCD facing 352

Orville seated at his desk looking at world globe at his left, August 17, 1946.
LC-BECK. Similar, facing forward: LC-BECK; U.S. Air Services, v. 33, Feb. 1948: 7

Orville seated at his laboratory desk with original 1901 wind-tunnel balance (lost since move from 1127 West Third Street to 15 North Broadway, December 6, 1916) found on December 9, 1946, in the attic of his laboratory, Dayton, December 13, 1946.
LC-BECK; MCFWP 203; MEFMF facing 119; U.S. Air Services, v. 32, Jan. 1947: 17

Orville with Col. and Mrs. Edward A. Deeds and other guests, Deeds Day Celebration, Denison University, Granville, Ohio, May 3, 1947.
MARCD facing 353. Same occasion: Mrs. Deeds and Orville only; MARCD following 324

Orville, half length, holding military aircraft model made by him.
Rotarian, v. 72, Apr. 1948: 8

Orville, head and shoulders, full face.
ANDWF 585

Orville seated with a trophy at his right and a photograph of the Wilbur Wright Monument, Le Mans, France, on wall of his Hawthorn Hill home, Dayton.
ANDWF 604

Orville in his laboratory at 15 North Broadway, Dayton, in December 1946, with a wind tunnel balance constructed in 1901.

Bishop Milton Wright
(November 17, 1828–April 3, 1917)

Bishop Wright, head and shoulders, clerical collar, black tie.
**Dayton Journal, Aug. 14, 1908; Dayton Journal,
June 13, 1909; THOOB facing 525**

Bishop Wright, head and shoulders, clerical collar, head turned
to right.
**Birmingham Ledger, Oct. 1, 1908; COCKDH following
168; HILBW 6**

Bishop Wright, head and shoulders, clerical collar, head turned
slightly to right, 1889.
**DHCUBC facing 416; EWBNM 4; KELMKH
b. 238–239; The Religious Telescope, Dec. 23, 1908: 8**

Oval portrait of Bishop Wright, head facing to left.
Chicago Record-Herald, Oct. 18, 1908: 3

Bishop Wright, head and shoulders, clerical collar, white tie,
facing left.
**ADAMSF 66; KRBCUBC 61; SMIN 31,299–A;
World's Work, v. 20, Aug. 1910: 13307**

Bishop Wright, head and shoulders, clerical collar, head turned
slightly to left, about 1909.
MCFWP 1 (from family photo)

Wright family group portrait, full length, standing: Lorin, Wilbur, Bishop Wright, Orville, and Charles Taylor, their mechanic.
Dayton Journal, May 14, 1909

Bishop Wright delivering invocation at ceremony in which gold
medals were presented to Wilbur and Orville, Dayton, June 18,
1909.
MILWA v. 2: 178

Bishop Wright, head and shoulders, side view, head turned to
right, Dayton, 1910.
**LC-BECK; Christian Conservator, May 16, 1917: 1;
Dayton Daily News, Apr. 2, 1917: 161; The Telescope,
Apr. 11, 1917: 1**

Bishop Wright, head and shoulders, front view, clerical collar, white tie, taken by Jan Reece, Dayton, June 1910.
LC-BECK

Bishop Milton Wright and Reuchlin Wright, photographed after witnessing flight by Orville, Fort Myer, Va., July 1, 1909.
Washington Herald, July 1, 1909: 1; Washington Post, July 2, 1909: 2

Bishop Wright, in receiving line next to Orville and Wilbur at Homecoming Celebration for them, Dayton, June 1909.
Collier's, v. 80, Aug. 20, 1927: 9

Distant high-altitude view of Bishop Wright during his first ride in an airplane, when Orville attained an altitude of 350 feet, May 25, 1910.
LC-W86-124

Bishop Wright, three-quarter length, facing left.
The Telescope, Dec. 31, 1914: 1

Bishop Wright, head and shoulders, facing left.
The Telescope, Apr. 1, 1917: 12

Bishop Wright, head and shoulders, facing right.
Missionary Monthly, v. 21, May 1917:1

Portrait painting of Bishop Wright, age about 50, by Don Wallace, from an original photograph.
ASHWB 10; Dayton News, Apr. 15, 1931; Dayton News, Apr. 17, 1931; MCMWB 40; MILWA v. 2: 98; Pop Sci, v. 144, Jan. 1929: 19; SMIN A4441-B; SMIN 31,299-A; U.S. Air Services, v. 16, Dec. 1931: 21; Vie grand air, v. 15, Apr. 3, 1909: 228

Bishop Wright, head and shoulders, clerical collar, white tie, head facing forward.
ANDWF 548

Group picture of Orville, Bishop Wright, Katharine, Earl N. Findley, and nephew Horace Wright, all seated, on the lawn of Orville's home, Hawthorn Hill, 1915.
LC-W86-164; MCFWP 205. Similar photos of group on porch, on steps, and on walk of Orville's home on same occasion with John R. McMahon and Pliny Williamson added: LC-W86-163; LC-W86-165; LC-W86-166

Katharine Wright Haskell
(August 19, 1874–March 3, 1929)

Katharine, age about five, standing, three-quarter length, posing for commercial photographer.
> **Pop Sci, v. 114, Jan. 1929: 18; SMIN A4441–C**

Katharine, head and shoulders, facing right, wearing white high collar dress with leg-of-mutton sleeves, taken about the time of her graduation from Oberlin College in 1898.
> **Birmingham Ledger, Oct. 1, 1908 (one of the first published photographs of Katharine); Dayton Daily News, May 13, 1909; Dayton Journal, June 13, 1909; Dayton Daily News, June 16, 1909; KELMKH b. 238–239; St. Louis Star, June 6, 1909. Similar: facing forward, COCKDH following 168**

Katharine lying on ground, covered by a blanket, her friend Harriet Silliman in chair nearby, in wooded area, at camp, 1899.
> **LC–W85–58**

Oberlin College reception, group photo.
> **LC–W85–13; LC–W85–14**

Katharine and Harriet Silliman, seated near fireplace, September 1899.
> **LC–W85–73**

Katharine and Harriet Silliman, busy in kitchen, September 1899.
> **LC–W85–74**

Katharine and Harriet Silliman, half length, smiling and facing each other.
> **LC–W85–11**

Katharine, Harriet Silliman, and Agnes Osborn in horse-drawn carriage across from Wright home, 7 Hawthorn Street, Dayton.
> **LC–USZ62–66293; LC–W85–37**

Group photos of Oberlin class of 1898, June 29, 1900.
> **LC–W85–33; LC–W85–34**

Orville with his father, Bishop Milton Wright, his sister
Katharine, his friend Earl N. Findley, and his nephew Horace
on the lawn of Hawthorn Hill in 1915.

Katharine with broad smile, head and shoulders, from an infor-
mal family snapshot, about 1900.
MCFWP 2; EWBNM 4

Photograph of Orville, Katharine, and Wilbur with Katharine
wearing large hat and long striped suit coat and striped skirt,
France, 1909.
**FWGWA 4; HILBW 55; Vie grand air, v. 15, Mar. 20,
1909: 195**

Orville and Katharine in the gondola of the balloon *Icare,*
piloted by Ernest Zens, about to take off, February 25, 1909.
**L'Aérophile, v. 17, Mar. 15, 1909: 139; HILBW
1909: 56**

Group photo including Louis Blériot, Paul Tissandier, Capt.
Paul N. Lucas-Girardville, Wilbur, Mrs. Hart O. Berg, Count
Charles de Lambert, and Katharine, Pau.
**Allg Auto Zeit, v. 10, Feb. 21, 1909: 39; HEGOV fac-
ing 97; Revue aérienne, v. 2, Feb. 25, 1909: facing 105;
Vie grand air, v. 15, May 29, 1909: 356**

Katharine Wright with Harriet Silliman, September 1899.

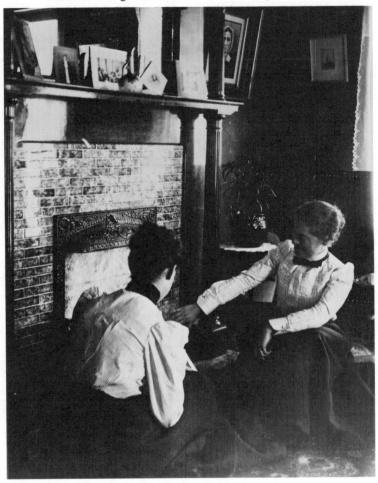

Orville, Katharine, and Wilbur promenading on the boulevard, Wilbur and Orville wearing dark suits, hats, and coats, Orville with cane, Katharine wearing large hat, suit, stole, and muff, Pau.

> **LC-BECK; Similar, Katharine without stole and muff and carrying pocketbook: Flight, v. 1, Mar. 20, 1909 (suppl.): 11; Vie grand air, v. 15, Jan. 30, 1909: 72**

Katharine seated in airplane next to Wilbur on the occasion of her first ride in an airplane, Pau, February 15, 1909.

> **LC-BECK; COCKDH following 168; Collier's, v. 80, Aug. 20, 1927: 8; MCMWB 220; MEFMF facing 103; MILWA v. 2: 172; SMIN 42,783–L**

Large group with Katharine, wearing large hat, long suit, stole, and muff, King Alfonso of Spain, in center facing right, and Orville, to the right of the king with a cane, at time of king's visit to Pau, February 20, 1909.

    LC-BECK. Similar, with king turned left toward Katharine: LC-BECK; World's Work, v. 20, Aug. 1910: 13307

Katharine, full length in long dark suit, stole, and muff, conversing with Pierre Gasnier and Hubert Latham, France.

    Aircraft, v. 1, Dec. 1910: 361

Group photo of Wright brothers and Katharine at luncheon as guests of Frank Hedges Butler, prominent balloonist, Carlton Hotel, London, May 3, 1909.

    MILWA v. 2: 177

Orville and Katharine en route home from Europe, at Plymouth, England.

    N.Y. Evening Telegram, May 5, 1909

Orville, Katharine, wearing hat covered with duster veil, and Wilbur on arrival from Europe, aboard ship *Kronprinzessin Cecilie,* New York, May 11, 1909.

    Am R Rs, v. 39, June 1909: 656; MILWA v. 2: 177; N.Y. World, May 12, 1909; SMIN 42,805-A. Similar: Katharine and Wilbur only, SMIN 42,804-G

Orville, Wilbur, and Katharine, with A. Holland Forbes, acting president of the Aero Club of America, on arrival from Europe, New York.

    Dayton Journal, May 11, 1909

Group photo taken when President William Howard Taft presented Wilbur, appearing at his right, and Orville, at his left, with Aero Club of America gold medals, Katharine wearing white dress also at the president's left, the White House, June 10, 1909.

    MCFWP 181; MARWBC 49; Aero Club Am Bul, v. 1, July 1912: 20–21; Pop Sci, v. 114, June 1929: 53; Washington Herald, June 11, 1909: 1; WRBR 13; YPHA 36

Group portrait of Wright family—including Milton Wright, Mrs. Milton Wright, Lorin Wright, Katharine, Reuchlin Wright, Orville, and Wilbur—gathered for Wright brothers' Homecoming Celebration, Dayton, June 1909.

    Dayton Herald, June 16, 1909

Katharine, at right, watches preparations for Orville's flight, Fort Myer, Va., July 30, 1909.

    Nat Geog Mag, v. 112, Aug. 1957: 268

Katharine, at left, in white dress, carrying pocketbook, with Orville, Fort Myer, Va., 1909.

    MILWA v. 2: 158

Katharine on right, in white dress and hat, Orville, in center, and friend, at left, Fort Myer, Va., 1909.
MILWA v. 2: 188

Katharine, head and shoulders, wearing striped suit, dark collar, and hat covered with duster veil.
Aircraft, v. 1, Mar. 1910: 21. Similar, three-quarter length: World's Work, v. 58, Dec. 1928: 80

Orville, Wilbur, and Katharine, side view, Belmont Park, N.Y., October 1910.
Aero blue book 1919: 28

Orville and Katharine, wearing leather jacket, cap, and goggles, in Wright airplane model HS, 1915.
LC–USZ62–56222; LC–W85–129; MCFWP 221

Katharine Wright, wearing a leather jacket, cap, and goggles, aboard the Wright Model HS airplane with Orville, 1915.

Orville, Katharine, and Lord Northcliffe, at presentation by Northcliffe to Orville of the Albert Medal of the Royal Society of Arts, Dayton, October 27, 1917.
Aerial Age Weekly, v. 8, Oct. 21, 1918: 294; Dayton News, Oct. 28, 1917:1

Percy MacKaye, Vilhjalmur Stefansson, Orville, Katharine, and Frederick H. Becker, pilot, in flying boat *Wilbur Wright.*
Dayton Daily News, Sept. 28, 1922

Percy MacKaye, Vilhjalmur Stefansson, Orville, and Katharine seated with bouquet of flowers in flying boat *Wilbur Wright,* christened by her in ceremony in New York, September 26, 1922.
U.S. Air Services, v. 7, Dec. 1922: cover

Katharine with Maj. Gen. Mason M. Patrick at door of Wright home, December 17, 1923.
Nat Aero Assn Rev, v. 2, Jan. 1, 1924: 1

Katharine in oval portrait, looking to right, head and shoulders, in news item when she was appointed an officer of France's Instruction Publique, March 10, 1924
Nat Aero Assn Rev, v. 2, May 1, 1924: 2

Katharine and Mrs. Mario Calderara, taken when Commander and Mrs. Calderara were Orville's house guests, Dayton, October 3–5, 1924.
Nat Aero Assn Rev, v. 2, Oct. 8, 1924: 4

Katharine, head and shoulders, wearing black dress with square neck, at time of her marriage to Henry J. Haskell (associate editor of the Kansas City *Star*), Oberlin, Ohio, November 20, 1926.
Dayton Journal, Nov. 20, 1926; Dayton News, Nov. 20, 1926

Views of Katharine Wright Haskell burial, Dayton, March 6, 1929.
Dayton Journal, Mar. 7, 1929

Photograph of oil paintings of Katharine presented to Wilbur Wright Junior High School, Dayton, April 29, 1938.
ANDWF 586; Dayton Journal, Apr. 29, 1938; Dayton News, Apr. 29, 1938

Wright Brothers Gliding Experiments and Flights

1900, Kitty Hawk, North Carolina

Views of Kitty Hawk, N.C., photographed by the Wright brothers in the vicinity of their 1900 camp, where they conducted their first gliding experiments in October.
> **LC–W85–89; LC–W85–93; LC–W85–103; LC–W85–104; LC–W85–106**

Kitty Hawk Bay viewed from Wrights' 1900 camp.
> **LC–W85–109; KELWB facing 148. Similar: LC–W85–108**

Hill between Kitty Hawk and Kill Devil Hill.
> **LC–W85–102**

Kill Devil Hill.
> **LC–W85–107**

Surf at Kitty Hawk.
> **LC–W85–83; LC–W85–94; LC–W85–95**

Captain William J. Tate, the Wrights' first host in Kitty Hawk, and family on porch of Kitty Hawk Post Office, which was also his home.
> **LC–USZ62–66298; LC–W85–87; MOORKH 118**

Captain Tate and wife standing in front of Kitty Hawk Post Office.
> **LC–W85–88; COCKDH following 168**

Home of Captain Tate, where the Wright brothers stayed until their camp was ready, September 13 to October 2.
> **U.S. Air Services, v. 28, Dec. 1943: 13**

Long-range view of Kitty Hawk Life Saving Station and Weather Bureau Station.
> **LC–W85–98**

Kitty Hawk seven-member lifesaving crew.
> **LC–USZ62–66295; LC–W85–91; LC–W85–92; Lithopinion, v. 6, Winter 1971: 63**

The Wright brothers' camp at Kitty Hawk,
North Carolina, in 1900.

Lifesaving crew at practice in ocean, distant view.
> LC-W85-99; LC-W85-100

Wright brothers' camp close to the village of Kitty Hawk, two
groups of scraggy trees to the left, side view of their tent at
right.
> LC-USZ62-56237; LC-W85-90; MCFWP 15;
> EWBNM 15; KELWB facing 138; U.S. Air Services,
> v. 28, Dec. 1943: 13; WODKH b. 34-35. Similar:
> LC-W85-105

Close-up view of Wright brothers' tent, a half mile from Captain Tate's home.
> LC-W85-101; U.S. Air Services, v. 28, Dec. 1943: 13

Tom Tate, son of Captain Tate's half-brother Daniel Tate, posing with drum fish in front of Wright 1900 glider.
> LC-USZ62-56239; LC-W85-86; MCFWP 16;
> EWBNM 15; MOORKH 119

Left side view of the Wright 1900 glider, before installation of
forward horizontal control surface, flying as a kite, tipped forward; Kitty Hawk Life Saving Station and Weather Bureau
buildings in background to the left.
> LC-USZ62-56238; LC-W85-96; MCFWP 14; Aero-
> sphere, 1943: CXXX; GSREA b. 44-45; GSEFM;
> GSPA 22; MCMWB 84; MILWA v. 2: 100; Sat Eve
> Post, v. 201, July 7, 1928: 11; SMIN A30, 905 1/2;
> SMIN 38, 530-L; W Soc Eng J, v. 6, Dec. 1901: 496,
> World's Work, v. 20; Aug. 1910: 13312

Left side view of glider flying as a kite, in level flight.
LC-USZ62-5645; LC-W85-97; HARFF 36;
HAWBHP 59

Crumpled glider wrecked by wind on Hill of the Wreck (named
after a shipwreck), October 10.
LC-USZ62-66264; LC-W85-85; MCFWP 17;
EWBNM 17; MOORKH 121

1901, Kitty Hawk, North Carolina

Kill Devil Hill views, including back side view and view from
top.
LC-W85-110; LC-W85-116; LC-W85-119

Wrights rebuilding their glider in wooden shed erected in July to
serve as a workshop and to house the glider in bad weather,
August.
LC-W85-114; MCFWP 18; EWBNM 22

Front view of the glider outside shed—the vertical "trussing
posts" visible on the lower wing—August.
LC-PWOW 120; MCFWP 20

Close-up and distant views of camp.
LC-W85-117; LC-W85-118

Wilbur with visitors and fellow campers in front of Wrights'
work shed: Edward C. Huffaker and Octave Chanute seated,
Wilbur standing, and George Spratt sitting on ground.
LC-W85-124; MCFWP 27; EWBNM 18; WODKH
b. 34-35

Group picture similar to preceding with Chanute, Orville, and
Huffaker seated at left and Wilbur standing.
LC-USZ62-66297; LC-W85-122; DOBOHA 162;
LOCA 275; MCMWB 100; MOORKH 123; SMIN 31,
205-B; SUBDF 166; U.S. Air Services, v. 28, Dec.
1943: 13; Vie grand air, v. 15, Apr. 17, 1909: 259

Front view of glider being flown as a kite, Wilbur at left side
and Orville at right.
LC-USZ62-65043; LC-W85-112; MCFWP 21

Side view of glider flying as a kite near ground, Wilbur at left
and Orville at right, glider turned forward to right and tipped
downward.
LC-USZ62-56234; LC-W85-121; MCFWP 22; FAA
World, v. 8, Jan. 1978: 12; HARFF 42; HAYPA 111;
Revue de l'aviation, v. 2, Jan. 1907: 8; Schweizer Aero-
Revue, v. 28, Dec. 1953: 421; Sci Am, v. 94, Apr. 7,
1906: 291; SMIN 41,153; SMIN 73-1859. Similar photo showing only front rudder: LC-W85-113

Wilbur in the camp building at Kill Devil Hill, before its remodeling. The skids and front rudder of the 1901 glider are suspended from the rafters at right.

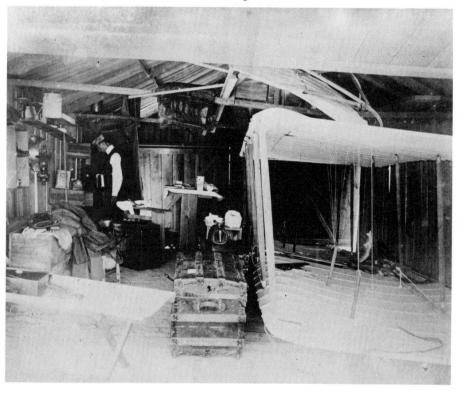

Glider soaring, photograph made from an out-of-focus, water-damaged negative.
LC–W85–126; MCFWP 23; W Soc Eng J, v. 6, Dec. 1901: 509

Front view of Dan Tate, at left, and Huffaker, at right, launching the glider with Orville or Wilbur in it.
LC–USZ62–65152; LC–W85–125; MCFWP 24; Aero Digest, v. 13, Dec. 1928: 1105; Aerosphere, 1943: CXXX; BBAKH; EWBNM 20; HAWBHP 60; Liberty, v. 53, Dec. 22, 1928: 16; MILWA v. 2: 101; Revue de l'aviation, v. 2, Jan. 1907: 10; SMIN 30, 906–E; SMIN A42, 413–F; SMINAR 1902: facing 139; W Soc Eng J, v. 6, Dec. 1901: 497

Orville at left wing end of upended glider, bottom view.
LC–USZ62–65097; LC–W85–115; MCFWP 19; GANAC 34; SMIN A42, 412–F; SMINAR 1902: facing 139; W Soc Eng J, v. 6, Dec. 1901: 507

A high glide, one of the few photos of the 1901 glider in free flight.

> LCPWOW 120; MCFWP 26; Flight, v. 1, Oct. 9, 1909: 621; SMINAR 1902: facing 142; W Soc Eng J, v. 6, Dec. 1901: 499

A low glide, glider turned diagonally to right close to ground.

> DOBOHA 162; Flight, v. 1, Oct. 2, 1909: 608; SMINAR 1902: facing 142; W Soc Eng J, v. 6, Dec. 1901: 500

Side view of glider in level flight almost overhead, moving to left, showing bottom wing and elevator, Wilbur piloting.

> LC-W85-123; MCFWP 28; Am Mag, v. 67, Apr. 1907: 619 (incorrectly dated 1902); BBAKH; EWBNM 20; Flight, v. 1, Oct. 16, 1909: 647; FRFH facing 35; HILBW 32; LOCA 268; Revue de l'aviation, v. 2, May 15, 1907: 9; SMIN 42, 296-A; SMIN A42, 412-H; SMINAR 1902: facing 143; SUBDF 167 (incorrectly dated 1902); W Soc Eng J, v. 6, Dec. 1901: 508; WODKH facing 35

Wilbur in prone position on glider just after landing, its skid marks showing behind it and, in foreground, skid marks from a previous glider landing.

> LC-W85-111; MCFWP 29; BBAKH; CLHAGW facing 128; EWBNM 21; GSREA b. 44-45; GSEFM; GSIA 38; HEGOV facing 65; Liberty, v. 53, Dec. 22, 1928: 18; MILWA v. 2: 100; SMIN A41, 153A; SMIN 42, 296; SMINAR 1902: facing 143; W Soc Eng J, v. 6, Dec. 1901: 504; World's Work, v. 20, Aug. 1910: 13312

1902, Kitty Hawk, North Carolina

Wilbur in Kill Devil Hills camp building before remodeling, interior crowded with supplies and equipment and skids and front rudder of 1901 glider suspended from the rafters at right, August 29.

> LCPWOW 120; MCFWP 35; COCKDH following 168; EWBNM 28; Life, v. 35, Dec. 7, 1953: 170; MOORKH 129; Pop Sci, v. 114, Apr. 1929: 43; WODKH facing 101

The "patent" beds built under the roof of the remodeled camp building, September 6.

> LCPWOW 120; MCFWP 37; Air Force, v. 36, Dec. 1953: 39; BBAKH

Kitchen of camp building with neatly arranged wall shelves holding dishes, canned foods, and other provisions.

> LC-USZ62-65138; LC-W86-5; MCFWP 38; Aero J, v. 20, July/Sept. 1916: b. 80-81; Air Force, v. 36, Dec. 1953: 39; BBAKH; EWBNM 29; KELWB b. 148-149; Pop Sci, v. 114, Apr. 1929: 43

The kitchen of the Wright camp at Kill Devil Hill, 1902.

Front view of Kill Devil Hill Life Saving Station, with four crew members wearing white hats and jackets standing in doorway and a boat near outer wall at right.
LC–W86–9; COCKDH following 168

Side view of Dan Tate, on left, and Wilbur, on right, flying the 1902 glider as a kite, September 19.
LC–USZ62–56242; LC–W86–40; MCFWP 39; BBAKH; Flight, v. 1, Oct. 23, 1909: 673; HAWBHP 63; KELWB b. 148–149; SMIN A38,722; Soaring, v. 38, May 1974: 27; W Soc Eng J, v. 8, Aug. 1903: 402; WIGLIG b. 548–549

Front view of Wilbur, on left, and Dan Tate flying the glider as a kite, September 19.
LCPWOW 120; MCFWP 40; SMIN 50, 325

Dan Tate, on left, Orville, and Wilbur carrying glider uphill (an unusual shot), October.
LCPWOW 120; MCFWP 46; DOBOHA 162; SMIN 33,951–G

A glide with the double-rudder machine moving to left, north slope of Big Kill Devil Hill, October 2.
LC-USZ62-56244; LC-W86-39; MCFWP 41; Am Aeronaut, v. 1, Jan. 1908: 9; GSAHS facing 81; GSREA b. 44-45; GSIA 39; HAWBHP 63; RGSPA, v. 14, Nov. 30, 1903: 1140; SMIN A42,412-E; Soaring, v. 38, May 1974: 31; W Soc Eng J, v. 8, Aug. 1903: 403

Front view of Orville landing the glider, showing sand spray thrown up by skids and right wing tip, October 2.
LCPWOW 120; MCFWP 42; RGSPA, v. 14, Nov. 30, 1903: 1141

Group of six, left to right: Octave Chanute, Orville, Wilbur, Augustus M. Herring, George A. Spratt, and Dan Tate, seated in front of glider at top of Little Hill, October 10.
LCPWOW 120; MCFWP 59; Aviation Quarterly, v. 2, No. 4: 359; COCKDH following 168; Pop Sci, v. 114, Apr. 1929: 42; RGSPA, v. 14, Nov. 30, 1903: 1136

Rear view of Wilbur gliding from No. 2 Hill west of camp building, October 10.
LCPWOW 120; MCFWP 51; Aviation Quarterly, v. 2, No. 4: 370; DOBOHA 162; GSREA b. 44-45; GSBHF 30; GSIA 39; GSPA; HAWBHP 65; HAYPA 113; RGSPA, v. 14, Nov. 30, 1903: 1138; SMIN A42,668a; Soaring, v. 38, May 1974: 34; W Soc Eng J, v. 8, Aug. 1903: 404

Wilbur gliding downhill to right, Dan Tate running beside machine, Big Kill Devil Hill, October 10.
LC-USZ62-66324; LC-W86-86; MCFWP 48; MEFMF facing 38; Soaring, v. 38, May 1974: 29

Left view of Wilbur gliding, Kitty Hawk Life Saving Station and Weather Bureau buildings in distance, October 10.
LC-W86-3; MCFWP 52; Aero J, v. 20, July/Sept. 1916: b. 80-81; Aviation Quarterly, v. 2, No. 4; 368; GSEFM; HAWBHP 65; SMIN A42,667-A

Wilbur in glider turning rapidly to left, October 10.
LC-USZ62-663323; LC-W86-6; Am Aeronaut, v. 1, Jan. 1908: 9

Wilbur moving forward in glider with a single rear rudder, north slope of Big Kill Devil Hill, October 10.
LCPWOW 120; MCFWP 50; Air Force, v. 36, Dec. 1953: 36; BBAKH; Flight, v. 1, Nov. 15, 1909: 722; Flying, v. 2, Dec. 1913: 11; GSAHS facing 96; GSREA b. 44-45; GSIA 39; GSPA 23; GSWB 7; HARFF 50; MCMWB 118; PEPHO facing 21; Pop Sci, v. 114, Mar. 1929: 42; TAPHF 23; W Soc Eng J, v. 8, Aug. 1903: 401

Wilbur gliding to right, with bottom of glider and Wilbur's legs visible, October 10.
LC–USZ62–56233; LC–W86–13

Side view of Wilbur gliding in level flight moving to right near bottom of Big Hill, October 10.
LC–USZ62–56235; LC–W86–12; MCFWP 44; Aero J, v. 20, July/Sept. 1916: b. 80–81; Lithopinion, v. 6, Winter 1971: 63; SMIN A42,412–C. Similar: Soaring, v. 38, May 1974: 26

Start of a glide, Wilbur in motion at left holding one end of glider—rebuilt with single vertical rudder—Orville lying prone in machine, and Dan Tate at right, October 10.
LC–USZ62–56227; LC–W86–1; MCFWP 43; ASHWB 28; Aviation Quarterly, v. 2, No. 4: 367; BBAKH; Flight, v. 1, Nov. 15, 1909: 722; GANAC 35; GSEFM; GSIA 39; GSWB 7; HARFF 49; HAWBHP 64; HILBW 31; MEFMF facing 38; SMIN A–4377–A; Soaring, v. 38, May 1974: 32; USAF 48617; W Soc Eng J, v. 8, Aug. 1903: 408; YPHA 32

Orville skimming the ground, dark shadows of wings visible in front of glider, October 10.
LCPWOW 120; MCFWP 45; Am Aeronaut, v. 1, Jan. 1908: 8; HILBW 28; Soaring, v. 38, May 1974: 34; W Soc Eng J, v. 8, Aug. 1903: 405

Glider shown turning rapidly to left, the first photograph of a Wright glider in a turn, October 10.
LCPWOW 120; MCFWP 49; RGSPA, v. 14, Nov. 30, 1903: 1139

Rear view of glider on ground after landing, operator still lying prone in glider.
LC–W86–4; RGSPA, v. 14, Nov. 30, 1903: 1137

Three-quarter rear view of glider on ground following landing, operator in prone position, Dan Tate at rear left end of glider.
SMIN 33,951

Glider in level flight skimming the ground, moving to left.
SMIN 33,951–E

Wilbur gliding down steep slope, in level flight to the right, Big Kill Devil Hill, October 10.
LC–USZ62–56228; LC–W86–11; LC–BAIN; MCFWP 47; Aero J, v. 20, July/Sept. 1916: b. 80–81; L'Aerophile, v. 11, Aug. 1903: 179; Am Mag, v. 67, Apr. 1907: 617; Aviation Quarterly, v. 2, No. 4: 360; DAIHF 1948 b. 104–105; GSREA b. 44–45; HGCA 45; HMSHSA facing 179; MILWA v. 2: 101; Sat Eve Post, v. 201, July 7, 1928: 10; SMIN A38,530–M; Soaring, v. 38, May 1974: 36; W Soc Eng J, v. 8, Aug. 1903: 406; World's Work, v. 20, Aug. 1910: 13312; World's Work, v. 56, Sept. 1927: 514; YPHA 32

Orville beginning a glide, with Wilbur at his right and Dan Tate at his left, on the sands of Kitty Hawk, October 10, 1902.

Wilbur gliding, in level flight, Dan Tate running to left of machine, October 10.
        LCPWOW 120; MCFWP 48; Am Aeronaut, v. 1, Jan. 1908: 10; RGSPA, v. 14, Nov. 30, 1903: 1138

Series of photographs of Wright gliding experiments taken by Octave Chanute's camera during Chanute's October 5-14 visit to Kitty Hawk, where he witnessed gliding experiments, October 8, 9, and 10.
        SMIN 33,950, -A, -C, -D, -L, -M; SMIN 33,951, -A, -B, -C, -D, -E, -F, -G, -J

Wilbur gliding, in level flight, single rear rudder clearly visible, October 17.
        LC-W86-10

Orville on left and Dan Tate at right launching glider downhill with Wilbur on board, October 18.
        LCPWOW 120; MCFWP 56; WODKH b. 160-161

Rear view of Wilbur making right turn in glide from No. 2 Hill, right wing tipped close to ground, October 24.

> LC–USZ62–56236; LC–W86–7; LC–BAIN; MCFWP 57; Aero J, v. 20, July/Sept. 1916: b. 80–81; Am Mag, v. 67, Apr. 1907: 624; Aviation Quarterly, v. 2, No. 4: 368; EWBNM 31; Flight, v. 1, Oct. 30, 1909: 693; GANAC 35; HARFF 51; HAWBHP 65; HILBW 29; MILWA v. 2: 101; Revue de l'aviation, v. 2, May 1907: 3; Sat Eve Post, v. 201, July 7, 1928: 10; SMIN A43,395–A; W Soc Eng J, v. 8, Aug. 1903: 409

Orville making right turn, showing warping of wings, hill visible in front of him, October 24.

> LC–USZ62–66323; LC–W86–8; MCFWP 58

1903, Kitty Hawk, North Carolina

Kitty Hawk camp from top of Big Hill.

> LC–W86–17

The 1903 machine and large camp building used for housing it and small building used as workshop and living quarters, Kill Devil Hills, November 24.

> LC–W86–15; LC–W86–16; MCFWP 63; Aero J, v. 20, July/Sept. 1916: b. 80–81; ASHWB 44; Aviation, v. 15, Dec. 17, 1923: 739; BBAKH; EWBNM 40; FAA World, v. 8, Jan. 1958: 14; Flying, v. 2, Dec. 1913: 6; HARFF 58; HAWBHP 66; KELMKH b. 238–239; MILWA v. 2: 102; SMIN 38,618–A; YPHA 33

Wilbur and Orville assembling the 1903 machine in the new camp building at Kill Devil Hills, October.

> LC–USZ62–65137; LC–W86–65; MCFWP 61; Air Force, v. 36, Dec. 1953: 39; BBAKH; Collier's, v. 80, Sept. 21, 1927: 18; EWBNM 40; Flying, v. 2, Dec. 1913: 10; MILWA v. 2: 100; Sat Eve Post, v. 201, July 7, 1928: 11; WODKH b. 160–161; YPHA 32

1903 machine, front view.

> LC–USZ62–56223; LC–W86–24; MCFWP 64; Airpost Journal, v. 50, Dec. 1978: 108; BBAKH; EWBNM 38; GSIA 48; HAWBHP 68; MILWA v. 2: 102; SMIN 38,618–B; USAF 48628; U.S. Air Service, v. 8, Dec. 1923: 26

1903 machine, side view.

> MCFWP 67; Aviation, v. 15, Dec. 17, 1923: 738; Aviation, v. 25, Dec. 1, 1928: 1725; BBAKH; DOBOHA 171; EWBNM 38; Flying, v. 2, Dec. 1913: 12; GSIA 48; GSWB 10; HAWBHP 68; KELWB b. 148–149; MARWBC front.; MILWA v. 2: 102; Sat Eve Post, v. 201, July 14, 1928: 19; SMIN A26, 767–A; USAF 10466 A.C.; USAF 19131; U.S. Air Service, v. 8, Dec. 1923: 26

1903 machine, rear view.
> MCFWP 65; Aero J, v. 20, July/Sept. 1916: b. 80–81;
> USAF 48627

1903 machine, three-quarter rear view, Orville standing beside airplane.
> MCFWP 66; Aero J, v. 20, July/Sept. 1916: b. 80–81;
> Aviation, v. 15, Dec. 17, 1923: 735; Flying, v. 2, Dec.
> 1913: 12; MILWA v. 2: 103; USAF 48629; U.S. Air
> Service, v. 8, Dec. 1923: 26

Right rear view (one of three pictures taken on this date) of one of the successful glides made October 21 with the 1902 glider, camp buildings in distance.
> LC–W86–63; LC–W86–64; MCFWP 62; ADAMSF 38;
> BBAKH; Cent, v. 76, Sept. 1908: 642; EWBNM 30;
> FAA World, v. 8, Jan. 1978: 9; KELMKH b. 238–239;
> Liberty, v. 18, Dec. 22, 1928: 18; SMIN A42,413–B;
> Vie grand air, v. 15, Apr. 17, 1909: 260

Three-quarter right front view of Wright glider descending from Big Hill, one of four photos of gliding activities on this date, when Wilbur made two glides and Orville two, October 27.
> LC–W86–34

"Living room" of camp, showing woodpile, carbide-can stove, and hanging rugs used to keep out drafts, November.
> 2LCPWOW 120; MCFWP 36

Track on Big Hill, Kitty Hawk, and north slope of Kill Devil Hill, December 14.
> LC–W86–18; LC–W86–56; LC–W86–57

Machine on track, with four men from Kill Devil Hill Life Saving Station who helped move it from the shed to the hill, two small boys with them, Big Kill Devil Hill, before the trial of December 14.
> LC–W286–21; MCFWP 68; Aviation Quarterly, v. 2,
> No. 4: 371; BBAKH; EWBNM 42; Flying, v. 2, Dec.
> 1913: 11; HAWBHP 69; HEGOV facing 80; SMIN
> 43,482; SMIN 73–859; WODKH b. 160–161

Wilbur in prone position in damaged machine on ground after unsuccessful trial of December 14.
> LC–USZ62–56224; LC–W86–19; LC–W86–20;
> MCFWP 69; Air Force, v. 36, Dec. 1953: 37; Airpost
> Journal, v. 50, Dec. 1978: 109; Am Legion Mag, Feb.
> 1969: 609; ASHWB 42; Aviation Quarterly, v. 2, No. 4:
> 372–373; BBAKH; EWBNM 43; GSWB 10; HARFF
> 61; HAWBHP 70; MARWBC 21; Nat Geog Mag, v.
> 104; Dec. 1953: 41; NOZWBC facing 171; SMIN
> A42,545–A; TMHA 46–47

First flight, 120 feet in 12 seconds, 10:35 A.M., December 17. Orville at the controls of the machine, lying prone on the lower wing with hips in the cradle which operated the wing-warping mechanism. Wilbur, running alongside to balance the machine, has just released his hold on the forward upright of the right wing. The starting rail, the wing-rest, a coil box, and other items needed for flight preparation are visible behind the machine.

LC–USZ62–6166A; LC–W86–35; LC–BECK; MCFWP 70; Aerosphere, 1943: CXIX; ANDWF 606; ASHWB 48–49; Aviation Quarterly, v. 2, No. 4: 376–377; BBAKH; DOBOHA 172–173; Cent, v. 76, Sept. 1908: 644; DAIHF 1948: b. 104–105; Flight Magazine, v. 40, Dec. 1953: 38; GSEFM; HAWBHP 70; MILWA v. 2: 104–105; Nat Geog Mag, v. 104, Dec. 1953: 740; SMIN A26,767–B; TAPHF 24–25; USAF 1382 A.S.; USAF 19130; World's Work, v. 20, Aug. 1910: 13313; YPHA 33

Orville piloting, third flight of December 17.

LC–USZ62–57823; LC–W86–37; MCFWP 72; Aviation, v. 15, Dec. 17, 1923: 740; Aviation Quarterly, v. 2, No. 4: 374; EWBNM 47; HAWBHP 71; HEGOV facing 80; SMIN 42, 545–D; USAF 48626

Distant view of Wright airplane just after landing, photograph taken from starting point, with wing-rest in the center of picture and starting rail at right, following fourth and last flight, December 17.

LC–USZ62–65094; LC–W86–38; MCFWP 77; Aviation Quarterly, v. 2, No. 4: 375; Flying, v. 2, Dec. 1913: 6

Close-up view of damaged 1903 machine, rudder frame broken in landing, on ground at end of last flight.

LC–USZ62–65098; LC–W86–23; MCFWP 78; Flying, v. 2, Dec. 1913: 36; HAWBHP 71; SMIN 42,545–B; SMIN 73–862

Albemarle Sound, taken on return of Wrights to Dayton from Kitty Hawk, December 21.

LC–W86–33

1904, Huffman Prairie, Dayton, Ohio

Orville and Wilbur with second power machine, wings shown in warped position, newly constructed wooden shed for it— Wrights' first hangar—nearby, Huffman Prairie, May.

LC–USZ62–56231; LC–W85–30A; MCFWP 79; Aero Digest, v. 13, Dec. 1928: 1107; Aerosphere, 1943: CXXXII; Bee-Hive, v. 28, Jan. 1953: 14; COCKDH following 168; HARFF 70; MEFMF facing 54; USAF 22440

Long-range view of machine on launching track, showing hangar nearby and hummocky ground of former swamp, June or July.
LC–W85–28; LC-BECK; MCFWP 81; HEGOV facing 113; KELWB b. 148–149; SMIN 42,538

Long-range view of machine on track, men on either side of machine, probably Wilbur and Orville, June or July.
LC–W86–55

Close-up view of machine on track, June or July.
LC–W86–27; MCFWP 80

Flight 19, covering a distance of 356 feet, machine close to ground, Orville piloting, August 5.
LC–W86–26; MCFWP 82; HARFF 73

Flight 29, machine close to ground, Orville piloting, covering a distance of 640 feet in 15 seconds, August 13.
LC–W86–54; MCFWP 83

Flight 30, machine close to ground, Wilbur piloting, flight covering a distance of 784 feet in 22¾ seconds, August 13.
LC–W86–51; MCFWP 84; SMIN 30,959–L; USAF 48631

Damaged machine at right of starting track at end of flight 31, Orville piloting, with tall, white-shirted man in foreground who may be Charles E. Taylor, Wrights' mechanic, August 16.
LC–USZ62–66552; LC–W86–29; MCFWP 85; WODKH b. 220–221

Long-range view of flight 69, in which Orville covered a distance of 358 feet in 1 minute 31 seconds, large tree in foreground, machine in distance, October 14.
LC–W86–50; LC-BECK: SMIN 42,771

Flight 82, Wilbur piloting at a considerable height, flying a distance of 2¾ miles, almost four circles of the field, the best and longest flight of the year, in 5 minutes 4 seconds, November 9.
LC–W86–52; Cent, v. 76, Sept. 1908: 645

Flight 85, Orville in flight over tree tops, covering approximately 1,760 feet in 40 ⅕ seconds, November 16.
LC–USZ62–56243; LC–W86–25; MCFWP 86; ASHWB 50; Cent, v. 76, Sept. 1908: 645; DOBOHA 174; EWBNM 54; GSEFM; GSIA 49; GSREA b. 128–129; GSWB 11; GSWFAF 11; HAWBHP 73; HAWBHP 121; MILWA v. 2: 107; Sat Eve Post, v. 201, July 14, 1928: 645; SMIN A3727; World's Work, v. 20, Aug. 1910: 13313

1905, Huffman Prairie, Dayton, Ohio

Start of the first flight of 1905, Orville at controls of machine, near hangar, with two figures in center of photo, probably Wilbur and Charles E. Taylor, and catapult launching device (its first appearance in a photograph), Huffman Prairie, June 23.

> LC–USZ62–66557; LC–W86–48; MCFWP 87; Cent, v. 76, Sept. 1908: 46; DOBOHA 174; SMIN 42,771–A; Vie grand air, v. 15, Apr. 24, 1909: 275; WODKH b. 220–221

Flight 23, front view of machine in flight to right, Orville at controls, making two complete circles of field in 2 minutes 45 seconds, September 7.

> LC–USZ62–66559; LC–W86–47; MCFWP 88; HAWBHP 73; SMIN 42,572. Similar photo: LC–W86–46

Side view of flight 41, showing the machine traveling to the right, with double horizontal rudder in front and double vertical rudder behind, as Orville flew 12 miles, September 29.

> LC–W86–104; MCFWP 89; Cent, v. 76, Sept. 1908: 647. Similar photo: LC–W86–43

Front view of flight 41, Orville flying to left at a height of about 60 feet, September 29.

> LC–W86–75; MCFWP 90; WODKH b. 220–221. Similar photos: LC–W86–41; LC–W86–42; LC–W86–44; LC–W86–45

Side view of flight 45, Orville flying to right close to ground, flight covering a distance of about 14.2 miles in 25 minutes 5 seconds, October 3.

> LC–W86–73; MCFWP 91

Side view of flight 45, Orville flying to left at a considerable height, October 3.

> LC–W86–74; MCFWP 92

Front view of flight 46, Orville flying at a height of 40 to 60 feet for a distance of about 20¾ miles in 33 minutes 17 seconds, October 4.

> Cent, v. 76, Sept. 1908: 648; DOBOHA 174

Right front view from below of flight 46, Orville turning to right, October 4.

> LC–W86–69; MCFWP 94; EWBNM 55; GSAHS front.; GSEFM; GSWFAF; GSIA 78; GSWB 11; HAWBHP 94; SMIN 43,482–A

Rear view of flight 46, Orville shown flying at a considerably higher altitude than in preceding front view, October 4.
LC–W86–105; MCFWP 93; Cent, v. 76, Sept. 1908: 648; DOBOHA 174; Vie grand air, v. 15, Apr. 24, 1909: 276; World's Work, v. 20, Aug. 1910: 13313. Similar photo: LC–W86–68; LC–W86–70; ADAMSF 42; MCMWB front.; Vie grand air, v. 15, Apr. 24, 1909: 276

Rear view of flight 46, Orville turning left, October 4.
LC–USZ62–66554; LC–W86–66; MCFWP 95; SMIN A317

Left front view of flight 46, last photographed flight of 1905, Orville shown turning to left, October 4.
LC–W86–67; MCFWP 96; ASHWB 54; FRFH facing 98; GSBHF 32; HARFF 81; MEFMF facing 55; SMIN A42,737G. Similar photos: LC–W86–49; LC–W86–71; LC–W86–72

1907, Miami River, Dayton, Ohio

Wilbur and Orville conducting experiments with two pontoons supporting a platform on which there was a 20 horsepower engine and two propeller screws, on the Miami River, Dayton, March 21.
LC-BECK; Aero Club Am Bul, v. 1, Apr. 1912: 7; Dayton Herald, Mar. 21; SMIN 43,093; USAF 8637

1908, Kitty Hawk, North Carolina

Long-range view of Wright brothers' camp and Kitty Hawk Bay.
LC–W86–79; LC–W86–83; LC–W86–84

View of camp from northeast showing conditions at time of Wilbur's arrival, April 10. The old 1902 building is at left, side walls still standing but roof and north end gone, and the remains of the 1902 glider are on the ground.
LC–W86–82; MCFWP 146; NOZWBC facing 87

View of camp building from northwest with old building to the left and newly constructed building on the right with window on east side and outside wall braces on west side of building visible.
LC–W86–80 Similar view at different angle: LC–W86–81

The remodeled 1905 Wright machine—altered to allow the operator to assume a sitting position and to provide a seat for a passenger—on starting track, Kill Devil Hills, May 11. Apparently this was the only photograph of this machine taken by the Wrights in 1908.
LC–USZ62–66555; LC–W86–78; MCFWP 147

Retouched photo of above Wright airplane in flight at Kill Devil Hills, copyrighted 1908 by the *New York Herald* and widely reprinted.

> **MCFWP 149; Illustrated London News, v. 132, June. 13, 1908: 849; New York Herald, May 20, 1908; New York Herald, May 29, 1908; New York Herald (Paris), May 29, 1908**

Distant view of Wright machine in level flight traveling to left, May 13 or 14. Original unretouched photograph of the machine in flight taken by James H. Hare, photographer for *Collier's,* published May 30.

> **MCFWP 148; Aero and Hydro, v. 7, Dec. 27, 1913: 155; L'Aérophile, v. 16, July 1, 1908: 250; Air-Scout, v. 1, Apr. 1911: 13; Collier's, v. 41, May 30, 1908: 19; Flugsport, v. 12, July 11, 1908: 350; Literary Digest, v. 36, June 13, 1908: 801; Sci Am, v. 98, May 30, 1908: 393; Van Norden Mag, v. 3, Aug. 1908: 49**

Distant three-quarter front view of Wright airplane in flight to left, right wing turned slightly downward.

> **L'Aérophile, v. 16, July 1, 1908: 251; Collier's, v. 41, May 30, 1908; Sci Am, v. 98, May 30, 1908: 393**

Series of photographs of a group of newspaper correspondents, including Byron R. Newton, of the *New York Herald,* William Hoster, of the *New York American,* P. H. McGowan, of the London *Daily Mail,* Arthur Ruhl, writer, and James H. Hare, photographer for *Collier's,* who secretly witnessed Wright flights at a great distance from a clump of trees.

> **Aero and Hydro, v. 7, Dec. 27, 1913: 155; Air-Scout, v. 1, Apr. 1911: 155; Collier's, v. 41, May 30, 1908: 18**

1908, Hunaudières Race Course, Le Mans, France

Léon Bollée, three-quarter length, factory owner at Hunaudières, who offered Wilbur the use of his facilities to set up his machine. Wilbur arrived in France May 29 to demonstrate Wright machine's fulfillment of duration and speed requirements of a contract made March 3 with Henri Deutsch de la Meurthe, representing a French syndicate.

> **EWWLM 4**

Front view of Léon Bollée's factory.

> **EWWLM cover**

Wright airplane assembled and mounted on truck in Bollée's factory.

> **EWWLM 9**

Close-up views of center section of Wright airplane as assembled in Bollée's factory.

> **EWWLM 7; EWWLM 24**

Léon Bollée seated in the Wright airplane testing the motor.
EWWLM 15

Wilbur, wearing cap and in shirt sleeves, conversing with Lt.
Frank P. Lahm in front of hangar housing Wright airplane, the
day of his first flight in France, August 8.
**Am Aeronaut, v. 1, Aug. 1909: 20; London Magazine,
v. 21, Feb. 1909: 618; SMIN 8198; U.S. Air Services,
v. 9, Aug. 1924: 29**

View of Wright airplane being towed by automobile from Bollée's factory to flying field.
**Aerosphere 1943: CXXXIV; EWWLM 10. Similar view
near factory: EWWLM 11**

Front view of Wright airplane outside hangar at Hunaudières.
Ill Aero Mitteil, v. 12, Aug. 26, 1908: 510

Three-quarter front view of Wright airplane in front of hangar.
**FRFH facing 178; L'Illustration, v. 132, Aug. 15, 1908;
108; LOUVA facing 394; SMIN 42,584; SMINAR
1910: b. 148–149; USAF 34094**

Three-quarter front view of Wright airplane on its handling dollies outside hangar.
GSIA 49; GSWB 19; LVTNA 308; PEPHO facing 40

Side view of Wright airplane in front of hangar.
**MCFWP 150; Graphic, v. 78, Aug. 15, 1908: 201;
HARFF 107; London Magazine, v. 21, Feb. 1909: 618;
SMIN 43,204; Vie grand air, v. 14, Aug. 15, 1908. Sim-
ilar: L'Aérophile, v. 16, Aug. 15, 1908: 325; Bee-Hive,
v. 28, Fall 1953: 28; Flight, v. 64, Dec. 11, 1953: 797;
LOUVA facing 394; SMIN 43,142–B; SMINAR 1910:
b. 148-149**

Close-up rear view of Wright airplane showing early propellers
in use in 1908.
**L'Aérophile, v. 16, Sept. 1, 1908: 338; GSIA 148;
GSWB 19; LOUVA facing 398. Similar: EWWLM 7**

View of Wright airplane being assembled at Léon Bollée's shop,
Hunaudières.
EWWLM 8; SMIN 76–128117

Right front view of Wright airplane on two-wheel carrier being
wheeled from hangar.
**Automotor, v. 13, Aug. 22, 1908: 1120; Flight, v. 1,
Mar. 20, 1909: 7; Graphic, v. 78, Aug. 15, 1908: 201;
Illustrated London News, v. 133, Aug. 15, 1908: 220;
SMIN 43,063–L**

Right rear view of Wright airplane being wheeled to launching
site.
SMIN 42,783–B

Wilbur seated at the controls of his airplane.
Flight, v. 64, Dec. 11, 1953: 796; Ill Aero Mitteil, v. 12, Aug. 26, 1908: 511; L'Illustration, v. 132, Aug. 15, 1908: 108; PEPHO facing 44; SMIN 42,783–C. Similar: L'Aérophile, v. 16, 1908: 324.

Left side view of Wright airplane being placed in position on launching rail for takeoff.
L'Illustration, v. 132, Aug. 15, 1908: 108

Right side view of Wright airplane on the starting track ready for takeoff. Standing at the left at the rear of the machine are Wilbur, Léon Bollée, and Hart O. Berg.
Automotor, v. 13, Aug. 22, 1908: 1121; EWWLM 13

Side view of Wright airplane on starting track ready for flight, launching derrick behind it.
EWWLM 17

Right rear view of Wright airplane at starting rail, launching derrick nearby at left.
L'Aérophile, v. 16, Dec. 1, 1908: 474; Allg Auto Zeit, v. 9, Aug. 22, 1908: 5; Revue aérienne, v. 2, Jan. 25, 1909: 55; VCAAF 56; Wiener Luftschiffer-Zeitung, v. 7, Nov. 1908: 218

Wright airplane on launching track ready for flight.
Deutsche Luftfahrer-Zeitschrift, v. 16, June 12, 1912: 290; HAWBHP 75; LECNA 414; LOUVA facing 360; MTWWDA facing 25; PEPHO facing 44; R Aero Soc J, v. 57, Dec. 1953: 778; SC–107939; SMIN A42,783–H; USAF 10477 A.C.; USAF 48642

View of launching derrick with six men at left pulling rope to raise weight to top of tower for use in takeoff, several photographers at extreme right.
COCKDH following 168: NOZWBC facing 89; SC–107931; SMIN 42,584–C

View of launching tower, Wright airplane on starting track behind it, group of men at right pulling rope to raise weight.
American Heritage, v. 11, Feb. 1960: 62; EWWLM 16

Close-up view of derrick used to start Wright airplane.
LOCA 270

Wilbur at top of starting derrick preparing launching device.
ADAMSF 53; EWWLM 12

Side view of Wright airplane on starting rail ready for flight, launching derrick at right, men pulling rope to raise weight.
L'Illustration, v. 132, Aug. 15, 1908: 108. Similar: Graphic, v. 78, Aug. 15, 1908: 201; LOCA 270

Right rear view of Wright airplane on flying field, three men at rear, group of men at right front of airplane.
SMIN 43,063–E

View of spectators sitting in race course grandstand waiting for Wilbur's flight.
L'Aérophile, v. 16, Aug. 15, 1908: 325; PEPHO facing 48

Left front view of Wilbur in flight over race course grandstand, August 8.
Autocar, v. 21, Aug. 22, 1908: Automotor, v. 13, Aug. 22, 1908: cover; GSEFM; GSBHF 40; GSIA 148; GSWB 19; London Magazine, v. 21, Feb. 1909: 617; SMIN 42,804–J; SMINAR 1910: facing 149

Left front view of Wilbur flying past airplane hangar and approaching racetrack grandstand.
L'Aérophile, v. 16, Sept. 15, 1908: 354; Flight, v. 1, Mar. 20, 1909: 157; Flugsport, v. 12, Aug. 26, 1908: 511; GSREA b. 272–273; LANFL 6; NOZWBC facing 161; PEPHO facing 45; SBNA 107; SMIN A3487; SMIN 42,446–H; SMIN 42,783–A

Front view of Wilbur in flight over racetrack grounds.
COCKDH following 168; SMIN 42,805

Right side view of Wilbur in flight circling the field three times in 3 minutes 43 seconds, before a crowd of about three thousand assembled at the racetrack, August 11.
MCFWP 151; L'Aérophile, v. 16, Aug. 15, 1908: 327; WODKH b. 220–221. Similar, close-up view: L'Illustration, v. 132, Aug. 15, 1908: 132

Wilbur in flight at end of launching track immediately after takeoff.
L'Aérophile, v. 16, Sept. 1, 1908: 339; GSIA 149; SMIN 43,056

Right side view of Wilbur in level flight over treetops.
GSWFAF 15; GSIA 42; SMIN 18,245. Similar: LECNA 415

Right front view of Wilbur in level flight.
LC-JONES; Graphic, v. 78, Aug. 15, 1908: 201; USAF 4099 A.S.

Long-range views of Wilbur flying at a considerable altitude.
EWWLM 20; EWWLM 21; EWWLM 22

Fleury (Hart O. Berg's chauffeur) and Wilbur examining wing of Wright airplane damaged in landing, August 13.
LC-BECK; MCFWP 153; COCKDH following 168; GSPA 32; MARWBC 47; SC–107933; WRBR 20

Left side view of Wright airplane, Wilbur and group of men at its left front inspecting damage.
SMIN 43,063–G

Wilbur directing workmen removing damaged wing.
MCFWP 152; COCKDH following 168; Illustrated London News, v. 133, Aug. 22, 1908: 251; NOZWBC facing 163; SMIN 10,877–A; SMIN 31,990–G

Wright airplane being disassembled.
SMIN 43,063–K; SMIN 43,064–E

Left front view of Wright airplane, left wing removed, Wilbur at center near machine in conversation with Hart O. Berg.
SC–107939; SMIN A42,584–B

Left side view of damaged Wright airplane.
SMIN 42,864; SMIN 43,663–K

Close-up view of left wing with outboard panels removed, two women at left inspecting damage.
SC–107934; SMIN 42,5395D

Front view of Wright airplane in front of hangar, mechanics repairing wing damaged on landing in accident on August 13.
SC–107940; SMIN 42,783–E

Side view of Wright airplane on two-wheeled carrier ready for transportation to a new flying field at Camp d'Auvours, Le Mans.
London Magazine, v. 21, Feb. 1909: 618; SMIN 43,063

Side view of Wright airplane on two-wheeled carrier ready for towing by automobile on left.
SMIN 43,064–L

Wright airplane on two-wheeled carrier being towed by Léon Bollée's automobile from the Hunaudières Race Course to Camp d'Auvours.
Allg Auto Zeit, v. 9, Sept. 19, 1908: 13; American Heritage, v. 11, Feb. 1960: 61; FWGMBH 3; London Magazine, v. 21, Feb. 1909: 618; MARWBC 27; SMIN 6800–F; SMIN A42,845–D. Similar: SMIN A3402; SMIN 42,846–E

1908, Camp d'Auvours, Le Mans, France

Partial view of flying field at Camp d'Auvours, showing spectators lined up at edge of field to witness flights by Wilbur, who had come there from the Hunaudières area seeking a larger, better place from which to fly.
U.S. Air Services, v. 9, Aug. 1924: 30

Interior view of part of hangar at d'Auvours which served as Wilbur's workshop, kitchen, and bedroom, August to December 1908.
MCFWP 167; SMIN A42,845–R. Similar view: Allg Auto Zeit, v. 9, Sept. 20, 1908: 11; L'Illustration, v. 132, Sept. 19, 1908: 189

Wilbur, full length, wearing cap, high collar, tie, and vested suit, black dog named Flyer lying at his feet.
MCFWP 166; ADAMSF 1909: 70; EWWLM 8; SMIN 42,709; YPHA 36

Group photograph of Deputy Jean Laroche, Mr. and Mrs. Lazare Weiller, Wilbur, and Henri Deutsch de la Meurthe.
L'Illustration, v. 132, Sept. 26, 1908: 212; PEPHO facing 84

Wilbur with two of his students, Capt. Paul Lucas-Girardville and Count Charles de Lambert, October.
SMIN 43,063–B

Group photo of Maj. B. F. S. Baden-Powell, Charles S. Rolls, Wilbur, and Frank Hedges Butler.
Autocar, v. 21, Oct. 31, 1908: 654; Illustrated London News, v. 133, Oct. 24, 1908: 561

Rear view of Wright airplane being placed on towing dollies, workmen at front of airplane.
SMIN 43,064–D

Right side view of Wright airplane being pulled to launching derrick by three workmen.
Bollettino della Società Aeronautica Italiana, v. 5, Dec. 1908: 412

Front view of Wright airplane following a flight, being towed back to starting point by automobile.
L'Illustration, v. 132, Sept. 19, 1908: 189; SMIN A43,064–A

Close-up rear view of the center section of the Wright airplane.
Bollettino della Società Aeronautica Italiana, v. 5, Dec. 1908: 413; Revue aérienne, v. 1, Nov. 25, 1908: 74

Right front view of Wright airplane, workman placing a towing dolly on underside of airplane to pull airplane to launching derrick.
Bollettino della Società Aeronautica Italiana, v. 5, Dec. 1908: 413

Close-up right rear view of Wright airplane on ground.
Aero Manual, 1909: 109; Conquête de l'air, v. 5, Nov. 1, 1908: 1

Wilbur carrying a section of launching track.
SMIN 43,064–F

Wilbur at apex of launching tower adjusting pulley.
        SMIN A42,846–F

Wright airplane on flying field being made ready for flight by
workmen, launching derrick at right.
        Autocar, v. 21, Dec. 19, 1908: 999

Three-quarter front view of Wright airplane, Wilbur seated at
controls ready for takeoff.
        FWGMBH 6

Left front view of Wright airplane on flying field following a
flight.
        Conquête de l'air, v. 5, Oct. 15, 1908: 5

Group of men, including French Minister of Public Works Louis
Barthou and Wilbur, walking across flying field to inspect
Wright airplane.
        L'Illustration, v. 133, Jan. 9, 1909: 36

Léon Bollée (back to camera) at front of Wright airplane explaining its operation to Louis Barthou.
        American Heritage, v. 11, Feb. 1960: 63

Close-up view of Wilbur seated at the controls of Wright
airplane.
        SMIN 42,534–B

Wilbur near Wright airplane explaining its operation to two interested men at either side of him, another in rear.
        **COCKDH following 168; U.S. Air Services, v. 13, Dec.
        1928: 29; YPHA 34**

Wilbur in level flight past the hangar and nearby roadway with
starting derrick at extreme right, September 5.
        **Allg Auto Zeit, v. 9, Sept. 13, 1908: 47; Automotor,
        v. 13, Sept. 12, 1908: 1209; Flight, v. 1, Mar. 20, 1909:
        13; Motor, v. 14, Sept. 8, 1908: 134; SMIN 10,879–C**

Ernest Zens, French balloonist and Wilbur's first European passenger, seated in Wright airplane with Wilbur with whom he
flew on September 16.
        **L'Aérophile, v. 16, Dec. 1, 1908: 470; Automotor, v. 13,
        Oct. 3, 1908: 1303; Flight, v. 1, Mar. 20, 1909: 11; Il-
        lustrated London News, v. 133, Oct. 3, 1908: 477;
        PEPHO facing 64; Revue de l'aviation, v. 3, Oct. 15,
        1908: 14; SMIN 10,879–G; SMIN A10,879–L; U.S.
        Air Services, v. 13, Dec. 1928: 32; VCAAF 57**

Wilbur in airplane approaching from the left and about to pass the starting derrick, crowd at left gazing up at him, at twilight, September 21. The flight lasted 1 hour, 31 minutes, 25⅘ seconds, establishing world flying records for duration and distance.

American Heritage, v. 11, Feb. 1960: 63; BIAFW facing 52; CHAHA 65; DOBOHA 196; L'Illustration, v. 132, Sept. 26, 1908: 212; MARWBC 23; MILWA v. 2: 148; SMIN 42,445–J; Vie grand air, v. 15, May 29, 1909: 355. Similar, without starting derrick: Allg Auto Zeit, v. 9, Oct. 3, 1908: 37; Motor, v. 14, Sept. 29, 1908: 252

Wright airplane approaching starting derrick from right in low-level flight on Wilbur's flight of September 21.

MCFWP 168; Allg Auto Zeit, v. 9, Oct. 3, 1908: 37; BIAFW facing 52; Revue aérienne, v. 1, Oct. 15, 1908: facing 9; R Aero Soc J, v. 57, Dec. 1953: 779; SMIN A3404

Front view of Wright airplane during flight of 54 minutes, 3⅕ seconds carried out in an especially strong and gusty wind, September 24.

Revue de l'aviation, v. 3. Oct. 15, 1908: 5

Side view from below of Wright airplane in level flight to right, Wilbur and passenger Franz Reichel flying for 55 minutes, 32⅕ seconds (this flight thus qualifying as one of the two stipulated in the Wright contract with Lazare Weiller), October 3.

Everybody's Magazine, v. 20, Jan. 1909: 112; LVTNA 316. Similar: Aviation, v. 25, Dec. 1, 1928: 1726; LOCA 207

Hart O. Berg seated in Wright airplane with Wilbur with whom he flew on October 7.

Illustrated London News, v. 133, Oct. 24, 1908: 561. Similar: Allg Auto Zeit, v. 9, Oct. 18, 1908: 31

Mrs. Hart O. Berg seated in Wright airplane with Wilbur with whom she flew as his first woman passenger on October 7, the first real flight made anywhere in the world by a woman.

L'Aérophile, v. 16, Nov. 1, 1908: 428; Allg Auto Zeit, v. 9, Oct. 18, 1908: 31; ASHWB 71; Bee-Hive, v. 28, Fall 1953: 28; GSEFM; GSIA 148; GSPA 33; HILBW 38; Illustrated London News, v. 133, Oct. 24, 1908: 561; London Magazine, v. 21, Feb. 1909: 623; PEPHO facing 76; SMIN 18,094–E; SMIN 31,246–H; SMIN 43,064–B

Frank Hedges Butler seated in Wright airplane with Wilbur with whom he flew as a passenger on October 8.

American Heritage, v. 11, Feb. 1960: 62; Autocar, v. 21, Oct. 31, 1908: 654; Illustrated London News, v. 133, Oct. 24, 1908: 561

Charles S. Rolls, founder of British Rolls-Royce automobile firm, seated in Wright airplane with Wilbur with whom he flew as a passenger on October 8.

> **Automotor, v. 13, Oct. 31, 1908: 1413; Illustrated London News, v. 133, Oct. 24, 1908: 561; R Aero Soc J, v. 57, Dec. 1953: 776**

Maj. B. F. S. Baden-Powell, president of the Aeronautical Society of Great Britain, seated in Wright airplane with Wilbur with whom he flew as a passenger on October 8.

> **Automotor, v. 13, Oct. 31, 1908: 1413**

Griffith Brewer, first Englishman to fly, seated in Wright airplane with Wilbur with whom he flew as a passenger on October 8.

> **Autocar, v. 21, Oct. 31, 1908: 654; Illustrated London News, v. 133, Oct. 24, 1908: 561; R Aero Soc J, v. 57, Dec. 1953: 776**

Maj. B. F. S. Baden-Powell, Charles S. Rolls, and Frank Hedges Butler photographed in front of Wright airplane on visit to Camp d'Auvours on October 8.

> **The Car, v. 27, Dec. 16, 1908: 256**

Right rear view of Wright airplane on flying field with group of people, including in center Dowager Queen Margherita of Italy, nearby in foreground to witness flights by Wilbur, October 8.

> **SMIN 42,845–C. Similar: American Heritage, v. 11, Feb. 1960: 63**

Group of people including Wilbur, Dowager Queen Margherita, and Hart O. Berg gathered near Wright airplane on October 8.

> **SMIN A42,846–G**

Side view of front elevator of Wright airplane, Wilbur on far side visiting with Dowager Queen Margherita, October 8.

> **Bollettino della Società Aeronautica Italiana, v. 5, Dec. 1908: 412; SMIN 42,845**

Mrs. Lazare Weiller seated in Wright airplane with Wilbur with whom she flew as a passenger on October 9.

> **Allg Auto Zeit, v. 9, Oct. 18, 1908: 31; L'Illustration, v. 132, Oct. 17, 1908: 261; LVTNA 314; Revue aérienne, v. 2, Nov. 25, 1908: 73**

Right front view of Wright airplane in level flight, Wilbur and passenger Prof. Paul Painlevé, mathematician and member of the French Institute, establishing a new world flying record of 1 hour, 9 minutes, 42⅘ seconds, October 10.

> **L'Aéronaute, v. 42, Jan. 15, 1909: 3; Allg Auto Zeit, v. 9, Oct. 17, 1908: 29. Similar, Wilbur just passing launching derrick visible below at right: Automotor, v. 13, Oct. 17. 1908: cover.**

Paul Doumer, member of the French parliament, seated in Wright airplane in preparation for flight as passenger with Wilbur, October 31.
DOBOHA 197

Full left side view of Wright airplane on launching track.
ADAMSF 47; SMIN 42,846–A. Similar, with Wilbur at rear right near rudder: BIAFW facing 24

Close-up left front view of Wright airplane on launching track, Wilbur kneeling between skids making adjustments to airplane.
SMIN 42,846–B

Wilbur in front of airplane elevator preparing to attach launching line to airplane.
SMIN 43,063–H

Wilbur in conversation with unidentified person in front of Wright airplane, third person approaching from right.
SMIN 43,064

Left rear view of Wright airplane on starting track, Wilbur between skids inspecting the motor before takeoff, two workmen standing by ready to swing the two propellers.
COCKDH following 168: Esso Air World, v. 6, Nov./Dec. 1953: 68; SMIN A3406; SMIN 42,584–A

Left rear view of Wright airplane at starting rail, Wilbur in shirt sleeves standing between skids at throttle of motor, workman near one propeller.
Esso Air World, v. 6, Nov./Dec. 1953: 69; FWGMBH 4; SMIN 42,845–E

Left front view of Wright airplane on launching track.
SMIN 43,063–C

Rear view of Wright airplane being prepared for takeoff by Wilbur, two assistants aiding and a large group of spectators in background, October 10.
SMIN 42,447–C

Front view of Wright airplane on launching rail, workmen active around airplane, launching derrick in background, large group of spectators observing preparations for flight on October 10.
R Aero Soc J, v. 57, Dec. 1953: 778

Right rear view of Wright airplane on ground, Wilbur on ladder adjusting rudders, Hart O. Berg standing nearest to wing.
SMIN 42,846

Front view of Wright airplane on starting rail with men nearby hoisting launching weight in preparation for takeoff.
SMIN A42,845–A

Left rear view of Wright airplane on ground at end of starting
rail, unsuccessful in taking off.
Allg Auto Zeit, v. 9, Oct. 3, 1908: 35

Right rear view of Wright airplane taking off from starting rail.
**GSWB 21; LVTNA 311; Revue aérienne, v. 2, Jan. 25,
1909: 56; Revue de l'aviation, v. 3, Sept. 15, 1908: 5;
Wiener Luftschiffer-Zeitung, v. 7, Nov. 1908: 218**

Left rear view of Wright airplane in low-level flight just after
takeoff from starting rail.
Allg Auto Zeit, v. 9, Oct. 3, 1909: 35

Right front view of Wright airplane immediately after takeoff,
the jettisonable undercarriage visible beneath the skids.
MCFWP 169; SMIN A3403

Left rear view of Wright airplane in flight just after takeoff.
SMIN 43,064–K

Side view of Wright airplane in level flight.
**GSAHS facing 128; GSEFM; GSREA b. 272–273; Lon-
don Magazine, v. 21, Feb. 1909: 622; Vie grand air,
v. 21, June 8, 1912: 400**

Full front view of Wright airplane in flight, witnessed by spectators in distant background and two unidentified men at extreme right.
SMIN 42,846–D

Right front view of Wright airplane, Wilbur in training flight
with Count Lambert, buildings visible in lower foreground.
LVTNA 311

Left front view of Wright airplane in level flight passing to the
right of the starting derrick at nightfall.
**Everybody's Magazine, v. 20, Jan. 1909: 111; London
Magazine, v. 21, Feb. 1909: 621. Similar: L' aviation illustrée, v. 1, Mar. 6, 1909: cover; HATWYF facing 33**

Left front view of Wright airplane in level flight above treetops.
**CHAHA 64; Revue de l'aviation, v. 3, Sept. 15, 1908: 6;
Wiener Luftschiffer-Zeitung, v. 7, Nov. 1908: 279**

Wilbur in flight turning to his left near edge of flying field.
**L'Aérophile, v. 16, Oct. 15, 1908: 398; L'Aérophile,
v. 16, Dec. 1, 1908: 475; Revue aérienne, v. 2, Jan. 25,
1909: 34**

Wright airplane in low-level flight, turning to right, with marker
flag, two men, and woman at lower right.
SMIN 43,055–E

Right front view of Wright airplane in flight over flying field,
only trees visible in far distance.
SMIN 43,147–A

Wilbur guides his plane past the starting derrick at Camp d'Auvours, Le Mans, France, at twilight on September 21, 1908, for a flight that established world records for distance and duration. National Air and Space Museum, Smithsonian Institution, photo no. A42445J.

Wright airplane in high-level flight on November 18, Wilbur flying to an altitude of 60 meters and winning the 25-meter altitude prize of the Aéro-Club de France.
> **MCFWP 170**

Wright airplane in high-level flight, Wilbur flying above a 100-meter balloon to an altitude of 115 meters, establishing a new world record and winning the altitude prize of the Aéro-Club de la Sarthe, December 18.
> **MCFWP 171; L'Aérophile, v. 17, Jan. 1, 1909: 12; American Heritage, v. 11, Feb. 1960: 62; DOBOHA 196; Fachzeitung für Automobilismus, v. 3, Jan. 17, 1909: 16; Graphic, v. 78, Dec. 26, 1908: 815; L'Illustration, v. 132, Dec. 26, 1908: 443; Ill Aero Mitteil, v. 13, Jan. 13, 1909: 3; Motor, v. 14, Dec. 29, 1908: 741; Revue aérienne, v. 2, Jan. 25, 1909: 58; Revue de l' aviation, v. 4, Jan. 1, 1909: 11**

Right front view of Wright airplane in flight passing an American flag raised on the Auvours flying field at the start of Wilbur's record-breaking flight (which won the Michelin Cup for 1908 and a prize of 20,000 francs) covering 123 kilometers, 200 meters in a time of 2 hours, 18 minutes, 33⅗ seconds, December 31.
> **L'Illustration, v. 133, Jan. 8, 1909: 36**

Wright airplane in flight near sundown and end of Wilbur's record-breaking flight, December 31.
> **HILBW 58**

1908, Fort Myer, Virginia

Wright airplane loaded on top of a military supply wagon being towed by automobile to the Fort Myer parade ground, Orville, in straw hat, standing on running board of car, Spencer Crane driving. Orville had arrived in Washington on August 20 to conduct acceptance test with Wright airplane for the U.S. Army.

MCFWP 156; Aero Digest, v. 11, Dec. 1927: 638; HAWBHP 156; Look, v. 2, Feb. 1, 1938: 56; Nat Geog Mag, v. 104, Dec. 1953: 742; SMIN A18,470; SMIN 42,290–G; TILLMU 35; USAF 486113

Wright airplane being transported from balloon shed to hangar, on parade ground, large military spherical balloon at extreme left.

MCFWP 157; Aero Digest, v. 11, Dec. 1927: 638; Bee-Hive, v. 28, Spring 1953: 21; CLHAGW facing 140; JOHHU 233; Nat Geog Mag, v. 112, Aug. 1957: 267; SMIN 42,287–D; TILLMU 57; USAF 5434 A.C.; USAF 49,589; U.S. Air Services, v. 29, Sept. 1931: 22

Wright airplane being transported across parade ground, large spherical balloon visible at right, many spectators on ground.

SMIN 42,284–E

Wright airplane on top of military supply wagon in front of hangar.

MCFWP 155; SMIN 42,286–G; TILLMU 34

Orville standing beside wagon used to transport Wright airplane at entrance to hangar.

SMIN 42,286–H; USAF 48610

Orville standing at wing tip of Wright airplane being removed from transport wagon.

MCFWP 154; SMIN 42,289–C

Close-up view of center section of Wright airplane showing bicycle-chain transmission, radiator, gas tank, seat, and controls.

MCFWP 158; ASMEJ, v. 30, Dec. 1908: b. 1642–1643; CLHAGW facing 168; JOHHU 240; ME-FMF facing 54; SMINAR 1908 b. 134–135; USAF 17497

Close-up view of center section of Wright airplane showing seat, motor, and skids.

SMIN 42,287–B

Close-up view of center section of Wright airplane showing control levers, motor, and fuel tank.

SMIN 42,290–B

Close-up view of center section of Wright airplane showing motor, radiator, and right propeller.

Aero Digest, v. 11, Dec. 1927: 640; HAWBHP 77; SMIN 42,290–E; USAF 48605

View of center section of Wright airplane from right wing tip between struts.
SMIN 42,290–D

Close-up view of controls of Wright airplane.
Aero Digest, v. 11; Dec. 1927: 640; Sci Am, v. 99, Sept. 26, 1908: 208; SMIN 17,132–A

Detail of strut fitting and warping wire pulley of Wright airplane.
USAF 48600

View of Wright airplane partly assembled in hangar.
SMIN 42,284–H

Close-up view of blinker between elevator planes.
Aero Digest, v. 11, Dec. 1927: 640; Sci Am, v. 99, Sept. 26, 1908; SMIN 42,286–E; USAF 48595

Close-up view of lower end of rudder assembly of Wright airplane.
SMIN 42,287

Close-up view of rudder and boom of Wright airplane.
Aero Digest, v. 11, Dec. 1927: 640; SMIN 42,287–A; SMIN 76–17483; USAF 48599

Close-up view of motor mounted in Wright airplane.
SMIN 21,862–A

Close-up rear view of Wright airplane showing propellers and bicycle-chain transmission.
ASMEJ, v. 30, Dec. 1908: b. 1642–1643; SMINAR 1908: b. 134–135

Close-up view of center section of Wright airplane showing radiator, gas tank, and seat.
ASMEJ, v. 30, Dec. 1908: b. 1642–1643; SMINAR 1908: facing 134

Close-up view of lefthand propeller in Wright airplane.
SMIN 6, 159–C

Side view of Wright airplane in hangar, spectators gathered around inspecting it.
SMIN 42,285–G; USAF 48601

Side view of Wright airplane in hangar, five maintenance personnel at side and in front of plane.
SMIN 42,284–H

Full left side view of Wright airplane on parade ground.
SMIN 42,285–E

The Wright airplane, on the parade grounds at Fort Myer, Virginia, with a military balloon behind it, is being readied for army test flights, September 1908.

Left side view of Wright airplane on parade ground, Fort Myer buildings in background.
SMIN 42,284–F

Right front view of Wright airplane in front of hangar, small group looking on at left.
SMIN 43,055–D

Left front view of Wright airplane on parade ground, small group of spectators at left.
SMIN 43,056–E

Left side view of Wright airplane being pulled by military personnel to starting point for flight.
SMIN 42,288–G

Side view of Wright airplane on starting track, launching tower at left, military personnel pulling rope to raise weight to top of tower.
SMIN 42,534

Right front view of Wright airplane on launching track, Charles W. Furnas and Charles E. Taylor standing at front.
SMIN 42,287–E; USAF 48587

Left side view of Wright airplane being rolled across parade ground to launching site.
SMIN 42,928–H

Left rear view of Wright airplane being rolled across parade ground to takeoff site.
SMIN 42,289–H

Front view of Wright airplane being rolled over parade ground by military personnel, several women walking in front, numerous spectators in rear.
SMIN 43,056–F

Left front view of Wright airplane in front of hangar, military personnel starting to roll airplane to starting point for flight.
Look, v. 2, Feb. 1, 1938: 56; SMIN 42,287–E; USAF 48609

Right front view of Wright airplane being placed on launching track.
SMIN 42,284–B

Side view of Wright airplane being placed on launching track, military personnel working in front of airplane.
SMIN 42,290–C

Rear view of Wright airplane in hangar as seen from outside, with reporters, photographers, and spectators gathered around entrance.
LC-JONES; SMIN 42,288; SMIN 42,290–F; USAF 9554 A.S.; USAF 243393

Front view of Wright airplane being wheeled from tent hangar.
TILLMU 58; SMIN 42,289–E. Similar: LC-JONES

View of crowd gathered to witness flights by Orville, launching derrick at extreme right, Fort Myer buildings in background.
LC-BAIN

Right front view of Wright airplane on parade ground at Fort Myer, spectators behind roped off area at rear.
LC-BAIN

Right front view of Wright airplane in hangar, two men working on it.
LC-BAIN

Front view of Wright airplane in front of hangar, group of spectators looking on at right rear.
LC-BAIN

Lt. Frank P. Lahm in front of his horse holding its bridle, conversing with Glenn Curtiss, crowds witnessing Wright flights in background.
SMIN 42,667–D; USAF 48594

View of monorail and tower used to start Wright airplane, Fort Myer barracks buildings in background.
Fly, v. 1, Nov. 1908: 6; SMIN 43,062–C

Right front view of Wright airplane on starting track, launching tower behind, spectators gathered around airplane.
Aero Digest, v. 11, Dec. 1927: 683; SMIN A17,132–B; TAPHF 34; USAF 48606

View of large crowd gathered around Wright airplane and launching tower, Fort Myer building in background.
SMIN 43,056–H

Wright airplane being placed on launching track.
SMIN 42,284–B; SMIN 42,290–C

Right front view of Wright airplane on launching track, Orville seen leaning over pilot's seat.
SMIN 42,290; USAF 243399

Left front view of Wright airplane on launching track, Orville at front of machine with Maj. George O. Squier and Lt. Thomas E. Selfridge.
HAWBHP 78; SMIN 42,288–A

Front view of Wright airplane landing.
SMIN 43,190

Orville and Augustus Post, Aero Club of America secretary, full length, in front of Signal Corps tent, September 5.
LC-JONES; SMIN 42,288–B; SMIN 42,289–G

Right front view of Wright airplane in flight, Fort Myer buildings in background, September 8.
ASMEJ, v. 30, Dec. 1908: b. 1642–1643; CLHAGW facing 168; APGAFM 36; Sat Eve Post, v. 201, July 14, 1928: 19; SMINAR 1908: b. 134–135; USAF 52661

Group photograph of high-ranking government officials and military officers gathered around Wright airplane awaiting flight by Orville.
LC-JONES: MILWA v. 2: 159; SMIN 31,246–F

Orville seated at the controls of the Wright airplane, with Lt. Frank P. Lahm, passenger, September 9.
SMIN 42,589

Wright airplane taking off from launching track on flight, September 9.
LC-BAIN

Front view of Wright airplane in flight, Fort Myer buildings and trees in background, Orville's flight of 6 minutes, 24 seconds with Lt. Frank P. Lahm, September 9.

LC-JONES; Aerosphere, 1943: CXXV; USAF 9593 A.S.; U.S. Air Services, v. 16, Sept. 1931: 22. Similar: USAF 9592 A.S.; USAF 16764

Group photograph of high-ranking government officials and military officers conversing and inspecting Wright airplane following flight of 6 minutes, 24 seconds by Orville with Lt. Frank P. Lahm, September 9.

LC-JONES; SMIN 42,255; U.S. Air Services, v. 16, Sept. 1931: 21

Front view of Orville's flight of 1 hour, 2 minutes, 15 seconds on September 9.

LC-JONES; MCFWP 159; SMIN 42,288-D

Front view of Orville in relatively low flight, with trees, grounds, and one of the gateway entrances to Fort Myer visible below, the flight lasting 1 hour, 2 minutes, 15 seconds, September 9.

LC-JONES; ASMEJ, v. 30, Dec. 1908: b. 1642-1643; Flight, v. 1, May 1, 1909: 251; HEGOV facing 81; GHUSAF 5; JOHHU 240; SMINAR 1908: b. 136-137; TILLMU 2; USAF 4282 A.S.

Right front view of Orville circling parade ground, Fort Myer buildings visible in background, September 9.

LC-JONES; MCFWP 161; ASHWB 62; ASMEJ, v. 30, Dec. 1908: b. 1642-1643; COCKDH following 168; Flight, v. 1, May 1, 1909: 251; MILWA v. 2: 156; SMINAR 1908: b. 138-139; USAF 4280 A.S.; YPHA 35. Similar, at higher altitude: CHBLWB facing 240; World's Work, v. 17, Nov. 1908: 10848

Side view of Wright airplane rising shortly after takeoff on flight of 1 hour, 2 minutes, 15 seconds on September 9.

LC-JONES; USAF 9580 A.S.

Wright airplane in flight over Fort Myer parade ground, fort buildings in background below, mounted cavalryman in foreground at right, September 9.

LC-JONES; Popular Aviation, v. 3, Dec. 1928: 12; SMIN 42,288-C; USAF 9577 A.S.

Seven views of Orville's flight of 62 minutes, 15 seconds on September 9.

World's Work, v. 17, Nov. 1908: 10849

Series of six photographs of Orville's flight of 1 hour, 10 minutes, 24 seconds, which set a new world flying endurance record, September 11.

USAF 9498 A.S.; USAF 9595 A.S.; USAF 9597 A.S.; USAF 9599 A.S.; USAF 9690 A.S.

Series of seven photographs of Orville's flight of 1 hour, 10 minutes, 24 seconds on September 11.
LC-BAIN

Right front view of Wright airplane on launching track ready for takeoff, Orville and passenger, Maj. George O. Squier, seated in airplane, September 12.
APGAFM 36; ASMEJ v. 30, Dec. 1908: b. 1642–1643; BUFJM 14; Everybody's Magazine, v. 20, Jan. 1909: 110; Flight, v. 1, May 1, 1909: 252; Ill Aero Mitteil, v. 12, Mar. 10, 1909: 171; SMINAR 1908: facing 138

Right front view of Wright airplane on launching track, Orville at front of airplane supervising preparation for takeoff with Maj. George O. Squier as passenger, September 12.
LC-JONES; MCFWP 162; LOOWGF 7; USAF 9587 A.S. Similar: CAIAF 3; FRFH facing 178; USAF 9588 A.S.

Front view of Wright airplane, Orville flying with Maj. George O. Squier as passenger, in the air 9 minutes, 6⅓ seconds, establishing a new world record for flight with two men, September 12.
LC-JONES; MCFWP 163; ASMEJ, v. 30, Dec 1908: b. 1642–1643; Everybody's Magazine, v. 20, Jan. 1909: 104; Flight, v. 1, May 1, 1909: 253; GSPA 36; GSWB 23; HAWBHP 77; Nat Aero Assn Rev, v. 3, Dec. 1925: 189; SMIN 42,204–A; SMINAR 1908: b. 138–139; TILLMU 41; USAF 4613 A.S. Similar: USAF 9583

Side view from below of Wright airplane in level flight overhead, September 12.
LC-JONES; ASMEJ, v. 30, Dec. 1908: b. 1642–1643; Flight, v. 1, May 1, 1909: 252; GSWFAF 16; GSIA 152; GSREA b. 272–273; GSWB 23; SMINAR 1908: b. 136–137. Similar, trees and road in background: ASMEJ, v. 30, Dec. 1908: b. 1642–1643; Flight, v. 1, May 1909: 252; SMINAR 1908: b. 136–137

Series of views of Wright airplane in flight—front, overhead, left side, right side, and underside.
SMIN 42,284 (A, D, J); SMIN 42,285 (C, F, H); SMIN 42,286 (A, F); SMIN 42,287 (C, G, H); SMIN 42,288–F; SMIN 42,289 (A, F); SMIN 42,290–H

Rear view of Wright airplane in flight.
MCFWP 160; SMIN 42,284–C; SMIN 76–17460

Orville in front of Wright airplane adjusting motor, Lt. Thomas E. Selfridge seated in airplane, September 17.
SMIN 31,990–A

Orville seated at controls of Wright airplane on starting track ready for takeoff, Lt. Thomas E. Selfridge, passenger, seated at his right, September 17.

> MCFWP 164; Aeronautics, v. 5, Apr. 1909: 145; Bee-Hive, v. 28, Jan. 1953: 12; CLHAGW b. 168–169; HAWBHP 80; SMIN 42,225–C; SMIN 42,286–D; SMIN 42,869–E; TILLMU 44; USAF 48608; WODKH b. 220–221; World's Work, v. 56, Sept. 1927: 518

1908, Fort Myer Accident, September 17

Crumpled wreckage of Wright airplane, Fort Myer, September 17, 1908. The airplane had crashed to earth from a height of about 75 feet after the propeller blade broke and the machine went out of control. Orville, seriously injured, is being removed from wreckage. Lt. Thomas E. Selfridge, his passenger, lies on ground to right, fatally injured. He died several hours later.

> MCFWP 165; ASHWB 66; CAIAF 2; GHUSAF 5; GSEFM; GSPA 36; JOHHU 245; KELMKH b. 238–239; Nat Geog Mag, v. 104, Dec. 1953: 143; SMIN 42,667–E; USAF 49588; YPHA 35

Men lifting wing of Wright airplane to remove Orville who was pinned beneath the wreckage.

> COCKDH following 168; SMIN 42,869–B; SMIN 42,869–C

Doctors examining Orville after removal from wrecked Wright airplane.

> SMIN 42,927

View of bottom wing of wrecked Wright airplane, elevators tilted above wing, crowd at left of picture gathered around Orville.

> SMIN 42,869

Orville being carried from flying field on a stretcher, bottom wing of wrecked Wright airplane visible in background, mounted cavalry officers and military personnel at right.

> Collier's, v. 80, Aug. 20, 1927: 9; SMIN 42,869–F

View of Wright airplane wreck immediately following crash, spectators lifting wings to remove Lt. Selfridge, pinned beneath the wreckage.

> COCKDH following 168; HMSHSA facing 187; KELMKH b. 238–239; SMIN 42,667–E; USAF 48588

Three men bending over Lt. Selfridge who is lying on ground after removal from airplane, spectators at right.

> COCKDH following 168; SMIN 42,869–A; Washingtonian, v. 14, Nov. 1978: 189

Physicians administering to Lt. Selfridge, who is lying on ground. Wright airplane is at left, four cavalry officers at center and right, group of spectators at left and in center.
SMIN 42,289–D

Lt. Selfridge on stretcher being removed from scene of accident. Crowd is gathered at left and behind it is a mounted cavalry officer.
SMIN 42,285–B; USAF 48613. Similar: SMIN 42,927–A

View of wreckage of Wright airplane, crowd gathered around on sides and at rear.
SMIN 42,927–E

View of wreckage of Wright airplane, group of bystanders and horse and buggy in foreground.
SMIN 42,290–A; SMIN 76–17456

Propeller tip broken in accident.
SMIN 42,1684; TILLMU 52; USAF 48612

Rear view of propeller removed from Wright 1908 machine.
SMIN 6159–G

Wright airplane fitting which broke, contributing to accident.
SMIN 42,688–C

Close-up view between wing panels of Wright airplane showing damage caused by accident.
SMIN 42,286

Close-up view of damaged skid on Wright airplane.
SMIN 42,284–G

View of wreckage of Wright airplane, right end of airplane tilted upward.
COCKDH following 168; Collier's, v. 42, Oct. 3, 1908: 11; Pop Sci, v. 114, May 1929: 50; Washingtonian, v. 14, Nov. 1978: 189; World's Work, v. 56, Sept. 1927: 519

Close-up view of Wright airplane wreckage, bottom wing visible with elevators projecting above wing.
Illustrated London News, v. 133, Oct. 3, 1908: 480; L'Illustration, v. 132, Oct. 10, 1908: 244; SMIN 42,286–B; SMIN 76–17454

Close-up view of wrecked Wright airplane, mounted cavalry officer and civilian passing by.
SMIN 42,285–D; SMIN 76–17482

View of wreckage of Wright airplane, mounted cavalry officers and spectators at right.
SMIN 42,927–C

1909, Pont-Long, Pau, France

Wilbur and Orville in front of hangar, Wilbur issuing instructions to several workmen on either side of them relating to the completion of the hangar to house the Wright airplane, other workmen seen at work on hangar in background. Wilbur, seeking a warmer climate to continue the training of his students Count Charles de Lambert, Capt. Paul N. Lucas-Girardville, and Paul Tissandier, went to Pau at the edge of the Pyrénées Mountains in southern France, arriving on January 14.
> SMIN 18,054–A. Similar, long-range view of hangar: L'Aviation illustrée, v. 1, Jan. 30, 1909: 4

Right front view of Wright airplane in front of hangar, small number of spectators gathered around inspecting airplane.
> L'Aviation illustrée, v. 1, Feb. 20, 1909: 5

Group photo at Pau, including Louis Blériot, Paul Tissandier, Capt. Paul N. Lucas-Girardville, Wilbur, Mrs. Hart O. Berg, Count Charles de Lambert, and Katharine.
> L'Aérophile, v. 17, Feb. 15, 1909: 85; Allg Auto Zeit, v. 10, Feb. 21, 1909: 39; Automotor, v. 14, Feb. 20, 1909: 217; CHAHA 66; Flight, v. 1, Mar. 20, 1909: 6; Graphic, v. 79, Feb. 20, 1909: 224; HAWBHP 81; HEGOV facing 97; Revue aérienne, v. 1, Feb. 25, 1909: facing 105; Vie grand air, v. 15, May 29, 1909: 356

Wilbur's students: Paul Tissandier, Capt. Lucas-Girardville, Count de Lambert.
> DOBOHA 187

Paul Tissandier, head and shoulders.
> PEPHO facing 120

Paul Tissandier on flying field, full length.
> Revue aérienne, v. 2, Apr. 10, 1909: 222; Vie grand air, v. 15, Apr. 24, 1909: 263

Paul Tissandier seated in Wright airplane.
> L'Aérophile, v. 17, Apr. 1, 1909: 158; L'Aviation illustrée, v. 1, Apr. 10, 1909: 4; The Car, v. 28, Mar. 31, 1909: 265; Fachzeitung für Automobilismus, v. 3, Apr. 4, 1909: 23; LOUVA facing 400; VCAAF 57

Wilbur at front of Wright airplane instructing Paul Tissandier in its operation.
> HILBW 50; MILWA v. 2: 172

Count de Lambert, full length, at edge of Wright airplane.
> Revue aérienne, v. 2, Apr. 10, 1909: 221; Vie grand air, v. 15, Apr. 24, 1909: 262

Count de Lambert seated in Wright airplane.
>L'Aérophile, v. 17, Apr. 1, 1909: 158; The Car,
>v. 28, Mar. 31, 1909: 265; Fachzeitung für Auto-
>mobilismus, v. 3, Apr. 4, 1909: 23; LOUVA facing 400;
>SBNA 120; VCAAF 57

Orville seated in Wright airplane instructing Count de Lambert,
seated at his right, in the operation of the airplane.
>Vie grand air, v. 15, Mar. 13, 1909: 167

Distinguished visitors to Pau, including Lord Arthur J. Balfour,
former prime minister of England, Lord Alfred Northcliffe, and
Lord Alfred Harmsworth, pulling on rope used to raise weight
to top of starting derrick. February 11.
>ADAMSF 93; Graphic, v. 79, Feb. 20, 1909: 224;
>R Aero Soc J, v. 57, Dec. 1953: 780; Vie grand air,
>Feb. 27, 1909: 135; YPHA 34. Similar: LVTNA 309

Group of five on flying field at Pau, Duke William of Manchester pointing out a feature of the Wright airplane at left to
Lord Balfour and Lord Northcliffe.
>COCKDH following 168

Lord Balfour and Lord Northcliffe in conversation with Wilbur
close to Wright airplane, Orville with back to camera.
>MILWA v. 2: 149. Similar without Orville: Graphic,
>v. 79, Feb. 20, 1909: 224

Lord Northcliffe and Orville at rear of Wright airplane.
>R Aero Soc J, v. 57, Dec. 1953: 780; SMIN 32,031

Lord Northcliffe and Lord Balfour, wearing winter overcoats, at
Pau to witness flights by Wilbur.
>LC-BECK (two similar photos); COCKDH following
>168

Capt. Paul N. Lucas-Girardville on flying field, full length.
>Revue aérienne, v. 2, Apr. 10, 1909: 224

Capt. Lucas-Girardville seated in Wright airplane.
>L'Aérophile, v. 17, Apr. 1, 1909: 158; The Car, v. 28,
>Mar. 31, 1909: 265; Fachzeitung für Automobilismus,
>v. 3, Apr. 4, 1909: 23

Wilbur at front of Wright airplane instructing Capt. Lucas-
Girardville in its operation.
>Graphic, v. 79, Feb. 20, 1909: 224

Wilbur in front of Wright airplane instructing Paul Tissandier,
Capt. Lucas-Girardville, and Count de Lambert in its operation.
>HILBW 37

Wilbur and Count de Lambert seated in Wright airplane ready
for takeoff.
>Ill Aero Mitteil, v. 13, Feb. 24, 1909: 142

Count de Lambert and Wilbur in front of the Wright airplane, Countess de Lambert seated in Wright airplane ready for flight with Wilbur on February 15.

L'Aérophile, v. 17, Nov. 1909: 483; Ill Aero Mitteil, v. 13, Feb. 24, 1909: 142; Vie grand air, v. 15, Feb. 27, 1909: 134

Katharine seated in Wright airplane next to Wilbur on the occasion of her first flight in an airplane, February 15.

LC-BECK; MCFWP 220; Collier's, v. 80, Aug. 20, 1927: 8; MCMWB facing 220; MEFMF facing 103; MILWA v. 2: 172; SMIN 42,783–L

Wilbur at front of Wright airplane adjusting motor.

SMIN 42,805–H

Right front view of Wright airplane being prepared for flight, Wilbur about to climb out from under machine after attaching launching rope.

Automotor, v. 14, Mar. 20, 1909: 337; Flight, v. 1, Mar. 20, 1909: 158

Wilbur, oilcan in hand, preparing Wright airplane for flight, Orville standing nearby at his right, several spectators observing activities.

Automotor, v. 14, Mar. 20, 1909: 136; Flight, v. 1, Mar. 20, 1909: 157

Wright airplane being pushed into hangar, small group on right, back of fence, watching.

SMIN 42,804–D

Front view of Wright hangar, with doors open to take out Wright airplane, Wilbur walking energetically, about to enter, and Charles S. Rolls's Rolls-Royce visible in front of hangar.

Automotor, v. 14, Mar. 13, 1909: 304

Close-up photo of Wilbur in leather jacket at side of starting rail arranging launching catapult tackle.

MCFWP 172; HMSHSA facing 179; SMIN 31,991; Vie grand air, v. 15, May 15, 1909: 1744; WODKH front.

Close-up view of center section of Wright airplane showing motor, fuel tank, and radiator.

Allg Auto Zeit, v. 10, Mar. 14, 1909: 42; Flight, v. 1, Mar. 27, 1909: 182

Right front view of Wright airplane being removed from hangar.

Allg Auto Zeit, v. 10, Feb. 14, 1909: 30; L'Aviation illustrée, v. 1, Feb. 20, 1909: 5; SMIN 42,961–C

Wright airplane on starting rail ready for takeoff, derrick in rear.

L'Aéronaute, v. 41, Mar. 15, 1909: 16; Revue aérienne, v. 2, Mar. 10, 1909: 156

Wilbur seated in Wright airplane, staring intently ahead, ready for takeoff.
SMIN 31,247–E

Wilbur making adjustments to starting rail, Orville looking on from right, Wilbur's three students at left.
Aeroplane, v. 85, Dec. 18, 1953: 811; Automotor, v. 14, Mar. 6, 1909: 263; Flight, v. 1, Mar. 6, 1909: 128. Similar: Allg Auto Zeit, v. 10, Feb. 14, 1909: 30; L'Aviation illustrée, v. 1, Feb. 20, 1909: 5; Revue de l'aviation, v. 4, Mar. 1, 1909: 37; SBNA 106

Wilbur and Orville, three-quarter length, Orville pointing cane toward Wright airplane.
Allg Auto Zeit, v. 10, Feb. 14, 1909: 30; Fachzeitung für Automobilismus, v. 3, Feb. 21, 1909: 22; Revue aérienne, v. 2, Feb. 25, 1909: 113

Wilbur holding aloft an anemometer for measuring wind speed, Orville looking on at his right, front of Wright airplane visible at extreme left.
COCKDH following 168; HILBW 43

Side view of Wright airplane being placed on launching rail in preparation for flight, workmen seen on all sides assisting in preparations, starting derrick visible at extreme right.
Esso Air World, v. 6, Nov./Dec. 1953: 68; R Aero Soc J, v. 57, Dec. 1953: 779

Left front view of Wilbur just taking off after pulling release lever, derrick seen at right with weight descending.
Automotor, v. 14, Mar. 20, 1909: 338; Flight, v. 1, Mar. 20, 1909: 159

Close-up view of crowd inside roped-off area on flying field looking up at Wilbur as he flies by overhead, men waving their hats to him as he approaches.
GSEFM

Left front view of Wilbur in flight with passenger.
GSWB 25; SMIN 42,446

Wright airplane in flight over hangar, crowd inside fenced-off area in front of hangar observing flight.
HILBW 53

Wilbur and Paul Tissandier seated in slightly damaged Wright airplane, resting on ground after faulty takeoff with rudder broken.
Vie grand air, v. 15, Feb. 13, 1909: 101

Wilbur and small group of spectators watching removal of rudder from airplane following accident.
The Car, v. 28, Feb. 17, 1909: 25

Wilbur flying with one of his pupils, Paul Tissandier, at Pau, France, January 1909. National Air and Space Museum, Smithsonian Institution, photo no. A42962–A.

Automobiles lined up outside fence at edge of flying field, occupants watching Wilbur in flight overhead.
MCFWP 173; SMIN A3400

Distant side view of Wilbur in flight, hangar, and large crowd witnessing flight in foreground.
SMIN A42,961–J

Wilbur with Paul Tissandier as passenger in flight over three horse-drawn carriages, occupants waiting at the edge of the flying field to witness flight.
**ASHWB 66; GSEFM cover; HARFF 110;
L'Illustration, v. 133, Feb. 27, 1909: 139; KELWB
facing 244; LVTDAO 82; MEFMF facing 118;
MILWA v. 2: 150: NOZWBC front.; SMIN
A42,962–A; SMIN 510A 34**

Wilbur explains the mechanism of his airplane to
King Alfonso XIII of Spain, seated at his right, during
flights at Pau, France, in February 1909.

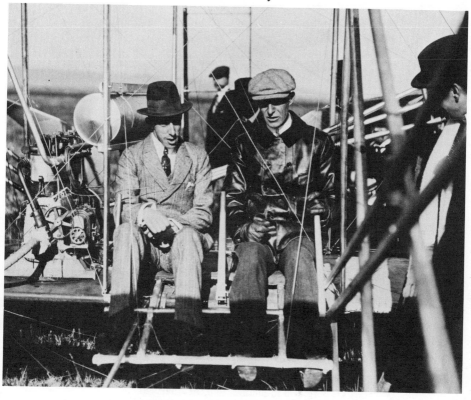

Large crowd assembled at flying field waving to Wilbur as he
flies overhead.
The Car, v. 28, Feb. 17, 1909: 25; SMIN A42,961–B

Wilbur in flight over a marsh near flying field, reflection of airplane seen in water.
Motor, v. 15, Mar. 30, 1909: 315

Wilbur with Capt. Lucas-Girardville in flight over hay cart
pulled by team of oxen.
LC-BECK; BUFJM 15; Collier's, v. 80, Sept. 24, 1927: 18; Graphic, v. 79, Feb. 20, 1909: 224; Liberty, v. 53, Dec. 22, 1928: 20; MAIKA facing 34; MILWA v. 2: 151

Wilbur in flight over three hay carts pulled by oxen in field
below.
COCKDH following 168; KELWB facing 244; NOZWBC facing 139; SMIN 31,246; SMIN A38,497–G

Wilbur flying with Capt. Paul N. Lucas-Girardville over a hay cart at Pau, France, in 1909.

King Alfonso XIII of Spain greeting Wilbur and Orville, with Hart O. Berg also in picture, Pau, February 20.
> **Allg Auto Zeit, v. 10, Feb. 28, 1909: cover; Autocar, v. 22, Feb. 27, 1909: 281; L'Aviation illustrée, v. 1, Feb. 27, 1909: 5; The Car, v. 28, Feb. 24, 1909: cover; Fly, v. 1, Apr. 1909: 12; Ill Aero Mitteil, v. 13, Mar. 10, 1909: 192; L'Illustration, v. 133, Feb. 27, 1909: 140; Revue aérienne, v. 5, June 10, 1912: 303; SBNA 112; SMIN 42,962**

Orville and Wilbur conversing with King Alfonso near the Wright airplane hangar.
> **L'Aérophile, v. 17, Mar. 15, 1909: 133; World's Work, v. 20, Aug. 1910: 13304**

Hart O. Berg, King Alfonso's equerry, with back to camera, Wilbur, King Alfonso, with back to camera, and Orville, with back to camera.
> **LC-BECK**

King Alfonso and his equerry with Orville and Wilbur, who are explaining mechanism of Wright airplane.
> **LC-BECK**

Wilbur in pilot's seat of Wright airplane, King Alfonso, and Orville pointing out a detail of the airplane.
Vie grand air, v. 15, Feb. 27, 1909: 133

Group picture with Katharine, King Alfonso, and Orville in center talking with him.
LC-BECK. Similar: LC-BECK; Allg Auto Zeit, v. 10, Feb. 28, 1909: 40; World's Work, v. 20, Aug. 1910: 13307

Wilbur speaking with King Alfonso (back to camera), Lord Alfred Northcliffe (in derby) behind him.
MCFWP 175

Close-up view of Wilbur seated in Wright airplane, King Alfonso seated at his right, Wilbur explaining mechanism of the Wright airplane to him.
Allg Auto Zeit, v. 10, Feb. 28, 1909: 39; COCKDH following 168; Fachzeitung für Automobilismus, v. 4, Mar. 7, 1909: 19; Motor, v. 15, Feb. 23, 1909: 113; NOZWBC facing 138; Vie grand air, v. 15, Feb. 27, 1909: 136

Wilbur seated in Wright airplane, explaining the use of lever releasing airplane for flight, King Alfonso and Orville standing nearby.
Airman, v. 8, Dec. 1964: 19; HILBW facing 47; KELWB b. 180–181; SMIN 43,147–E; SUBDF v. 2: 159. Similar: LOCA 273; side view; HILBW 59

King Alfonso with small group near flying field fence watching Wilbur in flight overhead, Wilbur approaching from left.
L'Aviation illustrée, v. 1, Feb. 27, 1909: cover; SBNA 109. Similar, more distant view: Allg Auto Zeit, v. 10, Feb. 28, 1909: 41; Automotor, v. 14, Feb. 27, 1909: 248; The Car, v. 28, Feb. 24, 1909: cover; Ill Aero Mitteil, v. 13, Mar. 10, 1909: 194; Motor, v. 15, Mar. 2, 1909: 183

Louis Barthou, French minister of public works, seated in Wright airplane conversing with Wilbur before a flight with him, February 22.
HILBW 52

Orville and Katharine with group gathered around the gondola of the balloon *Icare* as Orville and Katharine await ascension with French balloonists Ernest Zens and the Marquis Edgard de Kergariou, Pau, February 25.
COCKDH following 168

King Edward VII of England, walking with Wilbur and Orville to the Wright hangar, Pau, March 17.

> **ADAMSF 91; L'Aérophile, v. 17, Apr. 1, 1909: 157;
> Allg Auto Zeit, v. 10, Mar. 26, 1909: 39; ASHWB 73;
> The Car, v. 28, Mar. 24, 1909: cover; Collier's, v. 80,
> Sept. 24, 1927: 19; Flight, v. 1, Mar. 27, 1909: 184;
> Fly, v. 1, May 1909: 8; SMIN A42,783**

Orville and Wilbur with King Edward.

> **COCKDH following 168; Collier's, v. 80, Sept. 24,
> 1909: 19; Graphic, v. 79, Mar. 27, 1909; 393; Liberty,
> v. 5, Dec. 22, 1928: 20; MARWBC 42; MILWA v. 2:
> 170; SMIN 30,959–H; Vie grand air, v. 15, Mar. 27,
> 1909: 197. In reverse: YPHA 30**

Wilbur explaining the operation of his machine to King Edward, close-up view of airplane.

> **Graphic, v. 79, Mar. 27, 1909: 393; R Aero Soc J,
> v. 57, Dec. 1953: 785; SMIN A3466**

King Edward conversing with Orville, large group at side and at rear.

> **LC-BECK; Revue de l'aviation, v. 4, Apr. 1, 1909:
> cover; TAPHF 34**

King Edward accompanied by Lord Thomas Wilhelm Cunraven walking with large group on flying field to departure point for flight by Wilbur.

> **HILBW 51; SUBDF v. 1: 184**

King Edward and Orville with large group in front of the Wright hangar.

> **L'Aéronaute, v. 41, Apr. 15, 1909: 20; Fachzeitung für
> Automobilismus, v. 3, Mar. 28, 1909: 23; Vie grand air,
> v. 15, May 29, 1909: 355**

View of Wilbur in level flight at left of starting derrick, King Edward on opposite side behind derrick watching the flight, Orville in foreground center facing camera.

> **MCMWB 202; Pop Sci, v. 114, Feb. 1929: 42. Similar:
> Revue de l'aviation, v. 4, Apr. 1, 1909: 55**

Delegation from the French Chamber of Deputies examining starting rail on visit when they witnessed a flight by Wilbur, Pau, March 20.

> **L'Aérophile, v. 17, Apr. 1, 1909: 157**

Side view of Wright airplane in flight to left, Pyrenees Mountains in background.

> **Allg Auto Zeit, v. 10, Feb. 14, 1909: 29; Fachzeitung
> für Automobilismus, v. 4, Feb. 14, 1909: 24; Ill Aero
> Mitteil, v. 13, Mar. 10, 1909: 193**

Side view of Wright airplane in level flight, just turning to right, distant view of a road and spectators in background.

> **Flight, v. 1, Mar. 20, 1909: 160**

The Wright airplane being pulled by horses through the streets of Rome to the flying field at Centocelle, April 1909.

Left front view of Wright airplane in flight at considerable altitude, buildings and trees visible below, the Pyrenees Mountains seen in background.
> **L'Aviation illustrée, v. 1, Mar. 27, 1909: cover; The Car, v. 28, Mar. 24, 1909: cover; LVTNA 315; SBNA 94**

1909, Centocelle Field, Rome, Italy

Wright airplane being assembled in building in Rome, three workmen standing nearby. The Wrights had come to Italy to undertake the training of two Italian lieutenants, one from the Italian navy, the other from the army. Flights were made by Wilbur at Centocelle Field, April 15–27.
> **SMIN 42,962–D**

Wright airplane being assembled in Rome, Lt. Umberto Savoia watching Wilbur who is standing on box assisting several workmen.
> **SMIN 42,961–G**

Team of horses hauling the Wright airplane through streets of Rome to flying field at Centocelle, located 12 to 15 miles southeast of Rome. A group of civilians and two soldiers bearing rifles accompany the airplane.
MCFWP 176; SMIN 43,147–C. Similar: SMIN 42,962–E

Wright airplane on wagon en route to Centocelle Field, Lt. Umberto Savoia in foreground.
SMIN 42,961–F

Wright airplane on wagon arriving at Centocelle Field.
SMIN 42,962–H

Right front view of Wright airplane in hangar at Centocelle Field.
SMIN 42,961–E

Front view of Wright hangar at Centocelle Field, with truck nearby, crowd assembled.
SMIN 42,961–D

Front view of Wright airplane being taken out of hangar in preparation for flight.
Allg Auto Zeit, v. 10, May 2, 1909: 35; SMIN 37,774–D

Three-quarter rear view of Wright airplane in front of hangar at Centocelle Field, fence visible on left, a number of workers active in front of airplane.
SMIN 38,494–E

Three-quarter front view of Wright airplane being made ready for flight, Wilbur and Orville standing near airplane overseeing preparation with several Italian soldiers assisting.
L'Aéronaute, v. 42, May 15, 1909: 15; Allg Auto Zeit, v. 10, May 2, 1909: 35; SMIN 37,774–D

Three-quarter rear view of Wright airplane on field, workers active on side and in front of airplane.
ADAMSF 1909: 104

Three-quarter front view of airplane, Italian officers inspecting and discussing airplane.
SMIN 38,494–E. Similar: SMIN 38,494–F

Three-quarter front view of Wright airplane resting on starting rail.
SMIN 38,494–C

Wright airplane on launching track in front of hangar at Centocelle Field, weight being hoisted to top of derrick, crowd assembled at right.
SMIN 42,962–K

Wilbur ending a flight at dusk, Centocelle Field, April 1909.
National Air and Space Museum, Smithsonian Institution, photo
no. A38494B.

Wilbur working on Wright airplane at Centocelle Field.
L'Illustrazione Italiana, v. 36, Apr. 25, 1909: 433

Lts. Mario Calderara and Umberto Savoia at Centocelle Field,
where they received flying lessons from Wilbur, April 16–26.
L'Illustrazione Italiana, v. 36, Apr. 25, 1909: 433

Wilbur seated in Wright airplane with one of his Italian students, Lt. Mario Calderara.
SMIN 43,188–C

Three-quarter front view of Wright airplane with Lt. Mario Calderara, first Italian pilot, at the controls.
SBNA 15

Lt. Mario Calderara and Col. Mario Moris, head of the Italian
military service, standing in front of Wright airplane at Centocelle Field; Wilbur at extreme right in front of engine.
SMIN 43,188–A

Left front view of Wright airplane at Centocelle Field, Capt.
Alfred Hildebrandt of Berlin in dark suit in front of airplane
facing camera.
SMIN 43,188–B; SUBDF v. 1: 201

Close-up view of wing section of Wright airplane at Centocelle Field, Col. Mario Moris, and unidentified military man inspecting airplane.
SMIN 43,188

Katharine, Mrs. Hart O. Berg, Col. Mario Moris, and Lt. Mario Calderara at Centocelle field.
SMIN 42,962–C

Two photographers, backs turned, taking photo of Wright airplane beginning ascent from field.
SMIN 38,494–C

Close-up view of Wilbur in flight over Centocelle Field, flying to left, trees and building visible at left below.
Allg Auto Zeit, v. 10, May 2, 1909: 35; REPAT 8. Similar, at greater height and distance: Allg Auto Zeit, May 2, 1909: 35; Revue aérienne, v. 2, May 20, 1909: 289; World's Work, v. 20, Aug. 1910: 13310

Italian officers looking to left at Wright airplane in distance.
SMIN 38,494–F

Italian soldiers viewing Wright flight in far distance.
SMIN 38,494–C

Wilbur descending at approaching darkness, flying to right.
SMIN 38,494–B

Wilbur's flight at sunset with lighted windows of barracks visible below.
SBNA 117

Three-quarter rear view of Wright airplane positioned on starting track with soldiers on either end in preparation for takeoff. A captive balloon nearby is visible rising slightly above the airplane.
Der Motorwagen, v. 10, July 10, 1909: 525

Wright airplane in flight over Centocelle Field, a captive balloon with gondola and supporting ropes visible above the airplane.
Der Motorwagen, v. 10, July 10, 1909: 525

Front view of Wright airplane at high altitude flying over captive balloon.
FWGMBH 11

Wright airplane on track at Centocelle Field, photograph taken by Hart O. Berg from a military captive balloon.
MCFWP 177; DOBOHA 197; HILBW 33; Motor, v. 16, Aug. 10, 1909: 48; Revue aérienne, v. 2, Aug. 25, 1909: 487

Wright airplane leaving the starting rail, photographed from captive balloon, whose shadow appears at right.

MCFWP 178; DOBOHA 197; HILBW 35; Motor, v. 16, Aug. 10, 1909: 48; Revue aérienne, v. 2, Aug. 25, 1909: 488

Wright airplane beginning climb, its shadow visible below to its left, photographed from a captive balloon.

MCFWP 180; Motor, v. 16, Aug. 10, 1909: 48

Wright airplane in full flight to left, its shadow visible to right of picture, highway seen at top, photographed from captive balloon.

MCFWP 179; DOBOHA 197; HAWBHP 81; HILBW 36; Motor, v. 16, Aug. 10, 1909: 48; Revue aérienne, v. 2, Aug. 25, 1909: 489; SMIN 42,962–J

Three-quarter front view of Wilbur flying over flock of sheep grazing on field adjacent to the Centocelle Field grounds. The well-known aviation historian Charles H. Gibbs-Smith has determined that this widely used photograph is a fake, actually a superimposed photograph of Wilbur in flight at Le Mans, France, on August 8, 1908.

ASHWB front.; The Car, v. 28, Apr. 28, 1909: 407; PEOA 221; SMIN 3356; SMIN 32,425–A; SMIN 37,774–D; SMINAR 1910 facing 150

Orville and Wilbur walking with King Victor Emmanuel III of Italy between them at Centocelle Field, April 24, 1909.

Former Premier of Italy Sidney Sonnino seated in Wright airplane ready for his first flight, pilot Wilbur standing nearby in front of the airplane, April 16.
L'Illustrazione Italiana, v. 36, Apr. 25, 1909: 433

Italian Minister of Navy Admiral Giovanni Mirabello seated in Wright airplane at Centocelle Field, preparing to fly as a passenger with Wilbur, standing nearby, April 21.
L'Illustrazione Italiana, v. 36, May 2, 1909: 449

Wright airplane to the left of the starting rail just taking off with American ambassador to Italy, Lloyd C. Griscom, as passenger with Wilbur, April 24.
SMIN 38,494–C

Wilbur at a height of about 200 feet with Ambassador Griscom as passenger, buildings visible to left and trees in center below.
SMIN 38,494–F

Wilbur flying to left at a considerable height above Centocelle Field with Ambassador Griscom as passenger.
SMIN 38,494–F

Col. Mario Moris, head of the Italian military service, Ambassador Lloyd C. Griscom, and King Victor Emmanuel III of Italy, at Centocelle Field to see Wilbur fly, April 24.
SMIN 42,961–K

King Victor Emmanuel, Orville, and Wilbur standing in front of the Wright airplane, Centocelle Field.
SMIN 42,961–M

Orville, King Victor Emmanuel, Wilbur, and unidentified person at Centocelle Field.
SMIN 42,064–J

King Victor Emmanuel, camera in hand, walking and conversing with Orville and Wilbur on visit to Centocelle Field.
LC-BECK; Pop Sci, v. 114, May 1929: 48

Side view of King Victor Emmanuel conversing with Orville and Wilbur near starting derrick, Centocelle Field.
ADAMSF 106; SMIN 38,494–D

Front view of King Victor Emmanuel conversing with Wilbur and Orville, Centocelle Field.
SMIN 38,494–D

Wilbur about to climb into Wright airplane to join his passenger, Mrs. Frank Belleville, already seated in it, April 27.
London Daily Mirror, May 4, 1909: 8

1909, Fort Myer, Virginia

View of U.S. Army parade ground, Fort Myer, Va., Wright airplane visible in distance on ground, launching derrick to the left, large crowd gathered to witness flights. The flights conducted there in June and July were a continuation of the Wright brothers' government trials, interrupted by the September 17, 1908 accident that happened to Orville.
> **Fly, v. 1, Aug. 1909: 18. Similar: USAF 198232; World Today, v. 17, Sept. 1909: 932**

Series of Air Force photos of Wright brothers' flights, Fort Myer, Va., June-July.
> **USAF 198214–198253**

Series of twelve photographs, taken by James H. Hare, Fort Myer, of Wright brothers' activities, July.
> **Collier's, v. 43, July 17, 1909: 21**

Wilbur conferring with Charles Taylor.
> **MILWA v. 2: 188**

Orville, side view, conversing with sister Katharine and friend.
> **MILWA v. 2: 188**

Lt. Benjamin D. Foulois and Orville, full length, standing on parade ground.
> **LC-BAIN; YPHA 37**

Two groups of five people, senators and their wives, watching the Wright flights from flying field.
> **LC-BAIN**

German Ambassador Johann H. A. von Bernstorff and Maj. George O. Squier conversing beside Wright airplane rudders.
> **SMIN 42,667–D; USAF 48598**

Orville standing in doorway of hangar with soldier, Charles P. Taft (son of President Taft), and an unidentified man.
> **YPHA 37**

Left side view of Wright airplane being removed from hangar, Orville at left wing tip supervising removal.
> **SMIN 42,927–F**

Front view of Wright airplane being pulled away from hangar by military personnel.
> **SMIN 43,008–V**

Right side view of Wright airplane being pulled across parade ground by military personnel.
> **SMIN 43,008–G**

Right front view of Wright airplane being placed on starting rail by military personnel.
TILLMU 59; USAF 16773

Left front view of Wright airplane on flying field, spectators gathered around at left.
LC-BAIN

Close-up view of crowd of spectators gathered around Wright airplane on starting track ready for takeoff.
USAF 48611; World Today, v. 17, Sept. 1909: 934

Right front view of Wright airplane on launching track, Orville seated at controls.
SMIN 43,008–L

Right rear view of Wright airplane taking off from starting rail, Charles Taylor at right looking on.
MILWA v. 2: 159; YPHA 37. Similar, without Taylor: SMIN 42,927–D; World Today, v. 17, Sept. 1909: 934

Right front view of Wright airplane in flight, Fort Myer buildings visible in background below.
Am Aeronaut, v. 1, Sept. 1909: 85; Ill Aero Mitteil, v. 13, Sept. 22, 1909: 842

Wright airplane flying at a considerable height, launching tower visible in background below.
Am Aeronaut, v. 1, Sept. 1909: 85; Ill Aero Mitteil, v. 13, Sept. 22, 1909: 842

Front view of Wright airplane in flight over hangar and tents to the right.
SMIN 42,284–J

Side view of Wright airplane in level flight, trees in background below.
SMIN 42,286–C

Front view of Wright airplane in flight over Fort Myer parade ground, large crowd, many automobiles visible below in foreground.
LC-BAIN; Saturday Evening Mail, Aug. 7, 1909: 3; SMIN 43,008–J; SMIN 43,062–C; SMIN 43,062–D

Left front view of Wright airplane in flight at sunset.
Nat Geog Mag, v. 104, Dec. 1953: 743; World Today, v. 17, Sept. 1909: 931

Wilbur and Charles Taylor watching Orville in flight past launching tower.
Automobile, v. 2: July 8, 1909: 51; Nat Geog Mag, v. 104, Dec. 1953: 742; Nat Geog Mag, v. 112, Aug. 1957: 273. Similar: SMIN 42,055

Left front view of Wright airplane, in front of hangar, being prepared for a flight not made because of high wind, Orville and military personnel at front of machine, June 28.
LC-JONES; SMIN 44,833–F; USAF 9608 A.S.

Views of crowd of spectators on flying field, gathered around Wright airplane to witness a flight by Orville.
LC-JONES; USAF 9607 A.S.; USAF 9612 A.S.; USAF 9613 A.S.

Right front view of Wright airplane, Orville between skids making preparations for flight, June 28.
LC-JONES; SMIN 42,737–F; USAF 9606 A.S.; USAF 9609 A.S.; USAF 9618 A.S.; USAF 198220

Rear view of Wright airplane on flying field, the launching derrick used for starting flights at left, June 28.
LC-JONES; MCFWP 184; JOHHU 245; USAF 9611 A.S.; USAF 9614 A.S.; USAF 16771; USAF 16774

Views showing corner of hangar, barns, tent with men resting on ground outside, several mounted cavalrymen, Fort Myer area, June 28.
LC-JONES; USAF 9623 A.S.; USAF 9624 A.S.; USAF 9626 A.S.

Right front view of Wright airplane on flying field, June 28.
LC-JONES; USAF 9622 A.S.; USAF 9625 A.S.; USAF 9617 A.S. Similar: LC-BAIN

Right rear side view of Wright airplane in front of hangar, crowd at extreme right looking on, June 29.
LC-BAIN

Right front view of Wright airplane on starting rail, June 29.
LC-BAIN

Full front view of Wright airplane on starting track, starting derrick directly behind, man perched on top, barracks in background to left, June 29.
LC-JONES; Aerosphere, 1943; CXXI; COCKDH following 168; HEGOV facing 112; SMIN 42,670–A; USAF 9612 A.S.; USAF 16770. Similar, slight angle: CLHAGW facing 141

Right front view of Wright airplane on flying field, Orville between skids adjusting motor, June 29.
LC-JONES; USAF 9618 A.S. Similar: SMIN 43,008–A

Right front view of Wright airplane, Wilbur inspecting it, two military personnel at his left, two at his right, June 29.
USAF 198223

Right front view of Wright airplane, Orville seated at controls ready for takeoff, June 29. Four short flights were made on this date, highest altitude 25 feet.
> LC-BAIN

Right side view of Wright airplane in flight just above ground after leaving starting rail, June 29.
> LC-JONES; MCFWP 186; SMIN 43,523–A; USAF 9619 A.S.

Right front view of Wright airplane immediately following takeoff, June 29.
> LC-BAIN; SMIN 43,055–H

Right front view of Wright airplane on flying field, Wilbur wearing derby hat at near end, Orville standing between skids, June 29.
> LC-JONES; MCFWP 185; Aerosphere, 1943: CXXXV; DAFFA 19; GANAC 39; HAWBHP 83; LANFL 40; SMIN 30,959–E; USAF 9616 A.S.; USAF 198218

Side view of Wright airplane just taking off from starting rail, June 29.
> LC-BAIN; LC-JONES; SMIN 43,523–A; USAF 9619 A.S.; USAF 9620 A.S.

Front view of Wright airplane in flight above treetops to the left of the starting derrick, July 1.
> LC-BAIN. Similar, without starting derrick: LC-BAIN

Full right side view of Wright airplane on starting rail, July 2.
> LC-JONES; MCFWP 183; SMIN A42,670; USAF 9661 A.S.; USAF 16769

Front right side view of Wright airplane on starting rail ready for takeoff, launching derrick and Fort Myer buildings at left, July 2.
> LC-JONES; USAF 9655 A.S.; USAF 8646

Orville in flight making a short turn to left, launching derrick at extreme left, four military men at its base watching flight, July 2.
> Am Aeronaut, v. 1, Sept. 1909: 80; Sci Am, v. 101, Aug. 14, 1909; 112; SMIN 42,055; USAF 48596. Similar views at greater distance from launching derrick showing large groups watching flight: LC-BAIN; COCKDH following 168; HAWBHP 83; SMIN 42,699; USAF 9653 A.S.; USAF 9664 A.S.; USAF 48596

Right front view from below of Orville in flight, barracks visible below in background, July 2.
> LC-JONES; USAF 9656 A.S. Similar: LC-JONES; USAF 9662 A.S.

Left rear view of Wright airplane on ground following an accident which occurred when the ribs of the main plane were broken in passing over a dead tree and the machine fell, breaking the skids, July 2. Orville in dark suit stands near left wing tip. Lt. Frank P. Lahm, with raised riding crop, directs the removal of the machine.

LC-JONES; MCFWP 187; USAF 9658 A.S.

Wright airplane being returned to hangar following accident, July 2.

LC-JONES; USAF 9654 A.S.; USAF 9659 A.S.; USAF 9660 A.S.

Orville in flight over parade ground, military barracks in background, large tent at extreme right, a number of spectators sitting and standing observing flight, July 19.

LC-JONES; USAF 9665 A.S.; USAF 9669 A.S.

Side view of Orville in flight, hangar and tents in foreground below, several women standing observing flight, July 19.

LC-JONES; USAF 9666 A.S.; USAF 9668 A.S.

Wright airplane in flight as seen from below, July 19.

LC-JONES; MCFWP 188; USAF 9670 A.S.

Three distant views of Orville in flight, hangar and tents in foreground below, July 20.

LC-JONES; USAF 9715 A.S.; USAF 9718 A.S.; USAF 9720 A.S.

Five distant views of Orville in flight, July 20.

LC-JONES; HAWBHP 84; USAF 9716 A.S.; USAF 9717 A.S.; USAF 9719 A.S.; USAF 9721 A.S.; USAF 9722 A.S.

President William Howard Taft in the doorway of the Wright hangar on a visit, military personnel outside looking on, July 26.

LC-JONES; MILWA v. 2: 188; USAF 9714 A.S.

President Taft standing at front of tent observing Orville's flight, also witnessed by cabinet officers, high government officials, and nearby crowd, July 26.

HAWBHP 85; USAF 48604

Lt. Frank P. Lahm and Wilbur, full length, on flying field, July 27.

SMIN 43,055; YPHA 37

Right front view of Wright airplane being placed on starting rail, July 27.

LC-JONES; USAF 9678 A.S.; USAF 16773

Right front view of Wright airplane, Orville standing between skids talking with workman, July 27.

LC-JONES; USAF 9676 A.S.

Right side front view of Wright airplane on starting rail, Lt. Lahm and Orville conversing in front, Wilbur and Lt. Benjamin D. Foulois conversing in rear, July 27.

> **LC-JONES; KELWB b. 180–181; SMIN A41,140–A; USAF 9671 A.S.; U.S. Air Services, v. 24, Aug. 1939: 11; YPHA 37**

Right side front view of Wright airplane on starting rail, Orville standing by skid waiting for a lull in the wind, military personnel also around airplane, July 27.

> **LC-JONES; USAF 9679 A.S.; USAF 8649**

Left front view of Wright airplane, Lt. Lahm seated in it, Orville crouched between skids connecting the rope and weight to machine before takeoff, July 27.

> **World Today, v. 17, Sept. 1909: 933**

Right side front view of Wright airplane, Lt. Lahm and Orville, who is at controls, awaiting takeoff, July 27.

> **LC-JONES; MCFWP 180; COCKDH following 168; HAWBHP 84; SMIN 41,589; USAF 9672 A.S.**

Wilbur at base of starting derrick timing Orville's flight, military personnel also present, July 27.

> **LC-JONES; USAF 9673 A.S.**

Group photograph of the military Aeronautic Board which passed upon the flight of July 27.

> **LC-JONES; CLHAGW facing 169; GHUSAF 5; USAF 9675 A.S.**

Wright airplane on starting rail ready for takeoff, Orville at front making final adjustments, July 27.

> **LC-JONES; SMIN A42,668–B; USAF 9680 A.S.**

Left rear view of Wright airplane in flight of 1 hour, 12 minutes, 37 ⅘ seconds, July 27. Flight made by Orville and passenger Lt. Frank P. Lahm established new record for two-man flight and also fulfilled an army contract requirement for airplane by its remaining in the air for an hour carrying two persons.

> **LC-JONES; USAF 9679 A.S.; USAF 9681 A.S.; USAF 9682 A.S.**

Military personnel sliding dolly beneath skids of Wright airplane in front of hangar before pulling airplane to starting rail, Katharine at extreme right looking on, July 30.

> **Nat Geog Mag, v. 112, Aug. 1957: 268**

Left front view of Wright airplane in front of hangar, being prepared for flight, July 30.

> **LC-JONES**

Wright airplane in front of hangar, being made ready for transport to flying field, July 30.

> **LC-JONES; USAF 9685 A.S.; USAF 9691 A.S.**

Wilbur (left), Lt. Benjamin Foulois (center), and Orville (right) discussing the successful speed test flight of July 30, 1909, that covered a distance of about ten miles at Alexandria, Virginia.

Orville, Lt. Benjamin D. Foulois, and Wilbur walking along starting track, July 30.
LC-JONES

Wilbur and Orville discussing the Alexandria flight with Lt. Foulois, a flag used to mark the course of test flights between Fort Myer and Alexandria, Va., raised over Wilbur's shoulder, July 30.
LC-JONES; MCFWP 189; TILLMU 66; USAF 9690 A.S.; U.S. Air Services, v. 29, Aug. 1944: 14

View of photographers and spectators gathered to witness Orville's flight, Orville seen striding to right, Wright airplane and launching derrick at extreme right, July 30.
LC-JONES; USAF 9686 A.S.

Right front side view of Wright airplane on starting track, being prepared for takeoff, July 30.
LC-JONES; GHUSAF 5; TILLMU 62; USAF 9687 A.S.; USAF 9689 A.S.; USAF 9695 A.S.

Katharine Wright and her party watching Wright airplane in flight, a crowd of witnesses at far rear, July 30.
LC-JONES; USAF 9697 A.S.

Wilbur, wearing straw hat, high collar, tie, and vest, timing flight to Alexandria, July 30.
LC-JONES; USAF 9696 A.S.

Right front view of Orville in flight, with Lt. Benjamin D. Foulois as passenger-observer, rounding captive balloon on Shooter's Hill, Alexandria, turning point of the army speed test, July 30. An average speed of 42.583 miles per hour was achieved.
MCFWP 191; American Aeronaut, v. 1, Sept. 1909: 83; Collier's, v. 43, Aug. 14, 1909: 22; EWBNM 58; Fly, v. 1, Sept. 1909: 8; Saturday Evening Mail, Aug. 7, 1909; SMIN 21,337

Rear view of Wright airplane in flight, passing over four tents and shed in foregound, family of three walking away to left, mounted cavalryman at right, July 30.
LC-JONES. In reverse: SMIN A48,065–Q

1909, Germany (Tempelhof Field, Berlin, and Bornstedt Field, Potsdam)

Tempelhof Field, Berlin, where Orville conducted exhibition flights, August 3-September 18, 1909, to fulfill a contract made with the German newspaper *Lokal-Anzeiger.*
Die Woche, v. 11, Aug. 28, 1909: 479; Ill Aero Mitteil, v. 13, Sept. 8, 1909: 814

Right front view of Wright airplane after assembly in quarters of German Wright Company, Flugmaschine Wright.
Die Woche, v. 11, Aug. 28, 1909: 1478

Wright airplane on ground in front of hangar.
SMIN 42, 805–F

Close-up center section view of Wright airplane, showing two seats, controls, and transmission.
LC-HILDEBRANDT

Orville seated at controls of Wright airplane before takeoff at Tempelhof Field.
Die Woche, v. 11, Sept. 11, 1909: 1566

Control system of the Wright airplane as used in Berlin.
L'Aérophile, v. 17, Oct. 1, 1909: 439

Wheeling out Wright airplane in preparation for flight at Tempelhof Field.
LC-BAIN; Ill Aero Mitteil, v. 13, Sept. 8, 1909: 815; GSWB 25; SBNA 121; SMIN 42, 805–F; SMIN 43,008–B; SMIN 43,000–W; Sport im Bild, Sept. 10, 1909; Die Woche, v. 11, Sept. 11, 1909: 1566

Right front view of Wright airplane on launching track at Tempelhof Field, Orville making adjustments to machine before take off.

LC-HILDEBRANDT; SMIN 42,783–J; Sport im Bild, Sept. 10, 1909: 1001

Right front view of Orville in flight at Tempelhof Field, airplane at end of launching track during takeoff.

SMIN 612,783–F. Similar, when airplane is at slightly higher altitude: HAWBHP 86; SMIN 42,572–A

Left front view of Orville in flight at Tempelhof Field, mounted horseman in distance below.

SMIN 42,783–G

Right side view of Orville in Wright airplane in level flight across Tempelhof Field.

LC-HILDEBRANDT

Right front view of Wright airplane flying at a considerable altitude over Tempelhof Field, large crowd witnessing flight in foreground below.

LC-HILDEBRANDT

Rear view of Wright airplane in flight over Tempelhof Field, four spectators below at extreme left viewing flight.

Die Woche, v. 11, Sept. 11, 1909: 1565

Gen. Helmuth J. L. von Moltke, chief of the German general staff, Mrs. von Moltke, and Gen. von Kessel conversing with Orville on Tempelhof Field, September 4.

Die Woche, v. 11, Sept. 11, 1909: 1566

Group photo with Gen. von Moltke congratulating Orville following his first public flight in Germany, September 4. Katharine in center faces the two men.

MILWA v. 2: 200

Mrs. Alfred Hildebrandt seated in Wright airplane, preparing for flight, Orville standing between skids facing her, Capt. Alfred Hildebrandt at right looking on.

NOZWBC facing 5

Mrs. Hildebrandt, the first woman to fly as a passenger in an airplane in Germany, seated in Wright airplane with Orville before a flight with him of 8 minutes, 38 seconds, on September 9.

BRABSL 89. Similar, Mrs. Hildebrandt alone: Die Woche, v. 11, Sept. 18, 1909: 1610

View of large crowd assembled to witness flights by Orville at Tempelhof Field.

Die Woche, v. 11, Sept. 18, 1909: 1610

German Crown Prince Friedrich Wilhelm in conversation with Orville at Tempelhof Field, September 9.

Die Woche, v. 11, Sept. 18, 1909: 1609

Crown Prince Friedrich Wilhelm, Hart O. Berg, and Orville conversing near Wright airplane on Orville's return from a flight, Tempelhof Field, September 9.

LC-BECK (three slightly differing views); COCKDH following 168; Flugsport, v. 1, Sept. 17, 1909: 555; FWGWA 10; SUBDF v. 2: 139

Prof. Hugo Hergesell, University of Strassburg, seated in Wright airplane, for a flight with Orville who is standing in front between skids, September 13.

LC-HILDEBRANDT

Left front view of Orville in flight over Tempelhof Field, watched by group below including German empress and other high-ranking officials.

HAWBHP 86; SMIN 42,783-K

German empress and princess Viktoria Luise observing Orville's flight from their automobile, Tempelhof Field, September 17.

Berliner Lokal-Anzeiger, Sept. 20, 1909

Prince August Wilhelm and Prince Adalbert conversing with Orville close by the Wright airplane, Tempelhof Field, September 17.

Berliner Lokal-Anzeiger, Sept. 20, 1909

Orville flying over a captive balloon at Tempelhof Field as he breaks existing altitude record, rising to a height of 172 meters (565 feet), September 17.

LC-HILDEBRANDT; Berliner Lokal-Anzeiger, Sept. 20, 1909; Motor, v. 16, Sept. 28, 1909: 278; Die Woche, v. 11, Sept. 25, 1909: 1649

Mounted helmeted German military officer, wearing cape, observing flight by Orville.

LC-BECK: Air-Scout, v. 1, Jan. 1911: 17; SMIN 32,031-B

Large crowd, some waving hats to Orville as he passes overhead in one of his flights at Tempelhof Field.

L'Aérophile, v. 17, Sept. 15, 1909: 420; MCMWB 242; Die Woche, Sept. 11, 1909: 1566

Close-up photo of Orville in flight at Tempelhof Field, mounted horseman in distance below.

GSEFM

Orville standing next to Hart O. Berg at Wright airplane, a guard stationed at the right.

L'Aérophile, v. 17, Sept. 15, 1909: 420

German royal family present at Tempelhof Field to witness flights by Orville, September 17.

Berliner Lokal-Anzeiger, Sept. 20, 1909

Group photo at Tempelhof Field with Orville, Crown Prince Friedrich Wilhelm, and Katharine Wright posing in front of an early model German automobile.
LC-BECK; LOCA 275; YPHA 36

Crown Prince Friedrich Wilhelm, the first member of a royal family to ride in an airplane, photographed as a passenger with Orville on a flight of about 15 minutes, mounted helmeted German military personnel controlling large crowd below, Bornstedt Field, Potsdam, October 2. Having completed his exhibition flights at Tempelhof Field, Berlin, Orville moved to Bornstedt Field, a drilling ground for the Potsdam garrison, to give flying lessons to Capt. Paul Engelhard, retired German naval officer.
Vie grand air, v. 15, Oct. 9, 1909: cover

Orville riding with Crown Prince Friedrich Wilhelm in small four-passenger automobile. Crown Prince on left front seat is conversing with Orville who is seated next to German officer on rear left seat.
Vie grand air, v. 15, Oct. 9, 1909: cover

Orville is congratulated by the royal family, including Emperor Wilhelm II, the empress, and Princess Viktoria Luise, following a spectacular flight lasting 25 to 30 minutes, his last appearance in Germany, Bornstedt Field, Potsdam, October 15.
LC-BECK; FWGWA 11; MCMWB 242

1909, Governors Island, New York

Front view of Wright airplane in hangar on Governors Island, with group of spectators viewing the machine. The flights from Governors Island were made in fulfillment of a contract made by Wilbur providing for a series of flights during the Hudson-Fulton celebration to be held in New York in September and October 1909. These flights were the first over American waters.
HAHFC 1241; LOOWGF 9; SMIN 43,056–B

Three-quarter left front view of Wright airplane on drill field.
HAHFC 1245

Left front view of Wright airplane in front of hangar, attached canoe visible on underside of airplane.
SMIN 42,805–C. Similar: Aeronautics, v. 5, Nov. 1909: 180

Three-quarter front view of Wright airplane in front of hangar, showing canoe attached to underside of airplane, spectators in background, September 29.
LC-BAIN

Close-up three-quarter front view of Wright airplane in front of hangar, showing canoe attached to underside of airplane, a number of spectators visible in background, September 29.
LC-BAIN

Wilbur looks at the Wright airplane with a canoe attached to its underside at Governors Island, New York, October 4, 1909. National Air and Space Museum, Smithsonian Institution, photo no. A2330.

Close-up view of center section of Wright airplane in hangar.
SMIN A2330–B. Similar: SMIN 42,805–E

Three photographs of Wilbur, wearing derby hat, gray-vested suit, white collar, and tie, talking with several groups of men, military and civilian.
LC-BAIN

Side view of Wright airplane with canoe lashed to bottom, with Wilbur at side looking ahead toward starting rail.
CHBLWB facing 272; Harper's Weekly, v. 53; Oct. 16, 1909: 7 HMSHSA facing 186

Rear side view of Wright airplane with Wilbur looking at canoe attached to its underside.
HAHFC 1251; SMIN A2330

Front side view of Wright airplane showing attached canoe, and Wilbur facing camera.
Automobile Topics, v. 19, Oct. 9, 1909: 20

Three-quarter front view of Wright airplane with Wilbur in center facing camera. Officer at right is placing a wheel at one end of the lower wing in order to push the machine back to the hangar.
Am R Rs, v. 40, Nov. 1909: 557

Three-quarter front view of Wright airplane on drill field showing attached canoe on underside and American flag displayed near pilot's seat. Large crowd of spectators is assembled in front of the airplane and soldiers bearing rifles are standing guard in front and behind it.
SMIN 31,248

Close-up three-quarter front view of Wright airplane on drill field, Wilbur with cap, back to camera, examining the canoe attached to its underside, September 29.
LC-BAIN

Three photographs showing Wright airplane being removed from hangar and pulled into starting position by military personnel at field.
LC-BAIN

Photograph of ten soldiers pulling Wright airplane from hangar to drill field, canoe visible on underside of airplane.
HAHFC 1243; SMIN 42,804–A

Three-quarter front view of Wright airplane being examined by a number of cameramen and journalists.
SMIN A2330–A

Wilbur walking in front of Wright machine, attached canoe visible on underside of airplane, military personnel at rear.
SMIN 42,804–B

Wright airplane on launching track.
SMIN 43,008–M

Wilbur with towing dolly.
SMIN 43,055–G

Three-quarter front view of Wright airplane, attached canoe visible, Wilbur at front adjusting motor, Charles Taylor at rear adjusting propeller, preparatory to flight.
COCKDH following 168

Launching track and crowd of civilians and military personnel in foreground, Wright airplane at right of photograph.
SMIN 43,148–C

Side view of Wilbur starting his trip around Statue of Liberty, in low level flight over parade ground.
J Franklin In, v. 256, Dec. 1953: 495; LOOWGF 12

Wilbur in level flight above ship in the Hudson River.
New York Evening Mail, Sept. 29, 1909: 1

Wilbur flying over Hudson River as seen from Pennsylvania Railroad terminal building in Jersey City.
New York Tribune, Oct. 5, 1909

Photo taken from Jersey City showing Wilbur in flight against a background of New York City skyscrapers as he was returning to Governors Island.
Harper's Weekly, v. 53, Oct. 16, 1909: 1

Right side view of Wright airplane in flight over Governors Island.
SMIN 43,147

Wilbur flying to right on a course from Governors Island drill field around the Statue of Liberty on Bedloe's Island and back, September 29.
LC-BAIN

Two long-range views from Governors Island of Wilbur in Wright airplane at low level flight, the first flight over American waters, September 29.
LC-Bain

Wilbur flying to the left around the Statue of Liberty.
Harper's Weekly, v. 53, Oct. 9, 1909; New York American, Sept. 30, 1909: 1

Crowd watching Wilbur's flight around Statue of Liberty from Fort Castle William on Governors Island.
LC-BAIN

Crowd, many seated on grass, many reading newspapers as they wait, at Battery Park, New York, watching for Wilbur to come around Statue of Liberty in this first flight over American waters.
LC-BAIN

Crowd, standing behind chains at seawall, watching for Wilbur in his first flight over water around Statue of Liberty.
LC-BAIN

Wilbur in flight turning to right as airplane approaches landing on Governors Island.
New York Times, Oct. 10, 1909

Wilbur in Wright airplane returning to Governors Island at sunset, following flight around Statue of Liberty.
HAHFC 1249

Wilbur in level flight above drill field, moving to left on Governors Island, as he takes off on a flight of about 20 miles to Grant's Tomb and back, which lasted 33 minutes, 33 seconds, carrying a canoe on the underside of airplane as a safety precaution, October 4.

LC-BAIN; MCFWP 192; Am R Rs, v. 40, Oct. 1909: 521; Collier's, v. 80, Sept. 21, 1927: 18; HARFF 155; HAWBHP 87; SMIN 31,980–C. Similar, airplane tilted to right: LC-BAIN

Wilbur turning to right as he takes off from Governors Island on a flight to Grant's Tomb.

Aero, v. 1, Oct. 9, 1909: 366; The Car, v. 30, Oct. 13, 1909: cover; HAHFC 1247

Route followed by Wilbur in his Hudson River flight to Grant's Tomb.

Aeronautics, v. 5, Nov. 1909: 180

Wilbur turning to left as he takes off from Governors Island on his approximately 20-mile flight to Grant's Tomb.

CHBLWB facing 272; Harper's Weekly, v. 53, Oct. 16, 1909: 7

Wilbur taking off from Governors Island on his flight to Grant's Tomb, five cameramen at left of picture taking photographs.

SMIN A1136

Rear view of Wilbur taking off on his flight to Grant's Tomb.

COCKDH following 168; SMIN A2330–C

Wilbur flying up the Hudson River en route to Grant's Tomb, New York City skyline visible below.

Graphic, v. 80, Oct. 16, 1909: 489; SMIN 6800–1d; YPHA 37

Wilbur flying over a cargo ship and a tugboat sending out a dense cloud of black smoke over the Hudson River, October 4.

Harper's Weekly, v. 53, Oct. 16, 1909: 7

Wilbur in flight up Hudson River to Grant's Tomb, passing over German warship *Corsair* anchored in the Hudson River.

New York Evening Telegram, Oct. 4, 1909: 1

Wilbur flying over British warship *Arsyll* opposite Grant's Tomb.

New York Globe, Oct. 4, 1909: 1

Wilbur returning to starting point on Governors Island on his return flight from Grant's Tomb.

New York Evening Telegram, Oct. 4, 1909: 1

Wilbur on return from trip to Grant's Tomb flies over British warships in Hudson River.

LC-BAIN. Similar, enlarged: LC-BAIN

As Wilbur flew some twenty miles over the Hudson River to Grant's Tomb on October 4, 1909, New Yorkers had their first glimpse of an airplane in flight.

Wilbur photographed in flight from the top of Fort Castle William on Governors Island returning from Grant's Tomb.
New York World, Oct. 15, 1909: 1

Wilbur returning to Governors Island following trip to Grant's Tomb, the New York City skyline visible below at right.
New York World, Oct. 15, 1909: 1

Wilbur returning to Governors Island following trip to Grant's Tomb, the New York City skyline visible below at right.
Aero Club Am Bul, v. 1, July 1912: 21; Harper's Weekly, v. 53, Oct. 16, 1909: 1; NOZWBC facing 177; SMIN 43,148–B; WODKH facing 221; World's Work, v. 20, Aug. 1910: 13310

Wilbur approaching Governors Island following his trip to Grant's Tomb, the New York City skyline still visible on the right of the picture.
MCFWP 193; Am R Rs v. 40, Nov. 1909: 551; MILWA v. 2: 201; SMIN 31,980–G

Wilbur being congratulated on his successful flight to Grant's Tomb by Secretary William J. Hammer of the Aeronautic Committee of the Hudson-Fulton Celebration Committee.
New York Evening Sun, Oct. 5, 1909

Captain Dorcy, James M. Beck, Charles E. Taylor, Wilbur, and William J. Hammer gathered in front of the Wright airplane following Wilbur's flight up the Hudson River, October 4.
COCKDH following 168; U.S. Air Services, v. 17, Jan. 1932: 27

1909, College Park, Maryland

Left rear view of Wright airplane being prepared for flight by military personnel, October 1909. Wilbur arrived at College Park, Md., on October 5 to train Signal Corps officers in fulfillment of Wrights' contract with the War Department.
SMIN A48,870

Front view of Wright airplane on starting track being made ready for flight by military personnel, launching derrick at rear.
LC-JONES; USAF 2930 A.S.

Side view of Wright airplane with Wilbur preparing to start the engine.
Aeronautical Quarterly, v. 2, no. 1, 1976: 26

Wilbur and his student, Lt. Frederic E. Humphreys, in Wright airplane on starting rail getting ready for takeoff.
U.S. Air Services, v. 8, Dec. 1923: 15

Rear view of Wright airplane just taking off from starting rail.
Popular Aviation, v. 3, Dec. 1928: 15; USAF 2922 A.S.

1911, Kitty Hawk, North Carolina

View of Kill Devil Hill, where the first gliding experiments were conducted by the Wright brothers in 1900, Kitty Hawk, N.C., 1911. Orville, accompanied by his brother Lorin, his nephew Horace, and his friend Alexander Ogilvie, of England, arrived for the purpose of conducting gliding experiments with a glider resembling the Wright 1911 powered machine but lacking its motor, October10.
LC-W86-120; MCFWP 202

Crate containing Orville's 1911 glider being unloaded from wagon in front of camp building.
SMIN 42,970-B

Glider being assembled in front of camp building.
SMIN 42,970-A

Side view of glider inside camp building, ladder leading to sleeping quarters overhead visible at extreme right.
SMIN 42,683

Orville, back to camera, officiating in kitchen of camp, utensils visible hanging on wall.
R Aero Soc J, v. 57, Dec. 1953: 792

Front view of glider in front of camp building.
LC-W86–116; SMIN 42,683–D. Similar: LC-W86–114; corner of camp building only: LC-W86–114b

Instrument mounted on strut during 1911 gliding experiments.
SMIN 42,683–C

View of rudders and elevator of glider in front of camp building.
LC-W86–113; SMIN 42,683–A

Close-up view of rudders and elevator of glider in front of camp building.
LC-W86–112; SMIN 42,685–E

Close-up view of glider boom, Alexander Ogilvie behind it.
SMIN 42,971–A

Full front view of glider resting in sand dune, four persons standing at left of seat, two sitting at right of seat.
SMIN 42,971–D

Glider being prepared for flight by Orville and assistants, a number of reporters at right near glider.
LC-W86–107; MCFWP 198; USAF 48633

Close-up view of center section of glider showing Orville, in seat, turning right to adjust wires.
SMIN A52,375

Close-up view of center section of glider with Orville kneeling on seat of glider where he rested his arm, turning to his right to face camera.
SMIN A52,373

Orville, wearing topcoat and broad-brimmed hat, at end of glider, right arm outstretched to fasten a wire at upper wing of glider.
SMIN A52,376

Close-up view of center section of glider with Orville making adjustment to glider near seat, Alexander Ogilvie close by looking on.
SMIN A52,378

Orville at work on glider boom, Alexander Ogilvie assisting him at his right.
SMIN 42,971–E

Close-up view of center section of glider with Orville seated facing camera, unidentified person kneeling in front watching him.
Popular Mechanics, v. 16, Dec. 1911: 799

Orville on bended knee at right making repairs to glider, Alexander Ogilvie at left.
Aero, v. 3, Nov. 4, 1911: 94

Orville seated in glider making needed adjustments, Alexander Ogilvie looking on.
R Aero Soc J, v. 57, Dec. 1953: 790; SMIN 42,970–J

Wright glider being carried up hill over sandy area, two men at front of glider, one man at rear.
SMIN 42,970–F

Front view of glider being dragged up sand dune, cameraman ahead at right.
Aero J, v. 20, July/Sept. 1916: b. 80–81; BBAKH; SMIN 42,971–F

Glider being carried up hill, tail first, by three men, an unidentified man following at left.
Aero Club Am Bul, v. 1, Jan. 1912: 21; D Zeit Luft, v. 15, Nov. 29, 1911: 23; RIESW; SMIN A52,386

Three-quarter left rear view of glider in flight.
LC–W86–108; SMIN 42,413–C. Similar: LC–W86–110; LC–W86–111

Right rear view of glider descending and close to ground, Alexander Ogilvie aboard, onlookers at left.
Aero J, v. 20, July/Sept. 1916: b. 80–81; BBAKH (without spectators); R Aero Soc J, v. 57, Dec. 1953: 791; SMIN A42,970–D

Right rear view, from below, of glider at a considerable height.
SMIN 42,970–E

Left rear view of glider in flight at low altitude showing fixed vertical fin attached to a front strut.
LC–W86–118; HAWBHP 91; SMIN A42,683–B

Left side view of Orville gliding at a considerable height, in level flight.
Aero J, v. 20, July/Sept. 1916: b. 80–81; SMIN 42,970–G; USAF 48636; USAF 10471 A.C.

Left rear view of glider in flight at high altitude.
LC–W86–119; SMIN 42,971–B

Right rear view of glider descending from hill.
SMIN 42,971–C

Right side view of glider in flight at a considerable height.
SMIN 42,971. Similar: R Aero Soc J, v. 57, Dec. 1953: 792

Side view from below of Orville soaring, in level flight, spectators looking up at glider.
LC–USZ62–66609; LC–W86–117; MCFWP 200. Similar: D Zeit Luft, v. 15, Nov. 29, 1911: 23; RIESW; SMIN A52,381

Glider on left wing tip and tail turning over, with Orville hanging from struts, October 23.
MCFWP 201; Aero J, v. 20, July/Sept. 1916: b. 80–81; GLWB, b. 40–41; MILWA v. 2: 244; USAF 10470 A.S.

Glider turning a somersault with Orville clinging to it, Alexander Ogilvie racing from right to assist him.
Collier's, v. 48, Nov. 11, 1911: 20; MILWA v. 2: 244; Popular Mechanics, v. 16, Dec. 1911: 801

Orville seated in glider just before starting a glide, Alexander Ogilvie in front of glider on the right.
Aero, v. 3, Nov. 4, 1911: 94; Collier's, v. 48, Nov. 11, 1911: 20; SMIN A52,579

Right front view of glider in flight.
LC–USZ62–56250; LC–W86–101; MCFWP 199; Aerosphere, 1943: CXXXIX; GLWB b. 40–41; HAW-BHP 92; SMIN 17,132–C; SMIN 42,970–C; USAF 48634; USAF 10468 A.C. Similar: SMIN 42,413–D

Left front view of glider in flight.
SMIN 42,412; USAF 10472 A.S.

Right front view of glider in low flight over sand, Alexander Ogilvie at rear of glider.
SMIN 42,971–H

Right rear view of glider in flight over sand dunes, Orville aboard, 11 spectators at lower left of picture gazing up at glider, among them Alexander Ogilvie, Lorin Wright, members of the U.S. lifesaving crew, and men from the nearby lighthouse, on October 24. This flight lasted 9 minutes, 45 seconds, establishing a new soaring time record (exceeded in Germany 10 years later).
LC-BECK; Aero J, v. 20, July/Sept. 1916: b. 80–81; BBAKH; KELMKH b. 238–239; New York Herald, Dec. 16, 1923; R Aero Soc J, v. 57, Dec. 1953: 791; USAF 48635; USAF 10469 A.S.; U.S. Air Service, v. 7, Dec. 1922: 8

Left rear view of glider in flight, Alexander Ogilvie below machine, news cameramen in foreground.

Aero, v. 3, Nov. 4, 1911: 93; Aero Club Am Bul, v. 1, Jan. 1912: 21; Aeroplane, v. 1, Nov. 9, 1911: 544; Collier's, v. 48, Nov. 11, 1911: 20; D Zeit Luft, v. 15, Nov. 29, 1911: 23; Popular Mechanics, v. 16, Dec. 1911: 803; SMIN 43,061; SMIN A52,382. Similar: D Zeit Luft, v. 15, Nov. 29, 1911: 23; SMIN A52,385

Left rear view of glider descending from hill showing fin attached to front strut.

BUFJM 13; GSWB 29; RIESW; SMIN A52,383

Left front view of glider in level flight.

SMIN 42, 970–K

Left front view of glider in flight, Orville establishing a soaring record of 9 minutes, 45 seconds, October 24.

SMIN 42,412–B; USAF 10471 A.S.

Alexander Ogilvie, Orville, and Horace Wright standing in front of camp building.

SMIN 42,971–K

Lorin Wright, Alexander Ogilvie, and unidentified man near well at a Kitty Hawk residence.

SMIN 42,970

Group portrait taken in front of glider at Kill Devil Hill. Sitting: Horace Wright, Orville, and Alexander Ogilvie; standing: Lorin Wright, and group of journalists, including Van Ness Harwood of the New York *World,* Berges of the American News Service, Arnold Kruckman of the New York *American,* Mitchell of the New York *Herald,* and John Mitchell of the Associated Press.

LC–W86–106; USAF 48633

Orville, back to camera, in broad-brimmed hat, watching glider descending from hill, Alexander Ogilvie probably making the glide, camp building below visible in distance.

D Zeit Luft, v. 15, Nov. 15, 1911: 20; Sci Am, v. 105, Nov. 4, 1911: 405; Vie grand air, v. 21, June 8, 1912: 400

Orville sitting on deck of boat with an unidentified person and his brother Lorin, his nephew Horace, and his friend from England, Alexander Ogilvie.

SMIN 42,970–H; SMIN 42,971–J

Wright Airplanes

Photographs of earlier Wright airplane models are included in sections covering the early flights.

Signal Corps Machine, 1909

Left front view of Signal Corps machine flown by the Wright brothers at Fort Myer, Va., June-July 1909, the first airplane to be purchased by any government. The machine was subsequently presented to the National Museum and first exhibited there on October 26, 1911. It is now in the National Air and Space Museum, Washington.

> **USAF 75486; U.S. Air Services, v. 24, Aug. 1939: 11;
> U.S. Air Services, v. 29, Aug. 1944: 15**

Side view of Signal Corps machine with forward plane in position for elevating.

> **J U.S. Artillery, v. 33, Mar./Apr. 1910: facing 144;
> Professional Memoirs, v. 2, Jan./Mar. 1910: 100**

Close-up view of Signal Corps machine showing forward plane in position for depressing.

> **J U.S. Artillery, v. 33, Mar./Apr. 1910: facing 144;
> Professional Memoirs, v. 2, Jan./Mar. 1910: 101**

Side view of Signal Corps machine with wing tip warped to decrease lift.

> **J U.S. Artillery, v. 33, Mar./Apr. 1910: facing 146;
> Professional Memoirs, v. 2, Jan./Mar. 1910: 106**

Left front view of Signal Corps machine with wing tip warped to increase lift.

> **J U.S. Artillery, v. 33, Mar./Apr. 1910: facing 146;
> Professional Memoirs, v. 2, Jan./Mar. 1910: 105**

Close-up side view of Signal Corps machine showing arrangement of rear of airplane.

> **J U.S. Artillery, v. 33, Mar./Apr. 1910: facing 145;
> Professional Memoirs, v. 2, Jan./Mar. 1910: 103**

Series of photographs of Signal Corps machine installed in the West Hall of the Arts and Industries Building, Smithsonian Institution.
SMIN 24,066—SMIN 24,074

Left rear view of Signal Corps machine displayed in the West Hall, Arts and Industries Building, Smithsonian Institution.
Bee-Hive, v. 28, Spring 1953: 22; SMIN 24,071

Right rear view of the Signal Corps machine exhibited in the Power Hall, Arts and Industries Building, Smithsonian Institution.
SMIN 30,923

Right front view of the Signal Corps machine exhibited in the Power Hall, Arts and Industries Building, Smithsonian Institution.
SMIN 33,585; SMIN 39,097–B–X

Front view from below of Signal Corps machine displayed in the Arts and Industries Building, National Air Museum.
SMIN A44,631–A

Left side rear view of Signal Corps machine displayed in the Arts and Industries Building, National Air Museum.
SMIN A44,631–B

Right front view of Signal Corps machine decorated with wreath presented by the Early Birds on the 30th anniversary of the founding of the U.S. Air Force, August 1, 1907.
SMIN 33,907

Close-up view of center section of Signal Corps machine.
SMIN A3481

Close-up views of control levers, before replaced by wrist control lever, Signal Corps machine, displayed in Arts and Industries Building, 1911.
SMIN A37,875; SMIN A37,875–A; SMIN 37,991; SMIN 37,991–A

Model B, 1910–1911

Front view of model B, the first plane produced and sold in quantity by Wright Company, showing warping of the wings.
SMIN A48,522–G

Side view of model B.
GLWB, b. 40–41

Left front view of model B in factory.
Aerosphere, 1943: CXXVII; USAF 4479 A.S. Similar: SMIN 42,737

Left front view of model B on ground, Sgt. Stephen J. Idzack standing on right.
SMIN 45,472–F

Front side view of model B.
Sci Am, v. 103, Sept. 3, 1910: 180

Center section view of model B.
LC-JONES; Sci Am, v. 103, Sept. 3, 1910: 180

Orville, with group of students, standing by skids of a model B at Montgomery, Ala., 1910.
SMIN 42,688–G

Front view of model B in flight, student pilots watching it, Montgomery, Ala., 1910.
SMIN 42,689–A

Close-up view of center section of model B showing Arch Hoxsey standing on student pilot's shoulders to pour water into radiator, Montgomery, Ala., 1910.
SMIN 42,689

Close-up right rear view of model B, propeller being fastened on by two student pilots, Montgomery, Ala., 1910.
SMIN 42,689–B

Series of six views of Wright model B with personnel of Army Aero Squadron, Texas City, Texas, 1910.
USAF 35915–35920

Cornelius Vanderbilt, a Wright Company director, seated with Orville in model B at Belmont Park, N.Y., November 1, 1910. This was Vanderbilt's first flight, Orville reaching an altitude of 200 feet and circling the course six or seven times.
SMIN 43,062

Side view of Wright B on ground at Simms Station, Dayton, November 6, 1910. Orville is at left side of airplane, assisting in pulling it to starting point for a flight the next day to Driving Park, Columbus, Ohio, which was to be the first commercial cargo flight, carrying a bolt of silk.
SMIN 41,709

Left rear view of model B on ground near hangar at Simms Station, before flight to Columbus, Ohio, November 7, 1910.
SMIN 41,709–C

Right rear view of model B on field at Simms Station, before flight to Columbus, Ohio, November 7, 1910.
SMIN 41,709–D

Model B taking off from Simms Station carrying a bolt of silk to Columbus, Ohio, November 7, 1910. Orville in derby hat is in lower right corner of photo.
SMIN 41,709–B

Long-range view of model B in flight, Dominguez Field, California, 1910.
SMIN 34,116–H

Left front view of model B, maintenance crew around airplane, at Ft. Sam Houston, Texas.
CLHAGW b. 192–193

Front view of model B on ground, Simms Station, Dayton.
SMIN 42,688–H

Right front view of model B at Simms Station, Dayton, 1911.
Aerosphere, 1943: CXXXVIII; CAIAF 3; SMIN A4418–H; SMIN 42,737–D; USAF 22441

Left side view of model B in flight just above ground, Simms Station, Dayton, 1911.
LC-JONES; SMIN 42,688–F

Miss Jacqueline Cochran seated at the controls of the model B airplane in the Franklin Institute, Philadelphia.
Aerosphere, 1943: CXXVIII

Miss Lee Ya Cheng testing the control system of the model B airplane in the Franklin Institute.
Aerosphere, 1943: CXXIII

Right front view of model B on ground at Augusta, Ga., 1911.
LC-JONES; USAF 3825 A.S.

Center section view of model B with Lt. Thomas DeW. Milling seated in airplane and Lt. Henry H. Arnold standing in front of it, Augusta, Ga.
Nat Geog Mag, v. 112, Aug. 1957: 270

Center section view of model B, Capt. Charles DeF. Chandler at controls, College Park, Md., July 1911.
CLHAGW b. 192–193

Right front view of model B on ground at College Park, Md.
SMIN 42,690–E

Harry Atwood rising from White House grounds in model B airplane, July 14, 1911.
SMIN 31,291–B

Center front section of model B with Harry Atwood in pilot's seat.
SMIN 10,914–B

Wright model B in flight with Harry Atwood the pilot.
SMIN 30,959–B

Left front view of model B at Chicago International Aviation Meet, held August 12–20, 1911.
Aeronautics, v. 9, Sept. 1911: 93

Lt. Benjamin D. Foulois and Frank Coffyn flying across flying field at Ft. Sam Houston, Texas, 1911.
SMIN 45,474–B. Similar: SMIN 45,474–H

Inspection party gathered around model B airplane following accident, Ft. Sam Houston, Texas, 1911.
SMIN 45,474–G

Left front view of model B at San Antonio, Texas, 1911.
SMIN 45,472–H

Center section view of model B in hangar at San Antonio, Texas, 1911.
SMIN 45,471–C

Military personnel and civilians gathered around model B outside hangar, San Antonio, Texas, 1911.
SMIN 45,471–B

Frank Coffyn at the controls of the model B, San Antonio, Texas, 1911.
SMIN 45,473–A

Left front view of model B being pulled on to flying field at San Antonio, Texas, 1911.
SMIN 45,471–H

Lt. Benjamin D. Foulois and Frank Coffyn standing behind the left wing of the model B at San Antonio, Texas, 1911.
SMIN 45,474–K

Lt. Foulois working on the model B at San Antonio, Texas, 1911.
SMIN 45,472–A

Left front view of model B outside hangar, Lt. Foulois (second from right) and five military maintenance personnel in front of airplane, San Antonio, Texas, 1911.
MCFWP 209; GHUSAF 6; Nat Geog Mag, v. 112, Aug. 1927: 270; SMIN 34,794–B; TILLMU 90

Side view of model B, nosed-up, damaged in accident, San Antonio, Texas.
SMIN 45,472–K

Unloading Robert J. Collier model B, sent to replace damaged model B, San Antonio Texas.
SMIN 45,473–J

Collier Wright model B in flight at San Antonio, Texas, March 1911.
TILLMU 100

Lt. Benjamin D. Foulois and Philip O. Parmalee seated in model B at San Antonio, Texas, 1911.
SMIN 45, 472–C

Lt. Foulois standing in front of model B and Philip O. Parmalee seated inside, San Antonio, Texas, 1911.
SMIN 45,471–D

Left front view of model B, Lt. Foulois and Philip O. Parmalee standing in front of airplane, San Antonio, Texas, 1911.
SMIN 45,472–E

Lt. Foulois and Frank Coffyn in flight over flying field at San Antonio, Texas, 1911.
SMIN 45,473–C; SMIN 45,473–D; SMIN 45,474–A

Lt. Henry H. Arnold at the controls of a model B at the Wright Flying School, Dayton, 1911.
GHUSAF 4

Duval La Chapelle seated in a model B airplane at the Wright Flying School, Dayton, 1911.
SMIN A42,912–C; USAF 3557 A.S.

Ralph Johnstone seated in a model B airplane at the Wright Flying School, Dayton, 1911.
SMIN A42,912–A; USAF

Arthur L. Welsh seated in a model B airplane at the Wright Flying School, Dayton, 1911.
SMIN 42,912; USAF 22456

Close-up view of model B in hangar, mechanic adjusting an elevator guy wire.
SMIN 32,122–A

Robert J. Collier's model B airplane, 1911.
Aero Club Am Bul., v. 1, May 1912: 37; Air-Scout, v. 1, Mar. 1911: 11

Close-up view of front center section of model B, Lt. Benjamin D. Foulois and Philip O. Parmalee seated at controls.
Air-Scout, v. 1, Apr. 1911: 7

James H. Hare, photographer, and Philip O. Parmalee, pilot, in model B used for scouting purposes on the Mexican border.
Air-Scout, v. 1, Apr. 1911: 8

Wright model B equipped with pontoons being towed on Hudson River, New York, February 7, 1912.
SMIN 41,478–E

Model B in flight, College Park, Md., 1912. Lts. Thomas DeW. Milling and Henry H. Arnold are in airplane.
SMIN 34,794–A

Left front view of model B, the first army airplane in the Philippines, Ft. McKinley, March 1912.
CAIAF 5

George A. Gray flying model B at Grand Beach, Fla., January 1913.
SMIN A38,736

Front view of two Wright model B airplanes in front of tents which served as hangars, Augusta, Ga., 1915.
LC-JONES; GHUSAF 6; USAF 3828 A.S.

Front view of Wright model B in flight, Augusta, Ga., 1915.
LC-JONES; USAF 3833 A.S.

Nineteen students photographed in front of a model B airplane at the Wright School, Augusta, Ga., 1915.
LC-JONES; USAF 3833 A.S.

Marshall Earl Reid flying the reconditioned Wright model B from Camden Airport, New Jersey, December 17, 1934.
Aerosphere, 1943: CXXIII

Side and rear views of a modified model B displayed in the Air Force Museum, Dayton.
APGAFM

Model R (also called the "Roadster" and the "Baby Grand"), 1910

Full front view of model R, a one-place racer designed for speed and altitude competitions, first publicly shown at the International Aviation Tournament, Belmont Park, N.Y., October 22–30, 1910. This smaller version was called the "Baby Grand."
SMIN 9854; SMIN 34,115–C; SMIN 42,667–C; SMIN 43,523

Right front view of model R.
Aero Digest, v. 13, Dec. 1928: 1108; Aerosphere, 1943: CXXXVI; GSWB 29; SMIN 42,545–E; USAF 1354 A.S.; USAF 22439. Similar: SMIN 42,695–B; USAF 30303 A.S.

Left front view of model R.
Bee-Hive, v. 28, Jan. 1953: 15; SMIN 42,912–K; USAF 8655

Three-quarter rear view of model R.
Bee-Hive, v. 28, Spring 1953: 23; SMIN 34,115–H

Close-up rear view of center section of model R.
Aero Digest, v. 13, Dec. 1928: 1108; SMIN 42,926–A; USAF 22442

Three-quarter front view of model R with Orville at the controls, Belmont Park, N.Y., where he attained a speed of 77 to 78 miles an hour on October 25, 1910.
Aircraft, v. 1, Dec. 1910: 355; Air-Scout, v. 1, Dec. 1910: 15; AMHHF 143; GSWB 29; HARFF 202; New York Herald, Oct. 26, 1910: 1; SMIN 43,056. Similar: SMIN 9900-C; SMIN 43,061-E; without Orville, HAWBHP 90

Right front view of Wright "Baby Grand" on ground, Orville adjusting engine, Wilbur holding tail boom.
Air-Scout, v. 1, Jan. 1911: 19; SMIN A3486; SMIN A43,055-K; Town & Country, v. 1, Jan. 1911: 19

Close-up front view of model R, Orville adjusting motor.
SMIN 42, 927-J

Three-quarter front view of model R, Walter R. Brookins standing in front of engine.
Air-Scout, v. 1, Nov. 1910: 7

Close-up front view of model R, Arch Hoxsey standing by skid.
SMIN 43,009

Three-quarter front view of model R with James V. Martin at the controls.
Air-Scout, v. 1, Apr. 1911: 12

Front view of model R, Frank H. Russell, Wright Company manager, at the controls, Simms Station, Dayton, 1910.
MCFWP 210

Front view of model R, with Wilbur facing the machine and two assistants preparing to start propellers, Belmont Park, N.Y., 1910.
LC-BAIN

Model R airplane mounted on four-wheel carriage ready to be moved, assistants gathered around the airplane, Belmont Park, N.Y., October 1910.
LC-BAIN

Three-quarter front view of model R, with group of spectators at rear viewing the machine, Belmont Park, N.Y.
Flight, v. 2, Nov. 19, 1910: 958

Three-quarter front view of model R owned by Alexander Ogilvie, exhibited at London Aero Show, 1911.
Aero, v. 5, Apr. 1911: 17

Front view of model R with unidentified pilot at controls.
SMIN 38,532

Three-quarter front view of Wright "Baby" airplane built under license by the French firm, Astra, Societé de Constructions Aéronautiques, and equipped with Wright Bariquand et Marre motor, as exhibited at the Musée de l'air, Paris.
Pionniers, v. 8, Apr. 25, 1971: 29

Model EX, 1911

Three-quarter front and bottom view of reconstructed model EX *(Vin Fiz)* in National Air and Space Museum.
SMIN 31809–A

Rear view of reconstructed model EX in National Air and Space Museum.
SMIN 36,568

Three-quarter rear view of reconstructed model EX in National Air and Space Museum.
SMIN 36,584; SMIN 36,584–A

Three-quarter front view of modified model EX in flight, flying to left.
GSWB 27

Side view of modified model EX in low-level flight, flying to right, series of buildings visible below.
HAWBHP 90

Three-quarter rear view of model EX on beach, five unidentified men standing in front of wing.
SMIN 32–25–E

Model C, 1912

Three-quarter front view of experimental model C equipped with automatic stabilizer, Orville in pilot's seat.
MCFWP 212; SMIN 38,532–A. Similar: SMIN 42,978

Front view of model C with Orville at front of airplane conferring with Arthur L. Welsh and Robert Fowler, September 1911.
SMIN A4161–F

Three-quarter front view of model C in Wright Company factory, 1912.
SMIN 38,531–F; SMIN 42,737; USAF 48657

Three-quarter right front view of model C as exhibited at New York Aero Show, 1912
Aeronautics, v. 10, May/June 1912: 154; Fly, v. 4, June 1912: 13; SMIN 41, 178–K

Front view of model C (type C, M–1), Lt. Lewis H. Brereton at controls, College Park, Md., 1912.
CLHAGW facing 238

Center section view of model C (type C, M-1) with Lt. Thomas
DeW. Milling at controls and Lt. Henry H. Arnold standing in
front of airplane, June 1912.
SMIN 41,103

Center section view of model C (type C, M-1) with Lt. Leigh-
ton W. Hazelhurst at controls and Arthur L. Welsh, passenger,
June 1912.
SMIN 44,935–G

Front view of model C equipped with pontoons at Pasay on Manila Bay, Philippine Islands, 1913.
CAIAF 4; USAF 3148

Model D, 1912

Front view of military speed scout airplane, model D, on ground
at Simms Station, Dayton, 1912.
USAF 48650

Three-quarter front view of model D, facing right, on ground, at
Simms Station, Dayton, 1912.
SMIN 42,695–B; USAF 48648

Three-quarter front view of model D, facing left, on ground, at
Simms Station, Dayton, 1912.
**MCFWP 215; Aerosphere, 1943; CXLII; SMIN 42,695;
USAF 48649**

Left rear view of model D on ground with various components
of airplane labeled.
SMIN 42,791

Right front view of model D on ground at College Park, Md.
SMIN 42,690–E

Model CH, Early Twin-pontoon Version, 1913

Early CH model, with multiple-step pontoons, on ground, three-
quarter front view, near Miami River, Dayton, 1913.
USAF 48638. Similar: SMIN 38,527–E

Three-quarter front view of multiple-step version of model CH
resting on Miami River, Dayton, May 1913.
GLWB b. 40–41; USAF 48639

Orville testing the multiple-step version of model CH on Miami
River, near Dayton, 1913.
**MCFWP 213; Flying, v. 2, Sept. 1913; 21; NOZWBC
facing 35; SMIN 38,528–A**

Orville flying a Model E airplane at Dayton in 1913.

Side views of multiple-step version of model CH on Miami River, Dayton.
SMIN 38,528; SMIN 38,528–E; SMIN 38,528–G

Model CH with multiple-step pontoons beginning flight on Miami River, Dayton, and moving to left of picture.
Flying, v. 2, Sept. 1913: 21

Model CH, with multiple-step pontoons, beginning flight on Miami River, and moving to right of picture.
SMIN 38,528–B. Close-up view: SMIN 38,528–C

Orville flying at high altitude in test of model CH equipped with multiple-step pontoons over Miami River, Dayton, early May 1913.
Aircraft, v. 4, Sept. 1913: 153; Flying, v. 2, Sept. 1913: 20; SMIN 38,528–H

Orville flying at treetop level in flight test of model CH with multiple-step pontoons over Miami River, Dayton, early May 1913.
SMIN 38,528–H

Model CH with multiple-step pontoons flying near treetop level in test over Miami River, Dayton, early May 1913.
USAF 48640

Model CH, with Single Pontoon, 1913

Side view of model CH airplane with single pontoon, the first Wright hydroplane.
Aircraft, v. 4, Sept. 1913: 153; SMIN 32,121–A; SMIN 38,530–A

Side view of float of model CH single pontoon airplane.
Aeronautics, v. 13, July 1913: 11; Flight, v. 5, Sept. 6, 1913: 978

Front view of model CH resting in shallow water on the Miami River, Dayton, Orville seen in the pilot's seat.
MCFWP 214; Aircraft, v. 4, Sept. 1913: 152; Flight, v. 5, Sept. 6, 1913: 978; Flying, v. 2, Sept. 1913: 21; SMIN 38,528–F; USAF 48641

Three-quarter rear view of model CH resting in shallow water on the Miami River.
SMIN 38,528–D

Side view of model CH starting on the Miami River, moving to left.
Flight, v. 5, Sept. 6, 1913: 978

Model E, 1913

Three-quarter front view of model E with single pusher propeller, designed especially for exhibition flying.
Aircraft, v. 4, Nov. 1913: 210

Side view of model E.
Aeronautics, v. 13, Oct. 1913: 140–141. Similar: Aircraft, v. 4, Nov. 1913: 210

Front view of model E, center section only.
Aeronautics, v. 13, Oct. 1913: 140–141

Propeller end of model E.
SMIN 30,811

Model E in flight just off ground, flying to right.
SMIN 43,062–H

Front view of model E in flight, Simms Station, Dayton, 1913.
Aircraft, v. 4, Nov. 1913: 210; USAF 48647

Quarter front view of Orville flying model E at Simms Station, Dayton, 1913.
MCFWP 216; Aerosphere, 1943: CXLI; SMIN 30,811–G; SMIN 42,737–B; USAF 48646

Model F, 1913

Right side view of Wright model F military airplane, the first Wright machine with a fuselage, in factory in Dayton.
SMIN 42,682–B; USAF 48656

Full right side view of model F on ground.
SMIN 42,682–A; USAF 12930 A.C.

Full left side view of model F on ground.
SMIN A–48,824

Rear view of model F on ground, two mechanics at work on airplane.
SMIN 42,688–C

Right front view of model F on ground with pilot seated in airplane.
SMIN 42,682; USAF 48655

Right front view of modified model F on ground with ten mechanics holding airplane while engine is started.
SMIN 42,688–J

Right rear view of model F on ground with pilot ready for takeoff.
SMIN 42,688–D

Right front view of model F in flight over Simms Station, Dayton, 1913.
MCFWP 217; Aerial Age W, v. 1, Mar. 22, 1915: 8; Flying, v. 3, Oct. 1914: 267; SMIN 42,682; USAF 48655

Model G, 1913

Three-quarter front view of model G on ground facing to right, showing short hull and outrigger controls. The airplane was designed by Grover C. Loening under Orville's supervision and was the first deep-water flying boat produced by the Wright Company.
Aircraft, v. 4, Jan. 1914: 243

Three-quarter front view of model G in factory.
LC-BECK; USAF 48656

Side view of model G on ground at edge of water.
Flying, v. 2, July 1914: 181

Three-quarter front view of model G resting in water, facing right.
Flying, v. 2, July 1914: 181

Three-quarter front view of model G on Miami River, Dayton, facing to left, one man at each end of aircraft, Orville at right end.
MCFWP 218; Aeronautics, v. 13, Nov. 1913; 169; SMIN A38,527–A. Similar: front view: SMIN 38,527

Side view of model G in water facing right.
Aeronautics, v. 14, June 15, 1914: 170. Similar: Aircraft, v. 5, July 1914: 335; Sci Am Suppl, v. 78, July 25, 1914: 55

Three-quarter front view of model G in shallow water near shore, Orville and Grover Loening observing workmen at rear of airplane.
LOOWGF 37

Front view of model G in shallow water in Miami River with Orville in pilot's seat on the right and Oscar Brindley on left, unidentified man in water facing airplane.
Flying, v. 2, Jan. 1914: 21; SMIN A49,251–F; WRAMG 3

Three-quarter front view of model G resting in shallow water on the Miami River, Orville seated at controls, two men in water facing the airplane, one man standing on wing.
Aircraft, v. 4, Jan. 1914: 244

Left front view of model G on Miami River, four spectators on shore, two men standing in shallow water at rear of airplane, Dayton, November 1913.
LC-BECK; SMIN A42,912–F; USAF 22448

Side view of model G starting flight on Miami River, about to make a turn, moving to right.
LC-BAIN; Aircraft, v. 4, Jan. 1914: 243; Flying, v. 2, Jan. 1914: 20; WRAMG 3

Side view of model G in test on Miami River, Oscar Brindley at controls and accompanied by Grover Loening.
Aircraft, v. 4, Jan. 1914: 244

Front view of model G cruising to left, on Miami River, Dayton.
USAF 22450

Three-quarter front view of model G moving to left on Miami River, Orville at helm.
Aerial Age W, v. 1, Apr. 26, 1915: 129

Left and right side views of Harry N. Atwood seated in model G at edge of water at Toledo Beach, Toledo, Ohio, 1914.
Aero and Hydro, v. 8, June 27, 1914: 160

Front view of model G, Harry Atwood and Grover Loening seated in it, cruising on water at Toledo.
LOOWGF 35

Model G in flight over trees lining the banks of the Miami River, flying to right with Oscar Brindley at controls.
LC-BAIN; Aircraft, v. 4, Jan. 1914: 244; Flight, v. 6, Jan. 27, 1914: 56; Flugsport, v. 6, Feb. 4, 1914: 85; Flying, v. 2, Jan. 1914: 21; Sci Am, v. 109, Dec. 13, 1913: 458; SMIN 31,012; SMIN 76–19,217

Model H, 1914

Left front view of model H, a two-place military scout airplane, on ground at Simms Station, Dayton, 1914.
SMIN 42,912–P; USAF 48651

Left rear view of model H on ground, Simms Station, Dayton, 1914.
Aerosphere, 1943: CXLIV; SMIN 42,912–H; USAF 48651

Front view of model H in flight, Simms Station, Dayton, 1914.
MCFWP 219; SMIN 42,737–E; USAF 48652

High-altitude front view of model H in flight, Simms Station, Dayton, 1914.
SMIN 38,536–E; USAF 48653

Model HS, 1915

Three-quarter front view of model HS, a smaller version of the model H and the last Wright airplane with a double vertical rudder or pusher-type propellers, on ground at Simms Station, Dayton.
SMIN 42,737–P

Right front view of model HS on ground, Coronada Beach, Fla.
SMIN 42,688–E

Left side view of model HS on ground, Coronada Beach, Fla.
SMIN 42,688

Right side view of modified model HS on ground.
SMIN 42–688–A

Close-up left rear view of model HS on ground, Coronada Beach, Fla.
SMIN 42,688–B

Right rear view of model HS on ground, Coronada Beach, Fla.
SMIN 42,688–C

Front view of model HS in flight, Simms Station, Dayton, August 1914.
LC-BECK; Flight, v. 6, Nov. 20, 1914: 1133; Flying, v. 3, Oct. 1914: 267. Similar: two views, USAF 48654

Front view of model HS in flight, Simms Station, Dayton, March 1915.
LC-BAIN

Front view of model HS in flight, Augusta, Ga., 1915.
LC-Jones; MCFWP 220. Similar: USAF 3829

Left side view of model HS in flight, in slight dive.
SMIN 32,124–B; SMIN 34,290–G

Model K, 1915

Side view of model K, the first Wright design to have tractor propellers and ailerons with fuselage similar to that of the model G flying boat, in factory.
MCFWP 222; SMIN 45,253

Front view of model K, equipped with navy pontoons, in factory.
SMIN 44,432–G

Right-front view of model K in shallow water at naval base.
Aerosphere, 1943: CXLIV; SMIN 31,290–B

Side view of model K in shallow water at naval base.
SMIN 44,432–D

Three-quarter rear view of model K in shallow water at naval base.
SMIN 44,432–C; SMIN 44,432–E

Close-up side view of model K just starting flight with floats on water.
SMIN 44,432

Side view of model K rising from water.
Flying, v. 5, Sept. 1916: 336; SMIN 33,209–B

Model L, 1916

Front view of model L, the first Wright airplane to incorporate a single tractor propeller and the last model manufactured by the original Wright Company, on ground, Mineola, N.Y., 1916.
SMIN 42,681–C; USAF 341 A.S. Similar: SMIN 38,525–C

Wright Cycle Company, 1127 West Third Street, Dayton.

Four views of model L—front, side, three-quarter front, and rear views.

Aeronautics, v. 11, Aug. 16, 1916: 101; Aeroplane, v. 11, Aug. 30, 1916: 370; Flight, v. 8, Aug 10, 1916: 664; SMIN 31,838–A

Three-quarter rear view of Wright model L.

MCFWP 223; NOZWBC facing 49; SMIN 38,525

Three-quarter left front view of model L on ground.

Aerial Age W, v. 3, July 10, 1916: 508

Three-quarter right front view of model L on ground.

Aviation, v. 1, Aug. 1, 1916: 27; GLWB b. 240–241; SMIN 31,290–A. Similar: SMIN 31,290–H; USAF 340 A.S.

Right side view of model L on ground.

SMIN 38,525–D. Similar: SMIN 42,681–B

Right side view of model L on ground at Sheepshead Bay, N.Y.

Flying, v. 5, June, 1916: 199; SMIN 33,209–K; SMIN 42,681–B; USAF 339 A.S.

Close-up right rear view of center section of model L.

Aerosphere, 1943: CXLV; SMIN 42,681; USAF 1361 A.S.

Front view of model L in flight.

Flying, v. 5, July 1916: 245; SMIN 33,209–E

Bicycle Shop

The shop of the Wright Cycle Company was originally established in Dayton in 1892, located first at 1005 West Third Street, next at 1034 West Third Street, and finally at its best-known site 1127 West Third Street.

Orville and Edwin H. Sines, neighbor and boyhood friend, filing frames in back room of Wright bicycle shop, 1897.
LC–USZ62–65096; LC–W85–82; MCFWP 7; WRBR

Front view of bicycle shop, a gentleman and three ladies standing in front of it, 1127 West Third Street, Dayton.
Collier's, v. 80, Aug. 1927: 8; HMSHSA facing 178; MILWA v. 2: 99; Sat Eve Post, v. 201, July 7, 1928: 11; World's Work, v. 20, Aug. 1910: 13309

Front view of the Wright Cycle Company. The left half of the brick building and the frame building in the rear were occupied by the Wrights.
LC–BECK; MCFWP 8; Bee-Hive, v. 28, Jan. 1953: 5; BBAKH; EWBNM 4; MCMWB 68; Popular Aviation, v. 19, Dec. 1936: 17; Pop Sci, v. 114, Feb. 1929: 44; SMIN 41, 019; U.S. Air Services, v. 21, Aug. 1936: 15; YPHA 33

Photo of Wright shop purchased by Henry Ford, before removal to Dearborn, Mich.
Dayton News, July 1, 1936

Bicycle shop decorated with sign "Wright Bros. Built the First Airplane Here," American flag draped on either side, for observance of the 20th anniversary of first flight in 1903.
Aero Digest, v. 13, Dec. 1923: 1107; MILWA v. 2: 99; SMIN 42,928–C

Wright bicycle shop as restored in Greenfield Village, Dearborn, Mich., where it was dedicated on April 16, 1938, as a memorial to the Wrights.

Aero Digest, v. 32, May 1932: 12; Aerosphere, 1943: CXVIII; Am Legion Mag, v. 86, Feb. 1969: 16; ANDWF 607; ASHWB 16; Aviation W, v. 49, Dec. 13, 1948: Dayton Magazine, Aug. 1973: 36; Detroit News, Apr. 17, 1938: KELWB b. 180–181; SMIN 43,204–A; U.S. Air Services, v. 21, May 1938: 14

Interior view of the restored Wright bicycle shop, Dearborn, Mich.

ASHWB 35; Henry Ford Museum photo

Band saw in machine shop of the restored Wright bicycle shop.
Henry Ford Museum photo T38670B

Desk and chair in the office of restored Wright machine shop.
Henry Ford Museum photo T38670A

Drill press in restored Wright machine shop.
Henry Ford Museum photo T38670F

General view of the interior of restored Wright machine shop.
Bee-Hive, v. 28, Jan. 1953: 9; Henry Ford Museum photo T38670E; SMIN 43,204C

Lathe in restored Wright machine shop.
Henry Ford Museum photo T38670C

Reconstructed engine used to power the machinery in restored Wright machine shop.
Henry Ford Museum photo T38670D

Incidence Indicator

The incidence indicator was an instrument invented by Orville to show the angle of incidence of an airplane in flight, a contribution to the safe operation of an aircraft.

Early model of incidence indicator designed by Wrights.
Franklin Institute 2002; J Franklin In, v. 252, Aug. 1951: 192; SMIN 42,772–A

Wright incidence indicator manufactured by the Wright Company, Dayton, about 1913.
LC-BECK; Franklin Institute 2002; J Franklin In, v. 252, Aug. 1951: 192. Similar, with different name plate and with air vane at slightly different angle: MCFWP 231; Aero and Hydro, v. 6, Aug. 9, 1913: 380; Aeronautics, v. 12, Aug. 1913: 58; Aircraft, v. 4, Sept. 1913: 159; SMIN A3514; SMIN 42,772

Rear view of Wright incidence indicator.
SMIN A3513

Front and rear views of disassembled Wright incidence indicator.
SMIN A3515; SMIN A3516

Incidence indicator mounted on strut of Wright model E airplane.
SMIN A3512; SMIN 30,811

Motor

Wright motors included the original motor of 1903, an improved version used in the flights of 1904, a four-cylinder motor used in most Wright airplanes from 1908 until 1912, the eight-cylinder motor used in the Model R airplane at Belmont Park in 1910, and the six-cylinder motor, the last produced by the Wright Company, which was in general use after 1913.

View of the magneto side of the Wright four-cylinder motor as exhibited at the Second Annual Exhibition of the Aero Club of America in New York, December 1–8, 1906.
ACANA facing xxxv; Ballooning and Aeronautics, v. 1, Feb. 1907: 62; PEPHO facing 40; Sci Am, v. 95, Dec. 15, 1906: 449. Similar: Aero, v. 1, Nov. 5, 1910: 15; Aero Manual, 1909: 147; Aero Manual, 1910: 187; Aerosphere, 1939: 829; Allg Auto Zeit, v. 10, Mar. 26, 1909: 40; ANMAD 152; Flight, v. 1, Mar. 20, 1909: 161; GSIA 206; Rivista Tecnica di Aeronautica, v. 6, no. 3, 1909: 116; VOMLF 111

Series of six views of the Wright four-cylinder, 30-h.p. motor as used in the Wright 1909 military airplane.
SMIN A36,895—SMIN A36,895–E

Wright development motor no. 3, 1904–6, showing auxiliary exhaust port, and separate one-piece water-jacket block.
HWBETD 31

Right side view of the Wright four-cylinder motor used in the Wright 1909 military airplane.
SMIN A9900–A; SMIN 36,895–D

Magneto side of the Wright four-cylinder motor used in 1911.
LC–W86–93; LC–W86–94. Similar: HWBETD 26a

Left side front view of reconstructed Wright brothers' 1903 motor.

LC–W86–59; MCFWP 225; BLASF facing 64; EWBNM 33; Schweizer Aero-Revue, v. 28, Dec. 1953: 422; SMIN A38,496–G; SMINAR 1961: b. 358–359; WIGLIG b. 548–549; YPHA 32. Similar: ASHWB 38; Bee-Hive, v. 28, Jan. 1953: 7; HAWBHP 66; HWBETD 6; HGCA 53; NOZWBC facing 116; SMIN 38,626–B; TAYAP 12

Left rear underside view of Wright brothers' 1903 motor showing valve gear, camshaft, and flywheel.

Bee-Hive, v. 28, Jan. 1953: 8; HFGAUBTW 15; HWBETD 7; Science Museum 558/38; SMIN 38,626–F

Wright 1903 motor shown with the crankcase cover removed.

Bee-Hive, v. 28, Jan. 1953: 10; SMIN A38,626–H

Underside view of reconstructed Wright 1903 motor.

LC–W86–58; MCFWP 226; MARWBC 10; SAE Q Trans, v. 5, Jan. 1951: 9; SMIN 41,898–C; SMINAR 1961: b. 358–359

Views of cylinder, valve box, and gear mechanism for the Wright 1903 motor.

Bee-Hive, v. 28, Jan. 1953: 8; HWBETD 23; SMIN 38,628–G

Wright 1903 motor installed in the Wright 1903 airplane as exhibited in the Science Museum, London.

HWBETD 11

Center section view of Wright 1903 airplane when returned from England, 1948, showing controls and motor.

JUDAE facing 62; SMIN 32,125–F

Center section view of Wright 1903 airplane when returned from England, 1948, showing motor, controls, radiator, gas tank, and instruments.

Bee-Hive, v. 28, Jan. 1953: 9; MARWBC 9; Schweizer Aero-Revue, v. 28, Dec. 1953: 423; SMIN A38,387–C; SMIN 38,388; SMINAR 1961: b. 358–359

View of flywheel end of Wright motor at Carillon Park Museum, Dayton.

HWBETD 37d; SMIN A3773

Magneto side of Wright four-cylinder motor with crankcase cover removed.

HWBETD 37d

Left side view of Wright four-cylinder motor, 1909.

Aerosphere, 1939: 829; Aerosphere, 1943: CXXXVII; ANGAEE: 522; SAE Q Trans, v. 5, Jan. 1951: 11; SMIN 9900–B

Left front view of center section of Wright 1903 airplane when returned from England, 1948, with close-up view of controls, anemometer, stop watch, instrument assembly, and motor valves.
SMIN 38,387–E; SMIN 38,388–B

Rear view of Wright four-cylinder motor as installed in Wright 1903 airplane.
LC–W86–61; LC–W86–62; COCKDH following 168; DOBOHA 171; EWBNM 36; JOHHU 233

Rear view of Wright 1903 motor in shop, January 1, 1928, before its shipment to the Science Museum, London, on January 31, 1928.
LC–W86–60

Full right side view of Wright 30-h.p. motor manufactured by French firm Bariquand et Marre in 1908 as exhibited in the Musée de l'air, Paris.
Pionniers, v. 8, Apr. 25, 1971: 89

Full right side view of 30-h.p. Wright Bollée motor, 1909.
Science Museum 1382

Front and rear views of the Wright motor manufactured in Germany by the Neue Automobil-Gesellschaft at Oberschöneweide, as installed in a Wright airplane.
Zeitschrift der Verein der Deutscher Ingenieure, v. 54, May 1928: 888

Five views of the Wright 32-h.p. motor manufactured in Germany for the Flugmaschine Wright in 1910.
FWGWA 7–8

Charles Taylor's half-scale model of the Wright brothers' 1903 motor now in Wright brothers' collection in Greenfield Village, Dearborn, Mich.
SMIN 38,497–D

Reproduction of the Wright 1903 motor as mounted in a reproduction of the Wright 1903 airplane at the Wright Brothers National Memorial at Kitty Hawk, N.C.
HWBETD front.

Replica of the Wright 1903 four-cylinder motor in the Science Museum, London.
Aeroplane, v. 85, Dec. 18, 1953: 827

Series of six views of the Wright 6–60 motor, the six-cylinder motor in general use in Wright airplanes after 1913.
SMIN 44,091 - SMIN 44,091–E

Exhaust side view of the Wright 6–60 motor.
WCWAM 6–60: 3

Right side view of the Wright 6–60 motor.
Aeronautics, v. 13, Oct. 1913: 141; Aerosphere, 1939: 829; Aerosphere, 1943: CXLIII; ANGAAE 523; HWBETD 56; WCWAM 6–60: 2

Views of the Wright 6–60 motor: push-rod side, valve-port side, and crankcase with sump removed.
HWBETD 49; SMIN A3773–A; SMIN 45,598

View of the Wright 6–60 motor: cylinder assembly and valve parts; bottom side of piston; piston, piston pin, and connecting rod; valve mechanism; crankshaft; and flywheel.
HWBETD 52

View of Wright 6–60 motor mounted in Wright airplane.
Aero and Hydro, v. 7, Nov. 15, 1913: 87

View of Wright six-cylinder motor mounted in Wright model CH airplane, 1913.
SMIN 38,530–B

Charles Taylor and Fred A. Marshall photographed at ends of the Wright 6–60 motor.
Airway Age, v. 9, Dec. 1928: 38. Similar view of motor only: USAF 42110

Exhaust side view of Wright six-cylinder 6–70 motor with flexible flywheel drive.
HWBETD 56; SMIN A54,581

View of special Wright eight-cylinder motor used on the Wright model R airplane in International Aviation Tournament, Belmont Park, N.Y., October 1910.
MCFWP 229

View of intake side of Wright eight-cylinder motor.
HWBETD 48

Exhaust side view of Wright eight-cylinder motor.
HWBETD 48; SMIN 48,598

Close up rear view of Wright eight-cylinder motor, radiator, gas tank, and chain guide as used in Wright model R, 1910.
SMIN 42,668

Wright brothers' shop engine, 1901, showing governor and exhaust valve cam.
HWBETD 65

Orville Wright
Experimental Devices

The experimental devices developed by Orville in his later years when he was no longer associated with the original Wright Company were primarily related to aviation and were bequeathed to the Franklin Institute, Philadelphia, on his death in 1948. They are now in the Wright Brothers' Aeronautical Engineering Collection at the Franklin Institute.

Automatic landing device mounted in wing section, developed by Orville in 1943.
> **MCFWP 232; Franklin Institute 2015; J Franklin In, v. 252, Aug. 1951: 194**

Automatic electrical control device (1918–42) for airplanes.
> **MCFWP 234; Franklin Institute; J Franklin In, v. 252, Aug. 1951: 193**

Smoke apparatus and airfoils.
> **Franklin Institute 2005; J Franklin In, v. 252, Aug. 1951: 183**

Wind tunnel model of Gordon Bennett racer.
> **Franklin Institute 1991; J Franklin In, v. 252, Aug. 1951: 185**

Wind tunnel model of biplane with split flaps.
> **Franklin Institute 1992; J Franklin In, v. 252, Aug. 1951: 185; J Franklin In, v. 256, Dec. 1953: 522**

Wind tunnel model of Dayton Wright monoplane.
> **Franklin Institute 1990; J Franklin In, v. 252, Aug. 1951: 186**

Mud hooks for automobile wheels made by Orville in the 1920s.
> **Franklin Institute 2009; J Franklin In, v. 252, Aug. 1951: 188**

Lever cam and sleeve used in the 1903–5 airplane to control spark timing.
> **Franklin Institute 2000; J Franklin In, v. 252, Aug. 1951: 189; J Franklin In, v. 256, Dec. 1953: xii**

Foot control to Mea-magneto on the Wright 1910 biplane.
Franklin Institute 2000; J Franklin In, v. 252, Aug. 1951: 189; J Franklin In, v. 256, Dec. 1953: xii

Scale and weights made by Orville.
Franklin Institute 2010; J Franklin In, v. 252, Aug. 1951: 190

Experimental model of an electrical control device for airplanes.
Franklin Institute 1994; J Franklin In, v. 252, Aug. 1951: 193

Three-quarter front view of cypher machine.
Franklin Institute 2013; J Franklin In, v. 252, Aug. 1951: 195

Power unit used by Orville in 1910 to achieve automatic lateral stability.
J Franklin In, v. 252, Aug. 1951: 194

Bank indicator manufactured by the Wright Company, 1914.
LC-BECK; Franklin Institute 2007; J Franklin In, v. 252, Aug. 1951: 191; USAF 48656

Propeller

The propellers designed by the Wrights include the original one of 1903, the "taper tip" propeller of 1905, the "bent end" propeller of 1909-10, and the propeller used in 1911.

Front view of the propeller from Wright 1903 machine in the National Air and Space Museum.
MCFWP 129; Bee-Hive, v. 28, Spring 1953: 20; EWBNM 1; HAWBHP 67; SMIN 43,363-B

Side view of the Wright 1903 propeller.
SMIN 42,363-A

Rear view of the Wright 1903 propeller.
MCFWP 130; SMIN 42,363-C

End view of the Wright 1903 propeller, showing curvature of the blade.
MCFWP 131; SMIN 42,363-D

Front view of Wright 1905 intermediate "taper tip" propeller.
MCFWP 141; National Cash Register Company photo

Wright propeller mounted on Wright machine flown by Wilbur in France, 1908.
EWWLM 24

Propellers mounted on Wright machine, early 1909.
Autocar, v. 22, Mar. 2, 1909: 388

Group of finished and unfinished propellers in Flugmaschine Wright factory at Reinickendorf, Germany, about 1910.
FWGWA

Wright propeller of the "bent end" type, mounted on machine, late 1909 or 1910.
MCFWP 133

Front view of 1911 Wright "bent end" propeller in the National Air and Space Museum, showing canvas-covered tips.
MCFWP 134

End view of the 1911 Wright propeller, showing twisted appearance of the blade.
MCFWP 132

Side view of Wright 1911 propeller, entering edge at bottom, showing backward sweep of "bent end" blade.
MCFWP 135; SMIN 18,224–A

Rear view of 1911 Wright propeller.
MCFWP 136; SMIN 18,224–A

Wind Tunnel Experiments

Replicas of the wind tunnel used by Wilbur and Orville in their wind tunnel research in 1901–3 have been built and are on display in the Air Force Museum, Dayton; Carillon Park Museum, Dayton; Henry Ford Museum, Greenfield Village, Dearborn, Michigan; National Air and Space Museum, Washington, D.C.; and the National Memorial Museum and Visitor Center, Kitty Hawk, North Carolina. The original metal airfoils used by the Wrights in their research were willed to the Franklin Institute, Philadelphia.

Three-quarter left front view of replica of Wright brothers' wind tunnel located in workroom behind restored Wright brothers' bicycle shop, Henry Ford Museum, Greenfield Village, Dearborn, Mich. The Wright exhibit was dedicated April 16, 1938.
> **MCFWP 116; Am Legion Magazine, v. 86, Feb. 1969: 17; ANDWF 608; ASHWB 34; Bee-Hive, v. 28, Jan. 1953: 11; EWBNM 24; YPHA 33. Similar: front view, Aviation, v. 38, Aug. 1939: 21**

Left side view of wind tunnel replica in Henry Ford Museum showing metal-bladed fan in front which was used to force a current of air through the wind tunnel.
> **Greenfield Village photo A1319. Similar: right side view, Aviation, v. 38, Aug. 1939: 20**

Side view of replica of Wrights' 1901 wind tunnel as exhibited in the National Air and Space Museum.
> **Air Force, v. 36, Dec. 1953: 36; GANAC 34; SMIN 41,020**

Three-quarter front view of replica of Wrights' 1901 wind tunnel constructed under the supervision of Orville prior to World War II as displayed in the Air Force Museum, Dayton.
> **APGAFM 38**

The 1901 wind tunnel was located in a workroom behind the Wright bicycle shop, as shown here in the Greenfield Village restoration, Dearborn, Michigan.

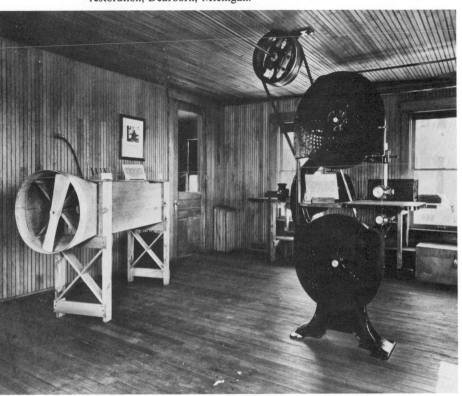

Side view of replica of Wrights' 1901 wind tunnel with a section of the wall cut away, showing the lift balance in position for a test, Carillon Park Museum, Dayton.
MCFWP 115; Carillon Park (Dayton) photo; KELWB b. 238–239; SAE Q Trans, v. 5, Jan. 1951: 4; SMIN A52,718; TAPHF 23; WODKH b. 100–101. Similar: SMIN A41,899–D

Three-quarter front view of replica of Wrights' wind tunnel on exhibit in Franklin Institute's Hall of Aviation.
J Franklin In, v. 252, Aug. 1951: 179

Three-quarter front view of replica of Wrights' wind tunnel in Wright Brothers National Memorial Museum and Visitors Center, Kitty Hawk, N.C.
National Aeronautics, v. 40, Dec. 1961: 5

Front view of balance for measuring lift of model airfoils in the 1901 wind tunnel experiments.
LCPWOW 240; MCFWP 30

Original Wright 1901 lift balance in Franklin Institute. Photograph shows balance as incorrectly assembled.

MCFWP 31; Franklin Institute photo; J Franklin In, v. 252, Aug. 1951: 176

Reproduction of lift balance used in 1901 wind tunnel with models of airfoils in testing position.

MCFWP 121; General Motors Inland Manufacturing Division (Dayton) photo; EWBNM 25; GANAC 34; HAWBHP 61; SAE Q Trans, v. 5, Jan. 1951: 5; Schweizer Aero-Revue, v. 28, Dec. 1928: 420; SMIN 9576; SMIN 41,899–B; WODKH b. 100–101

Reproduction of 1901 drift balance for measuring drag/lift ratio of Wright model airfoils.

MCFWP 122; EWBNM 25; Franklin Institute photo; General Motors Inland Manufacturing Division (Dayton) photo; J Franklin In, v. 252, Aug. 1951: 176; SAE Q Trans, v. 5, Jan. 1951: 5; SMIN 41,899–C

Reconstruction of Wrights' wind-tunnel balancing vane.

MCFWP 119; General Motors Inland Manufacturing Division (Dayton) photo; SAE Q Trans, v. 5, Jan. 1951: 3; Schweizer Aero-Revue, v. 28, Dec. 1953: 420; SMIN 41,899

Reconstruction of the Wrights' "recheck" vane, used to check the lifting characteristics of square planes.

MCFWP 120; General Motors Inland Manufacturing Division (Dayton) photo; SAE Q Trans, v. 5, Jan. 1951: 7; SMIN A–41,899–A

Close-up side view of reconstructed Wrights' wind tunnel with a portion of the intake cone cut away to show the large wind straightener and the smaller honeycomb straightener behind it, Carillon Park, Dayton.

MCFWP 117; Carillon Park (Dayton) photo

Reconstruction of Wrights' wind tunnel with portion of side wall cut away to show workings of wind-tunnel apparatus inside, Carillon Park, Dayton.

Carillon Park (Dayton) photo

Reconstruction of Wrights' bicycle-wheel testing device for comparing lift characteristics of model surface against flat-plate resistance.

MCFWP 118; Bee-Hive, v. 28, Spring 1953: 24; Carillon Park (Dayton) photo; HAWBHP 61; SAE Q Trans, v. 5, Jan. 1951: 3; Schweizer Aero-Revue, v. 28, Dec. 1953: 419; SMIN 41,899–E

Collection of 1901 model airfoils, a comparative grouping with test specimens one-fifth actual size.

MCFWP 127; General Motors Inland Manufacturing Division (Dayton) photo; HAWBHP 62; SAE Q Trans, v. 5, Jan. 1951: 6; SMIN A41,898–D

Collection of model airfoils used in the Wrights' December 1901 wind tunnel experiments.
J Franklin In, v. 252, Aug. 1951: 178

Wind tunnel airfoils used in the wind tunnel experiments of 1901. Thirty-eight of the original airfoils are in the Franklin Institute, Philadelphia.
LCPWOW 120; MCFWP 123; MCFWP 124; MCFWP 125; MCFWP 126. Seven of the airfoils in MCFWP 124 are reproduced in WODKH b. 100–101

Wax model airfoils used in Orville's 1919–21 wind tunnel tests.
Franklin Institute 1985; J Franklin In, v. 252, Aug. 1951: 181

High-lift airfoils used in Orville's 1921–22 wind tunnel tests.
Franklin Institute 1984; J Franklin In, v. 252, Aug. 1951: 181; J Franklin In, v. 256, Dec. 1953: 522

Shaper for making wax model airfoils for Orville's 1917 wind tunnel.
MCFWP 231; Franklin Institute 1995; J Franklin In, v. 252, Aug. 1951: 181; J Franklin In, v. 256, Dec. 1953: 522

Orville seated and looking at original Wrights' wind tunnel lift balance, misplaced when moved December 6, 1916, and rediscovered in attic of Orville's laboratory in Dayton, December 9, 1946.
Science News Letter, June 4, 1949: 355

Three-quarter front view of the Orville Wright wind tunnel he designed in 1916 to conduct aerodynamic experiments during World War I at wind velocities exceeding 160 miles per hour.
APGAFM 38

Wright Company

The Wright Company was incorporated on November 22, 1909. The Wright Company factory was completed in November 1910 and a duplicate factory building was erected in 1911. The buildings continued in use until the Wright Company was sold, October 15, 1915.

Series of nine interior views of the factory of the French firm of Astra, Societé de Constructions Aeronautiques, Paris, which was building Wright airplanes in 1909 under license from the Wright brothers.
 L'Aviation illustrée, v. 1, May 29, 1909: 1

Exterior.view of Wright Company factory, Dayton, 1910.
 World's Work, v. 20, Aug. 1910: 13311

Exterior end views of Wright Company factory, Dayton, 1911.
 LC–W86–98; LC–W86–127; SMIN 38,530–C; SMIN 38,531–B

Exterior side views of Wright Company factory, Dayton, 1911.
 LC–W86–95; LC–W86–96; Aircraft, v. 2, Sept. 1911: 246; HAWBHP 94; SMIN 3830–O

Interior views of Wright Company factory, Dayton, including views of the assembly of wing frames, biplane strut construction, elevator and rudder frame construction, and runner construction.
 Allg Auto Zeit, v. 10, Mar. 26, 1909: 41; LOUVA facing 164, 170, 402, 404; SBNA 83 (two views)

Series of interior views of Wright Company factory, Dayton.
 WADC 252372–252383

Series of interior views of Wright Company factory, Dayton.
 SMIN 32,120–E; SMIN 32,122–Q; SMIN 36–323–A; SMIN 38,524–E; SMIN 38,530–B; SMIN 38,530–J; SMIN 38,531–A

Interior view of Wright Company factory, Dayton, 1911, showing three airplanes in process of assembly.
 MCFWP 211; GHUSAF 11; HAWBHP 96

General Assembly Department, Wright Company factory, Dayton, 1911.

**Aero Digest, v. 13, Dec. 1928: 1109; WADC 22443.
Similar: HAWBHP 94; NOZWBC facing 116; WADC 252376**

Interior view of Wright Company factory, Dayton, showing assembled Wright model B in background and wheels, struts, and skids in foreground.

HAWBHP 95; SMIN 42,689–G

Propeller and Rib Department, Wright Company factory, Dayton, 1911.

Bee-Hive, v. 28, Spring 1953: 24; SMIN 38,531

Wing construction at Wright Company factory, Dayton.

LOOWGF 32

Interior view of Wright Company factory, Dayton, two wing sections in foreground.

HAWBHP 96; SMIN 31,291; World's Work, v. 20, Aug. 1910: 13311

Interior view of Wright Company factory, Dayton, showing wing panel of a Wright model B in foreground in process of being covered.

HAWBHP 95; SMIN 42,689–D

Exterior and interior views of Flugmaschine Wright factory at Reinickendorf, Germany, near Berlin.

FWGWA 10, 12–13

Six interior views of Flugmaschine Wright factory, Reinickendorf, Germany.

Ill Aero Mitteil, v. 13, Dec. 1, 1909: 1077–1080

Home

The first Wright home, located at 7 Hawthorn Street, Dayton, Ohio, was occupied by the Wright family from 1871 to 1914. Orville Wright lived at Hawthorn Hill from April 1914 until his death in 1948.

Parlor of Wright home, 7 Hawthorn Street, Dayton, occupied by the Wright family 1871–78 and October 1885–April 1914.
LC–W85–80; MCFWP 6

In 1900, the Wright family home was the house at 7 Hawthorn Street, Dayton.

Christmas tree in Wright home, 1900.
   LC–USZ62–66296; LC–W85–45; LC–W85–46

Side view of home, taken from rear.
   LC–W85–59

Photograph of Hawthorn Street taken by Charles E. Taylor
from porch of Wright home.
   LC–W85–31; LC–W85–32

Front view of home with trees in leaf.
   MCFWP 5. Similar: LC–W85–38; EWBNM 2

Front view of home with trees bare and bicycle resting against
front fence at right gate, about 1900.
   **LC–W85–64; LC–W85–65; Bee-Hive, v. 28, Jan. 1953:
   4; HFGAUBT 10; KELMKH b. 238–239; MOORKH
   109; SMIN 43,204–B; YPHA 33**

The parlor of the Wright home at 7 Hawthorn Street as it was
about 1877.

Front view of home similar to above but without bicycle.

> **BBAKH; Collier's, v. 80, Aug. 20, 1927: 8; MCMWB 68; MILWA v. 2: 98; Vie grand air, v. 15, Apr. 3, 1909: 228; World's Work, v. 20, Aug. 1910: 13309. Similar, enlarged: ASHWB 12**

Dayton home of Wright brothers as restored by Henry Ford and set up in Greenfield Village, Dearborn, Mich., and dedicated April 16, 1938.

> **Detroit News, Apr. 17, 1938; EIDWHS facing 10; U.S. Air Services, v. 23, May 1938: 13; U.S. Air Services, v. 28, Dec. 1943: 27**

A Christmas tree in the Wright home, 7 Hawthorn Street, in 1900.

Corner of Wright living room as restored in Greenfield Village.
   Dayton Herald, Apr. 15, 1938

Right front summer view showing driveway approach to
Hawthorn Hill, Oakwood home occupied by Orville from April
1914 until his death in 1948.
   **LC-BECK; BBAKH; U.S. Air Services, v. 34, Feb.
   1949: 13**

Front summer view of Hawthorn Hill.
   ANDWF 588

Front winter views of Hawthorn Hill.
   **LC-W86-151; LC-W86-152; LC-W86-153;
   LC-W86-154; LC-W86-155; KELMKH b. 238-239**

Group picture showing close-up views of porch, steps, and
grounds, Hawthorn Hill, 1915.
   **LC-W86-163; LC-W86-164; LC-W86-165;
   LC-W86-166**

In 1914, Orville Wright moved to Hawthorn Hill in Dayton,
where he lived until his death in 1948.

Family, Friends, and Associates

Composite photograph of Wright family, head and shoulders, Susan Koerner Wright and Bishop Milton Wright in center, surrounded by their children, Wilbur, Katharine, Lorin, Reuchlin, and Orville, early 1900s.
NOZWBC facing 67

John G. Koerner, maternal grandfather of the Wright brothers, head and shoulders.
MCFWP 40; HILBW 5; SUBDF v. 1: 165

Susan Koerner Wright, mother of the Wright brothers, head and shoulders, from an ambrotype taken just before her marriage to Bishop Milton Wright, November 24, 1859.
LC-BECK; COCKDH following 168; U.S. Air Services, v. 16, Dec. 1931: 21

Susan Koerner Wright, age 40, head and shoulders.
HILBW 5

Susan Koerner Wright, about 44 years old, head and shoulders.
LC-BECK; MCMWB 40

Bertha Wright, niece of the Wright brothers, daughter of Lorin Wright, age five, January 1901.
LC-W85-2; LC-W85-3

Harold W. and Bertha Ellwyn Steeper, family photographs.
ANDWF 553-554

Helen Wright, niece of the Wright brothers, daughter of Reuchlin Wright, age 12, January 1901.
LC-W85-4; LC-W85-5; LC-W85-6; Lithopinion, v. 6, Winter 1971: 61

Herbert Wright, nephew of the Wright brothers, son of Reuchlin Wright, age eight.
LC-W85-24; LC-W85-25

Herbert Wright, age eight, and Milton Wright, son of Lorin Wright, age nine.
LC–W85–17; Lithopinion, v. 6, Winter 1971: 61

Horace (Bus) Wright, nephew of the Wright brothers, son of Lorin Wright.
LC–W85–12; LC–W86–160

Horace Wright, head and shoulders.
MARWBC 50

Horace Wright family photos.
ANDWF 573

Ivonette Wright, niece of the Wright brothers, daughter of Lorin Wright, age three.
LC–W85–15

Ivonette Wright, age five, three-quarter length.
LC–W85–16

Ivonette Wright, head and shoulders.
MARWBC 50

Ivonette Wright, head and shoulders.
Dayton, U.S.A., Aug. 1973: 34

Ivonette and Harold S. Miller family photo.
ANDWF 562

A composite photograph from the early 1900s shows the Wright family with, from left to right, Wilbur, Katharine, Mrs. Milton Wright, Loren, Bishop Milton Wright, Reuchlin, and Orville.

Leontine Wright, niece of the Wright brothers, daughter of Lorin Wright, age one year.
LC–W85–24; LC–W85–25; Lithopinion, v. 7, Winter 1971: 61

Leontine Wright, three-quarter length.
LC–W86–162; Lithopinion, v. 6, Winter 1971: 61

Lorin Wright, brother of Wilbur and Orville, seated holding his children, Horace, Ivonette, and Leontine.
LC–W85–12

Lorin Wright pulling Leontine, age three, on sled, January 27, 1901.
LC–W85–39; LC–W85–40

Lorin Wright family photographs.
ANDWF 558

Mrs. Lorin (Lou) Wright, half length, January 1901.
LC–W85–18; LC–W85–19

Milton Wright, nephew of Wright brothers, son of Lorin Wright, probably age nine, copy photograph.
LC–W85–29; LC–W85–30

Milton Wright, Ivonette Wright, and Leontine Wright seated on sled, January 29, 1901.
LC–USZ62–66294; LC–W85–41; LC–W85–42

Milton Wright family photographs.
ANDWF 560

Reuchlin Wright, brother of Wilbur and Orville, age 40, head and shoulders, January 1901.
LC–W85–22; LC–W85–23

George Reeder, relative, called Uncle George, head and shoulders.
LC–W85–9

Carrie Kayler Grumbach, member of the Wright household for nearly half a century, head and shoulders, and Charles Grumbach, head and shoulders.
ANDWF 587

Mrs. Emma Dennis, Orville's cousin, head and shoulders.
Detroit News, Jan. 24, 1937

Mr. and Mrs. Lindemuth, farmers, at Shoup's Mill, near Dayton.
LC–W85–66; LC–W85–67; Lithopinion, v. 6, Winter 1971: 60

Clarence "Grandpa" Liv and Alonzo "Teddy" Tucker at back of Wright brothers bicycle shop.
LC–W85–27; Lithopinion, v. 6, Winter 1971: 59

Neighbor, Daniel Henderson, in front of Wright home.
LC–USZ62–66290; LC–W85–28

Eleanor and Billy Prentiss and Enyart Cruke, Wright neighbors.
LC–W85–169; LC–W85–170; Lithopinion, v. 6, Winter 1971: 59

Hart O. Berg, business associate of the Wrights, seated at desk in his office.
HILBW 60

Léon Bollée, factory owner at Hunaudiéres, France, who provided Wilbur with facilities for setting up his machine in 1908, half length.
EWWLM 4

Wilbur and Léon Bollée, three-quarter length, outside Bollée's factory.
COCKDH following 168; EWWLM 5

Griffith Brewer, longtime personal friend of Orville, head and shoulders.
Aeronautics, v. 17, Nov. 27, 1919: 488

Griffith Brewer, half length.
BRFYF front.

Orville and Griffith Brewer sitting on the porch of Orville's home at Hawthorn Hill, Dayton, 1912.
BRFYF facing 96

Orville and Griffith Brewer, full length, Huffman Prairie, Dayton, 1914.
BRFYF facing 97; R Aero Soc J, v. 57, Dec. 1953: 791

Walter R. Brookins, neighbor, first civilian student of the Wright brothers and member of the Wright Exhibition Company.
Blue Book of Aviation, 1932: 85

Octave Chanute, friend and most important correspondent of Wrights, half length, sitting.
MCFWP 9

Octave Chanute, half length, sitting, 1908.
MCFWP 142

Wilbur, in derby hat and overcoat, with Frank T. Coffyn, Wright Exhibition Company flier, in cap and jacket, New York, 1912.
MILWA v. 2: 245; SMIN 42,805–D; World's Work, v. 58, Dec. 1928: 84; YPHA 72

Col. Edward A. Deeds, president of the National Cash Register Company, Dayton, and friend of Orville's, head and shoulders.
Who's Who in American Aeronautics, 1925: 39

Earl N. Findley, editor, journalist, and longtime friend of Orville's, head and shoulders.
U.S. Air Services, v. 41, July 1956: 4

Earl N. Findley, head and shoulders.
American Aviation, v. 2, Jan. 1, 1939: 2

Orville and Henry Ford, full length, on porch at 7 Hawthorn Street, Dayton, October 27, 1936, at time of negotiation for removal of house and Wright shop to Dearborn, Mich.
LC-BECK

Charles F. Kettering, president and director of General Motors Corporation and friend of Orville's, head and shoulders.
Who's Who in American Aeronautics, 1925: 67

Col. Edward A. Deeds, Orville, Henry Ford, and Charles F. Kettering, seated.
MARCD following 344

Henry Ford, Orville, and Charles F. Kettering at banquet following dedication of the Wright home and bicycle shop in Greenfield Village, April 16, 1938.
American Aviation, v. 1, May 1, 1938: 10

Group photo of A. D. Etheridge, John T. Daniels, Capt. William J. Tate, witnesses of early Wright flights at Kitty Hawk, N.C., and Orville at dedication of Wright brothers home and bicycle shop in Greenfield Village, April 16, 1938.
American Aviation, v. 1, May 1, 1938: 10. Similar: EIDWHS facing 26

Grover C. Loening, early Wright Company engineer and friend of Orville's, head and shoulders.
Who's Who in American Aeronautics, 1925: 75

Orville with group of veterans of 1908-9 U.S. Army airplane trials at Fort Myer, Va., at dedication of Wright brothers home and shop in Greenfield Village, April 16, 1938.
EIDWHS facing 36

Two early Wright flying students, Capt. Kenneth Whiting, U.S.N., Gen. Henry H. Arnold, with Orville and Col. Edward A. Deeds.
MARCD facing 252

Edwin H. Sines, neighbor of the Wright brothers and partner in their early printing business, in printing office, 1897.
LC-W85-79

Edwin H. Sines and Orville, backs to camera, in back room of Wright brothers bicycle shop, 1897.
LC–W85–82; MCFWP 7; WRBR 3

Edwin H. Sines, age 66, head and shoulders.
Dayton Herald, Feb. 9, 1938; Dayton Journal, Feb. 9, 1938: 16; Popular Aviation, v. 22, June 1938: 40

Captain William J. Tate, host of the Wright brothers at Kitty Hawk, N.C.
U.S. Air Services, v. 28, Dec. 1943: 29–30

Captain William J. Tate.
Collier's, v. 122, Dec. 25, 1948: 27

Charles E. Taylor, machinist and Wright brothers' mechanic, head and shoulders, wearing cap.
Pop. Sci, v. 114, Apr. 1929: 43; U.S. Air Service, v. 8, Dec. 1923: 13

Charles E. Taylor, half length.
Slipstream, v. 9, May 1928: 9

Charles E. Taylor, head and shoulders, examining motor part.
ANDWF 616; Colliers, v. 122, Dec. 25, 1948: 27

Charles E. Taylor, age 70, working on scale model of Wright 1903 motor.
Bee-Hive, v. 28, Jan. 1953: 8; Dayton Journal, Apr. 17, 1938: SMIN 38,495–B

Charles E. Taylor, head and shoulders.
SMIN 38,649

Dayton Homecoming, 1909

Celebrations honoring the Wrights were held in Dayton, May 13 and June 17-18, 1909.

Scenes on May 13, when thousands greeted Wilbur, Orville, and Katharine in Dayton on their return from European trip, including views of crowds, Dayton Union Station scenes, and photograph of Wrights in carriage drawn by four white horses in which they were driven to their home.
Dayton Journal, May 14, 1909

A parade on June 17, 1909, marked the beginning of a two-day celebration staged by the city of Dayton to honor the Wright brothers on their homecoming.

Views of reception for Wrights on their return from Europe, Dayton, May 13.
Dayton Daily News, May 14, 1909

Court of honor for two-day celebration to honor Wright brothers, Dayton, June 17–18.
COCKDH following 168; Dayton Daily News, June 10, 1909: 1; Dayton Herald, June 15: 1; Greater Dayton, July 1909: 11; USAF 22460. Similar, with night illumination: Greater Dayton, July 1909: 12; World's Work, v. 20, Aug. 1910: 13308

Dayton *Daily News* "Wright Brothers Welcome Home Edition," containing numerous photographs.
Dayton Daily News, June 15, 1909

Scenes from the opening morning exercises of the Wright brothers celebration, June 17.
Dayton Herald, June 18, 1909

Photographs of Wright homecoming ceremonies, Dayton, afternoon and evening, June 17.
Dayton Daily News, June 18, 1909: 1

Third Regiment Ohio National Guard and regulars from Fort Thomas in Grand Parade led by Third Regiment Band of Sidney, Ohio.
Greater Dayton, July 1909: 23; MCFWP 182

Bishop Milton Wright delivers the invocation at homecoming ceremonies in Dayton on June 18, 1909. National Air and Space Museum, Smithsonian Institution, photo no. 8677.

Scenes from Wright homecoming celebration, June 18.
Dayton Journal, June 19, 1909

Wilbur and Orville in formal attire with Prince Albert coats and silk hats at homecoming celebration, June 18.
Dayton Journal, June 19, 1909

Bishop Milton Wright delivering invocation at beginning of ceremonies in which gold medals are presented to Wilbur and Orville, Wilbur and Orville standing behind him on platform, June 18.
Aeronautics, v. 5, Aug. 1909: 43; Dayton Journal, June 19, 1909; Harpers, July 3, 1909: SMIN 8677

Front view of Wilbur and Orville in formal attire on reviewing stand.
Aero Club Am Bul, v. 1, July 1912: 21; COCKDH following 168; MOORKH 166–167; SMIN 31,980–F

Gov. Judson Harmon speaking for the State of Ohio as he presents the Wright brothers with the Gold Medal of the State of Ohio. Behind him on the platform sit Wilbur and Orville, Bishop Wright, and elder brothers Reuchlin and Lorin.
MILWA v. 2: 179; SMIN 31,980–B; World's Work, v. 20, Aug. 1910: 13305; YPHA 36

Human flag formed by 2,000 school children to honor Wrights on reviewing platform.
LC-BAIN; Dayton Herald, June 16, 1909: Greater Dayton, July 1909: 18

Nine photographs of Wright celebration by James H. Hare of *Collier's,* Dayton, June 17–18.
Collier's, v. 43, July 3, 1909: 4

Pictorial account of homecoming celebration honoring Wrights, Dayton.
Harper's, v. 53, July 3, 1909: 7

Medals and Trophies

After the successful flights of the Wrights in France, where Wilbur won many cups and trophies, numerous awards and honors were conferred on Wilbur and Orville for their achievements, first in France and then in Great Britain. On their triumphant return from Europe in 1909, national, state, and city medals were awarded them in the United States.

Photographs of 15 of the numerous medals and trophies awarded to Wilbur and Orville in 1908 and 1909 in recognition of their invention and development of the airplane.
> **The Wright Company *vs*. Herring Curtiss Co. and Glenn H. Curtiss, Complainant's Record-Appendix, New York, 1912, p. 17**

Obverse and reverse of gold medal voted to the Wright brothers "in recognition of their distinguished service to Aeronautical Science" by the Aeronautical Society of Great Britain on November 9, 1908.
> **Aero J, v. 13, Jan. 1909: facing 2; Daily Graphic, May 4, 1909; R Aero Soc J, v. 57, Dec. 1953: 781; SMIN 30,953–F**

Bronze art object, representing the Muse of Aviation, designed by Louis Carvin, presented to Wilbur by Aéro-Club de la Sarthe, Le Mans, May 1, 1909.
> **L'Aérophile, v. 17, Jan. 15, 1909: 39; Allg Auto Zeit, v. 9, Dec. 13, 1908: 19; Autocar, v. 22, Jan. 23, 1909: 123; The Car, v. 27, Jan. 13, 1909: 398; 1908: 19; Vie grand air, v. 15, May 29, 1909: 356**

Front view of Muse of Aviation as displayed on a table in Orville's home, Hawthorn Hill, Dayton.
> **LC–W86–167; LC–W86–173**

Rear view of Muse of Aviation as displayed in Orville's home.
> **LC–W86–168; LC–W86–172**

Front view of Muse of Aviation displayed in a specially constructed niche in Orville's home.
> **LC–BECK**

Front view of Michelin Cup, the work of Paul Roussel, offered
for the first time in 1908, won by Wilbur on December 31,
1908, at Camp d'Auvours, Le Mans.

> **L'Aérophile, v. 17, May 15, 1909: 234; Fachzeitung für
> Automobilismus, v. 3, May 16, 1909: 24; SMIN
> 37,774–B; Vie grand air, v. 15, May 22, 1909: 340**

Aero Club of America gold medals voted Wrights at a meeting
of the Aero Club, November 2, 1908, and presented to them at
a White House ceremony on June 10, 1909. The medals were
designed by sculptor Victor D. Brenner and were struck at the
Philadelphia Mint. The obverse side bears busts of Wilbur and
Orville with their names and the dates and places of their most
successful individual flights. The reverse shows one of the
Wright airplanes in flight with the seal of the Aero Club at the
bottom.

> **LC-BAIN; ACAWMB; L'Aérophile, v. 17, June 1, 1909:
> 255; Ill Aero Mitteil, v. 13, July 14, 1909: 628;
> MILWA, v. 2: 104–105; Numismatist, v. 22, May 22,
> 1909: 134; SMIN 5678–D; SMIN 5678–E; World's
> Work, v. 56, Sept. 1927: 526**

Congressional Medal awarded to the Wrights on March 4, 1909,
and presented to them at a ceremony in Dayton, June 18, 1909.
The obverse of the gold medal, designed by Charles E. Barber
and George T. Morgan of the United States Mint, shows busts
of the Wright brothers, their names, and the inscription "in
recognition and appreciation of their ability, courage, and
success in navigating the air." The reverse shows a winged figure
with a torch, the Genius of Aviation, in flight and the inscription
"shall mount up with wings as eagles."

> **LC-JONES; ACAWMB; FAHAMUSM 245; Harper's,
> v. 53, July 3, 1909: 7; MILWA, v. 2: 180; Numismatist,
> v. 22, Aug. 1909: 231–232; SMIN 31,299–B**

The Langley Medal designed by J. C. Chaplain and awarded the
Wrights by the Smithsonian Institution, February 10, 1909, "for
advancing the science of aerodromics in its application to
aviation by their successful investigations and demonstrations of
the practicality of mechanical flight by man" and presented to
them in a ceremony at the Smithsonian Institution, February 10,
1910. Obverse has names of Wilbur and Orville in center, the
year 1909, and "Aerodromics." The reverse has words "per
Orbem."

> **LC-JONES; MILWA v. 2: 180; SMIN 23,967;
> SMINAR 1910: facing 104; USAF 3570 A.S.**

The Wright brothers' medals—nation, state, and city.

> **Dayton Daily News, June 16, 1909; MOORKH 160**

State of Ohio medal designed and executed by A. Newslat,
presented to the Wrights, June 18, 1909, by Gov. Judson
Harmon.

> **Greater Dayton, July 1909: 17; MOORKH 160**

City of Dayton medal presented to Wrights by Mayor Edward
E. Burkhart, June 18, 1909.
> **LC-BAIN; Dayton Herald, June 10, 1909: MOORKH
> 160**

Collier Trophy awarded to Orville for the year 1913 "for the
development of the automatic stabilizer," announcement made
in Dayton, February 5, 1914.
> **Flying, v. 3, Feb. 1914: 6; MILWA, v. 2: 231**

National Aeronautic Association 20th anniversary of flight
medal, presented to Orville in Dayton, December 17, 1923.
> **Nat Aero Assn Rev, v. 2, Jan. 1, 1924: 1**

Wright brothers medal in Hall of Fame series, designed by Paul
Fjelde, issued on May 7, 1967, when commemorative tablets and
busts of Orville by Paul Fjelde and of Wilbur by Vincent
Glinsky were installed in the Hall of Fame for Great Americans
at New York University.
> **HFGAUBTW 21**

Wright brothers coin-medal issued by National Commemorative
Society. Sculpted by Albino Manca. Obverse shows busts of Orville and Wilbur in center with their names and dates around
outer edges. Verso has airplane with inscription, "First flight,
Kitty Hawk, Dec. 1903."
> **FAHAMUSM 11**

Aero Club of America gold medals, designed by sculptor Victor
D. Brenner, were presented to the Wright brothers at the White
House on June 10, 1909.

Wright Brothers' Medal awarded by the Society of Automotive Engineers "for meritorious contribution to aeronautic engineering." Obverse has Wright airplane in center and reverse has space for name of awardee.

SMIN 31,187-A

Wright Brothers Memorial Trophy, to be awarded annually in memory of the Wright brothers by the National Aeronautic Association, is presented for the first time on December 17, 1948. The trophy is a miniature silver replica of the Wright brothers' 1903 powered airplane, mounted on a replica of the commemorative boulder at Kitty Hawk that marks the takeoff point for the Wrights' first flights.

SMIN 38,920

Monuments and Memorials

Continuing tribute has been paid to the Wrights in the building and dedication of markers, memorials, and monuments in their honor—in France at Auvours, Hunaudières, Le Mans, and Pau and in the United States at Dayton, Ohio, Governors Island, New York, Kitty Hawk, North Carolina, and New Castle, Indiana.

The Auvours monument, a simple stone marker erected in 1913 bearing Wilbur's name with a bird poised in flight above, commemorating Wilbur's flights at Camp d'Auvours, France, in 1908, front and three-quarter front view.
Légion d'honneur, v. 1, Apr. 1933: 209

Wilbur Wright monument at Le Mans, France, the work of sculptor Paul Landowski and architect Paul Bigot, which was dedicated July 17, 1920. Views of the large gathering of prominent Frenchmen and Americans at the unveiling of the forty-foot-high monument in the Place des Jacobins, with the Cathedral of St. Julien in the background. The figures of Wilbur and Orville are carved in bas-relief at the base and, at the summit, is an allegorical figure, a man reaching to the skies, as if straining to overcome the restrictions of earth.
Aerial Age W, Sept. 13, 1920: 8; Flying, v. 9, Sept. 1920: 530; L'Illustration, v. 56, July 24, 1920: 69

Wilbur Wright monument at Le Mans, three-quarter front view.
LC-BECK; Aero Digest, v. 25, Dec. 1928: 1780; L'Illustration, v. 56, July 24, 1920: 68; Légion d'honneur, v. 1, Apr. 1933: 206; MARWBC 5; Le Monde illustré, v. 27, July 24, 1920: 63; SMIN 31290–K; U.S. Air Service, v. 4, Nov. 1920: 21; U.S. Air Service, v. 8, Dec. 1923: 18

Three-quarter front view of the Wilbur Wright monument at the studio of the sculptor, Paul Landowski. At the left are Sidney B. Viet, President, Paris Chapter, National Aeronautic Association, and Baron Paul d'Estournelles de Constant, President, Wilbur Wright Monument Committee, and at the right is Paul Landowski.
MILWA v. 2: 83

Wilbur Wright monument with Cathedral of St. Julien in background. Etching, by Caroline Armington.
MILWA v. 1: 6

The base of the Wilbur Wright monument, three-quarter front view, with the sculptor, Paul Landowski, standing to the left.
L'Illustration, v. 56, July 24, 1920: 69

Base of the Wilbur Wright monument showing the Wright airplane and the figures of Wilbur and Orville in bas-relief, with notable dates in their flying careers inscribed.
Le Monde illustré, v. 27, July 24, 1920: 63

Wright brothers monument, Pau, France, dedicated January 30, 1932, to commemorate the first flights of Wilbur at Pau in 1909 and the training of the first French aviators there. The monument, a slender shaft, was the work of the Pau sculptor Ernest Gagard and shows the likenesses of Wilbur and Orville and a representation of one of their first machines in flight. The inscription reads, "Ici, en 1909, Wilbur Wright fit ses premiers vols."
Légion d'honneur, v. 1, Apr. 1933: 212

Scene at dedication of Pau monument, January 30, 1932, with French officer and French aviation personnel to right of monument.
L'Illustration, v. 181, Feb. 6, 1932: 164; Revue des Forces aériennes, v. 4, Apr. 1932: 1

The French 36th Aviation Group, to whose care the Wright monument was entrusted, saluting it as they march past at the dedication ceremonies, January 30.
National Aeronautics Magazine, v. 10, May 1932: 16; U.S. Air Services, v. 17, Apr. 1932: 32

American Ambassador Walter Edge speaking under specially decorated canopy to group gathered for the dedication ceremonies at Pau monument, January 30.
National Aeronautic Magazine, v. 10, May 1932: 16

Memorial tablet honoring Wilbur at Henry County Memorial Park, New Castle, Ind. Erected by the Phi Delta Kappa Fraternity on April 15, 1923, the marker is located on the spot where the farmhouse of Bishop Milton Wright originally stood. The inscription reads, "Wilbur Wright—aeronaut and pioneer of heavier-than-air aviation."
Dayton Journal, Dec. 17, 1933: 1; Dayton Journal, May 4, 1937: 1; SMIN 13,470–A; SMIN 13,470–C; WIWRM

Simple stone memorial marking the site of Wilbur's flights at Hunaudières Race Course, Le Mans, France, in August 1908. On the stone are simple diagrams of the Wright airplane and launching pylon and inscriptions in French and English recording Wright flight events at the site.
Aeroplane, v. 95, Aug. 8, 1928: 190

Orville, Sen. Hiram Bingham, and Amelia Earhart at the unveiling of a granite memorial erected by the National Aeronautic Association on December 17, 1928. The boulder has a
bronze plaque bearing the inscription "The First Successful
Flight of an Airplane Was Made from This Spot by Orville
Wright, December 17, 1903, in a Machine Designed and Built
by Wilbur Wright and Orville Wright."
> **Aeronautic Review, v. 7, Jan. 1929: 5; Aeronautic Re-
> view, v. 10, July 1932: 15; BBAKH; Washington Star,
> Dec. 30, 1928. Orville only: MCMWB 306**

Marble shaft honoring the Wright brothers erected at Kitty
Hawk, N.C., at the Capt. William J. Tate homesite where the
first Wright experimental gliders were assembled.
> **BBAKH; U.S. Air Services, v. 13, Dec. 1928: 33**

Sen. Hiram Bingham unveiling the memorial to the Wright
brothers at the spot where the first flight was made,
December 17, 1903.
> **Aeronautic Review, v. 7, Jan. 1929: 4**

Bronze and granite marker unveiled on December 17, 1954, on
Governors Island, N.Y., by Early Birds to commemorate historic
flights to and from Governors Island, the first by Wilbur on September 29, 1909. A bronze propeller cast from a wooden one
used by the Wrights in 1909 is mounted on one side of the
monument.
> **SMIN A 48,798**

Wilbur and Orville Wright Memorial, Dayton, Ohio

Long-range front views of Wilbur and Orville Wright Memorial,
dedicated on August 19, 1940, on Wright Brothers' Hill, Dayton, overlooking the site of Huffman Prairie where the Wrights
experimented with their airplane of 1904 and 1905. The bronze
tablet on the front of the 30-ton pink granite column is crowned
by a winged torch symbolizing the Wrights' research and
achievements.
> **SMIN A48,799; WADC 78238–78240, 78242**

Close-up front views of Wilbur and Orville Wright Memorial,
Dayton, Ohio.
> **WADC 78241, 78245**

Three-quarter front views of Wilbur and Orville Wright Memorial, Dayton, Ohio.
> **BBAKH; APGAFM 7; SMIN A 48,797; WADC 78246,
> 78247; WRBR 16**

Close-up front view of bronze tablet on Wilbur and Orville
Wright Memorial, inscribed with their names and achievements.
> **WADC 78237**

Close-up view of bronze tablet at Wilbur and Orville Wright Memorial, inscribed with names of 119 of "Pioneer Flyers Who Were Trained at Wright Brothers Field."
WADC 2978

Close-up view of bronze tablet at Wilbur and Orville Wright Memorial, inscribed with achievements of Wrights at nearby Huffman Prairie in 1904–1905.
WADC 78244

Col. Edward A. Deeds presiding at the dedication of the Wilbur and Orville Wright Memorial before its unveiling.
MARCD following 352

Col. Edward A. Deeds eulogizing the Wrights at dedicatory exercises for the Wilbur and Orville Wright Memorial, August 20, 1940. Orville is seated nearby with Gen. Henry H. Arnold at his left and Navy Capt. Kenneth Whiting at his right, both former flying pupils of the Wright School.
U.S. Air Services, v. 25, Sept. 1940: 11

NCR [National Cash Register] *Factory News* special issue giving pictorial account of the Wilbur and Orville Wright Memorial dedicatory exercises.
NCR [National Cash Register] Factory News, Aug./Sept. 1940: 1–6

Wright Brothers National Memorial, Kitty Hawk, North Carolina

Winning design in competition for Wright memorial at Kitty Hawk, N.C., site.
Dayton Journal, Feb. 28, 1930; New York Times, Feb. 23, 1930: ix, 14; Pencil Points, v. 11, Apr. 1930: 304–305

Aerial views of Kitty Hawk, N.C., first flight area, including Wright Brothers National Memorial.
Aeronautic Review, v. 6, Dec. 1928: 188, 191, 192: BBAKH; National Aeronautics, v. 40, Dec. 1961: 6; SMIN A52,719

Ruth Nichols unveiling Wright Brothers National Memorial, November 19, 1932, in the presence of Orville and high-ranking government officials.
New York Times, Nov. 20, 1932; SC–98159

Orville with members of his family and relatives in front of Wright memorial when it was dedicated, November 19.
SMIN 42,288–H

Long-range views of Wright memorial.
LC-BECK; Life, v. 113, Nov. 10, 1941: 113; New York Times Magazine, Dec. 11, 1932: 4

Close-up front view of Wright memorial with visible inscription reading "Wilbur Wright, Orville Wright. In commemoration of the Conquest of the Air."
BBAKH; HEGOV facing 112; KELMKH b. 238–239

Side view of the Wright memorial.
Airlanes, Nov. 1937: cover; HWMHD 3. Similar: HAWBHP 100

Corner views of the Wright memorial.
BBAKH; GLWB facing 41; SMIN 31,684–C; SMIN 38,902; USAF 62465; U.S. Air Services, v. 22, Dec. 1937: 4; U.S. Air Services, v. 24, May 1939: 13

Stainless steel doors of the Wright memorial ornamented with eight panels symbolizing various steps in human efforts at mechanical flight.
HWMHD 10; Technology Review, v. 41, Jan. 1939: cover

Front view of Wright memorial with group of visitors on steps on day of dedication, November 19.
SC–99158; SMIN 31,290–A; SMIN 42,412–G

Wright Memorial as viewed on December 14, 1953, when United States, United Nations, and International Goodwill flags were flown nearby as part of the observance of the 50th anniversary of the 1903 flights by the Wright brothers.
SMIN A52,723

Aircraft in flight over Wright memorial.
Airlanes, Nov. 1937: 4; BBAKH; EWBNM facing 1; EWBNM 62; USAF 13876 A.C.

Museum and Visitors Center and rebuilt Wright brothers' 1903 hangar and living quarters at the Kitty Hawk memorial.
National Aeronautics, v. 40, Dec. 1961: 4; SMIN A4345. Hangar and living quarters only: Society of Architectural Historians Journal, v. 13, Oct. 1954: 29

Reconstructed Wright brothers' 1902 kitchen.
Society of Architectural Historians Journal, v. 13, Oct. 1954: 29

Art

From the days of Wilbur's early flights in France in 1908 until the present time, the Wrights have been the subject of numerous works of art, including busts, etchings, mural paintings, portraits, and, in particular, depictions of their famous first flight at Kitty Hawk, North Carolina, on December 17, 1903.

First flight of the Wright brothers on the sands of Kitty Hawk, December 17, 1903, machine on ground, Orville at controls, Wilbur at one end, four witnesses of flight at other end. Watercolor by Albert E. V. Brenet.
CHAHA facing 46

First flight, December 17, 1903. Front view of airplane landing, Wilbur running behind, five witnesses nearby looking on from rear, Wright camp buildings in background to left of picture. Painting by Melbourne Brindle. Presented to the National Air and Space Museum, December 17, 1948.
Collier's, v. 122, Dec. 25, 1948: 10; SMIN 38,596CN; Sperryscope, v. 11, Winter 1949: cover

First flight, December 17, 1903. Wilbur is shown running in the foreground with side view of airplane in flight, witnesses of flight following at left rear. Painting by Arlo Greer.
Air Force, v. 36, Dec. 1953: cover

First flight, December 17, 1903. Three-quarter front view of airplane, Orville at controls, Wilbur running at rear, three witnesses and camp buildings at right. Painting by Charles H. Hubbel, one of a series painted for use on Thompson Products, Inc., calendars, and first appearing in the calendar for January 1941.
Aero Digest, v. 67, July 1953: 65

First flight, December 17, 1903. Side view of airplane in flight with Wilbur running at side, five witnesses at rear left looking on. Painting in the Franklin Institute Museum, Philadelphia, by William Heaslip, 1933.
Aerosphere, 1943: CXXIX; J Franklin In, v. 256, Dec. 1953: cover; AOPA Pilot, v. 3, Dec. 1960: 27

Orville and Wilbur Wright, as depicted by an illustrator in 1909 in the *Livre d'or de la conquète de l'air.*

First flight, December 17, 1903. Mosaic mural in lobby of Dayton Convention and Exhibition Center, Dayton, Ohio, reproducing the historic photograph, the original glass-plate negative of which is in the Library of Congress collection. Unveiled December 15, 1972, the 60- by 20-foot mural consists of 163,000 one-inch square tiles manufactured in Italy, each tile bearing one of eighteen symbols related to the story of the Wright brothers. Detailed reproductions are shown of the eighteen symbols, which were designed to convey graduated shades of light and, used with black and white tiles, present, when viewed from a distance, a total picture of the flight.
Dayton USA, v. 9, Dec. 1972: 20

First flight, December 17, 1903. Side view of airplane in flight just above ground, Wilbur running behind. Painting by Harvey Kidder.
HSAFPHA 3

First flight, December 17, 1903. Airplane is seen descending with Wilbur and witnesses following at rear and Wright camp building visible in background. Painting by John T. McCoy, Jr.
KELWB (Ballantine Books ed., 1975): cover; Life, Dec. 7, 1953: 162–163; SMIN 45,010

Kitty Hawk scene, likenesses of Orville and Wilbur in background, Wright machine behind them at lower left, sand dunes seen in background. Painting in John Hancock Mutual Life Insurance collection, Boston.
American Heritage, v. 5, Winter 1954: 41

Birth of aviation in the United States. Close-up view of Wright airplane flight, Orville at controls, Wilbur running alongside. Fresco painting forming part of the rotunda frieze in the United States Capitol, by Allyn Cox, completed in 1953.
CWAUSC 301

First flight, December 17, 1903, Orville at controls, Wilbur running alongside the right wing tip, five witnesses following close behind, Wright camp buildings and sand dunes at left. Painting by Frank Wootton.
Valerie Woolman, The Road to Kitty Hawk (Alexandria, Time-Life Books, [1980]) endpapers

Front view of Wright airplane in level flight, Wilbur piloting, at twilight, the rays of the setting sun reflected in clouds above and on parts of airplane, Camp d'Auvours, September 21, 1908. Painting by Serafino Macchiati.
Vie grand air, v. 11, Nov. 28, 1908: b. 366–367

Wilbur, head and shoulders. Lithograph by Jacques Weismann, made at Camp d'Auvours, France, October 31, 1908.
L'Aérophile, v. 16, Dec. 1, 1908: 469; Avia, v. 2, June 15, 1912: 40; La Revue aérienne, v. 1, Nov. 25, 1908: 25

Wilbur. Side view of bust by French sculptor Louis Carvin, completed February 1909.
LC-BECK

Wilbur. Louis Carvin holding bust.
Vie grand air, v. 15, Feb. 27, 1909: 135

Wilbur and Orville. Busts by Louis Carvin, Royal Aeronautical Society, London.
Ill Aero Mitteil, v. 13, Mar. 10, 1909: 192; Motor, v. 15, Mar. 2, 1909: 174

Busts of Wilbur and Orville by Louis Carvin. Composite photograph.
Flight, v. 1, May 1, 1909: 244

Wilbur in flight at Camp d'Auvours, France, 1908, side view. Watercolor painting by Georges Scott.
LOCA facing 278

Wilbur, half length, seated, tan cap, dark suit, green tie, high collar. Oil portrait from life by Jules Alfred Hervé-Mathé, Le Mans, France, in 1908, presented to the Smithsonian Institution, 1950.
NPG; SMIN 41,096

Wilbur Wright Monument, Le Mans, France, with Cathedral of St. Julien in background. Etching by Caroline Armington.
MILWA, v. 1: 6

Lt. Frank P. Lahm's first flight on September 9, 1908, at Fort Myer, Va., with Orville. Side of airplane on track with pylon at rear with Lt. Lahm and Orville seated in airplane and military personnel and spectators at side and at rear. Painting by Richard Green. Air Force Art Collection.
HSAFPHA 5

Front view of Wright airplane in flight, Paul Tissandier as passenger with Wilbur, Pau, 1909. Painting by Tom O'Donnell.
MARWBC cover

Orville and Wilbur, head and shoulders.
LOCA 271; Vie grand air, v. 15, Mar. 20, 1909: cover

Wilbur in Wright airplane in flight over Centocelle Field, Rome, April 1909, spectators viewing flight gathering in right foreground. Drawing by A. Bianchi.
Graphic, v. 79, May 1, 1909: 576

Wright brothers at Fort Myer, Va., July 30, 1909. Orville and Wilbur are conversing with Army officers, with Wright airplane and pylon in background and numerous spectators and man with camera at left. Painting by T. McCoy, Jr.
HSAFPHA 7

Wilbur's flight of September 29, 1909, from Governors Island around the Statue of Liberty and return. Wright airplane is shown in flight over water with parade ground and barracks on Bedloe's Island, anchored ships and ferry boats visible below, the Statue of Liberty in left foreground. Painting by Harper Goff.
Esquire, v. 25, May 1946: 49–50

Lts. Henry H. Arnold and Thomas DeW. Milling standing in front of a Wright model B airplane at Aeronautical Division's training field at College Park, Md., about 1912. Painting by John T. McCoy, Jr.
HSAFPHA 11

Orville, head and shoulders, side view facing right. Etching drawn from life by Oscar Cesare.
New York Times Magazine, Feb. 1, 1925: 8; SMIN 39, 043–H; U. S. Air Services, v. 12, Sept. 1927: 22; In reverse: World's Work, v. 56, Sept. 1927: 513

Wilbur, head and shoulders. Drawing by Samuel J. Woolf.
World's Work, v. 56, Sept. 1928: 512

Wilbur and Orville. Plaster busts by Dayton sculptor Seth M. Velsey, later to be cast in bronze for the Army Aeronautical Museum, Dayton. The bronze busts were installed in the rotunda of the Army Aeronautical Museum, June 15, 1937.
Dayton Journal, Jan. 17, 1937

Orville and Wilbur. Life-size bronze busts by Seth M. Velsey, Air Force Museum, Dayton.
APGAFM

Youth gazing up at Kitty Hawk monument to Wright brothers. Drawing by H. M. Mueller.
Airlanes, Nov. 1937: 5

Wright brothers. Painting by Arthur Lidov from a portrait photograph by Hollinger & Company, 1907, donated to the Institute of the Aeronautical Sciences.
Collier's, v. 122, Dec. 25, 1948: cover; SMIN A3419. Similar, silhouette in reverse: SMIN A3421

Orville. Bronze, life-size bust made from life by Oskar J. W. Hansen, 1931. Presented to Smithsonian Institution, January 27, 1950.
NPG; SMIN 38,463 to 38,463–E; SMIN 42,460 to 42,460–D

Wilbur. Bronze, life-size bust by Oskar J. W. Hansen, 1949. Presented to Smithsonian Institution, January 27, 1950.
NPG; SMIN 38,904 to 38,904–D

Wilbur. Bust by Oskar J. W. Hansen, resting on table at presentation ceremonies, January 27, 1950. Dr. Alexander Wetmore, Secretary of the Smithsonian Institution, the sculptor, and the donors, Mr. and Mrs. Elmer F. Wieboldt, grouped around it.

SMIN A38,875–A. Similar, with Grover Loening, Maj. Gen. Grandison Gardner, Rear Adm. Alfred M. Pride, and Alexander Wetmore grouped around table: SMIN A38,875

Wilbur and Orville, three-quarter length seated. Photograph of oil painting by Dwight Mutchler, unveiled and dedicated, December 17, 1959, and hung in the Ohio State Capitol Building.

LC–USZ62–20780 (copy negative)

Wilbur, at left, and Orville, at right, at the base of the Wright Brothers National Memorial, Kitty Hawk, N.C. Bronze busts by Oskar J. W. Hansen.

National Aeronautics, v. 40, Dec. 1961: 5

Wilbur and Orville in bas-relief and the caption "They Taught Us To Fly," with, in background, the gliders which the Wrights flew on the Kitty Hawk dunes in 1901, 1902, and 1911. Bronze memorial plaque by Capt. Ralph S. Barnaby, unveiled December 17, 1963, for display at the Wright Brothers National Memorial, Kitty Hawk, N.C.

Soaring, v. 28, Mar. 1964: 8

Wilbur, head turned to left, grey business suit, high collar on shirt, red tie, loosely tied, pearl stickpin. Oil portrait by Efrem Melik. Presented to National Air Museum by Flight Safety Foundation, April 8, 1964.

NPG; SMIN 72–11299–CN

Orville. Oil portrait by Efrem Melik. Presented to National Air Museum by Flight Safety Foundation, April 8, 1964.

NPG; SMIN 72–11300–CN

Wilbur. Bust by Vincent Glinsky. Orville. Bust by Paul Fjelde. Installed in the Hall of Fame for Great Americans at New York University, May 7, 1967.

NPG; HFGAUBTW 2

Wilbur and Orville, portrait montage with views of Wright Dayton bicycle shop, Wright 1903 airplane, 1903 Kitty Hawk camp buildings, and wind tunnel in background. Painted by George Akimoto.

American Aviation Historical Society Journal, v. 23, Winter 1978: cover

Caricatures and Cartoons

Caricatures and cartoons dealing with the Wright brothers appeared primarily in the years 1908-10, first on the postcards which were popular following Wilbur's successful public flight at Hunaudières, France, on August 8, 1908, and later in the European press and in the American press when the Wrights were honored after their return from Europe in 1909.

One of the earliest caricatures of Wilbur in France, by Charles Lucien Leandré. Wilbur is depicted as composed of mechanical parts, sitting on a cloud held up by a cone inscribed "aide-toi et Dieu t'aidera," holding in his right outstretched hand a model of the Wright airplane.
Le Rire, journal humoristique, Sept. 5, 1908, No. 292: colored lithograph on cover

Caricature of Wilbur at Camp d'Auvours by Daniel T. de Losques. Wilbur, giant-size, bare-headed, wearing trousers, high collar, and tie, is in shirtsleeves, a launching derrick in background to his right.
GCDCA 110; Le Figaro, Oct. 4, 1908

Caricature of group pulling rope to raise weight to top of derrick, side view of Wright airplane in background, Wilbur at extreme right looking on, by Leo Maix.
GCDCA 110

French toy resembling "Little God Billiken," a caricature of Wilbur by C. Giris. Wilbur is seated in simplified Wright airplane, head projecting above it. The toy was shown at the Salon des Humoristes, Paris, spring 1909.
Allg Auto Zeit, v. 9, Nov. 22, 1908: 36; Dayton Journal, Dec. 8, 1908; GCDCA 110

Promotional item entitled "L'Aéro-cap; chapeau extra léger," a caricature of Wilbur dressed in his customary flying cap and jacket, signed P. Narco. Wilbur is seated at controls of a frail wingless flying device supported by four French hats, another hat below seat, buildings seen in background below.
COCKDH following 168

Caricature of Wilbur by Mich. Wilbur, head and shoulders, at left, wears a checkered cap, cigarette in mouth, and an attractive smiling woman close by at his right gazes at him admiringly.
ADAMSF 85; Vie parisienne, v. 46, Nov. 14, 1908: cover

Caricature of Wilbur by Mich. Wilbur, three-quarter length, wears a checkered cap, hands in pockets, at left, and an attractive smiling woman, wearing large hat and carrying parasol, approaches him from right.
ADAMSF 95; Vie parisienne, v. 46, Nov. 28, 1908: 857

Cartoon entitled "For the Conquest of the Air" by Charles Lupin depicts competition between the French school of aviation and the American school. Wilbur stands with spear in hand and Wright airplane on back, while Lazare Weiller represents the Americans attacking from right and Henri Farman and one of the Voisin brothers, bearing a French type airplane, attack from left.
GCDCA 159; Revue aérienne, v. 1, Dec. 10, 1908: 128

Caricature of Wilbur sitting on ground holding and working on airplane wing above, Léon Bollée at left looking on, Orville, Hart O. Berg, a workman, and several guards behind him and at right. One of many postcard caricatures of Wilbur popular in France in the winter of 1908-9.
MCFWP 174

Caricature of Wilbur by Leo Maix, Wilbur looking up to his left at Wright airplane tied to string he holds. This particular postcard caricature was sent from France by Wilbur during Orville's flights at Ft. Myer with written message, "I'll Tie a String to You Next Time to Keep You from Going Too High or Too Far. It's Too Much Trouble to Break Your Records. Will."
KELMKH b. 238–239

Caricature of Wilbur at the Paris Automobile Show by Mich. Wilbur, broad smile, is seated at controls of airplane and a woman, head only, beams a bright light at exhibit area below.
Vie parisienne, v. 46, Nov. 28, 1908: 662–663

Cartoon of Wilbur and Orville, flying, their wings attached, an eagle on land screaming. Caption: "Let the Eagle Scream. She Hatched 'Em."
New York Herald, Paris, Dec. 22, 1908

Caricature of Wilbur by Yves Marevery.
Allg Auto Zeit, v. 10, Mar. 5, 1909: 35; Revue aérienne, v. 2, Jan. 25, 1909: facing 97

Caricature of Wilbur, facing left, wearing checkered cap, low white collar, black jacket (his hand is in the pocket), white trousers, and French style shoes. Pen-and-ink drawing by Fox, 1909.
BIAFW 3

Caricature of Orville, facing left, black moustache, hair visible beneath bowler hat, wearing two-button longcoat, hand in pocket, and French style shoes. Pen-and-ink drawing by Fox, 1909.
BIAFW 4

Caricature of Wilbur by M. Lourdey. Wilbur is seated at controls of airplane, and a woman wearing lacy hat and carrying parasol faces him.
GCDCA 110; Journal amusant, Apr. 10, 1909

Caricature of Wilbur and Léon Bollée by Maresco. Wilbur, attired in boxing togs and gloves, faces Bollée, similarly attired.
Vie grand air, v. 15, May 22, 1909: 340

Caricature statuette of Wilbur, who sits astride abbreviated airplane skids with tail at end, with wings projecting from his shoulders.
SBNA 107

Cartoon of Wilbur in shirt sleeves, hammer in hand, sitting on high stool, and Orville in business suit, derby hat, seated at table. Both, airplane parts in hands, are repairing a propeller with old wooden preserve boxes.
Revue aérienne, v. 2, June 25, 1909: 363

Caricature of Wilbur by Mich entitled "The Man and the Machine." Wilbur, three-quarter length, wearing coat, hand in pocket, faces right, and both his head and Wright airplane are encircled.
Aero Manual, 1909: 34; Aero Manual, 1910: 34

Caricatures of the leading aviators in France by Robert Dick, dated Paris, 1910. Wilbur and Orville appear first in a column of 13 flyers.
CHAHA 53

Caricature of well-known people in France helping to pull up the weight to the top of the starting derrick, Wilbur standing at the far right in his usual cap.
GSPA 33

Caricature entitled "Aviators and Their Machines" showing Wilbur with elongated cap, Count Charles de Lambert, and Paul Tissandier, each encircled. Wright airplane is in flight above them.
Aero Manual, 1910: 79; Motor, v. 17, Mar. 8, 1910: 161

Fans bearing caricatures of Wilbur.
Fachzeitung für Automobilismus, v. 3, Mar. 21, 1909: 21

Humorous sketch of Wilbur in flight with J. L. Breton, deputy for the department of Cher, Pau, France, March 20, 1909, by A. de Broca.
L'Aérophile, v. 17, Apr. 15, 1909: 171

Caricature of Wilbur by Mich. He wears a high collar, tie, and cap and has his left hand in his trouser pocket.
PEPHO facing 98

Silhouette of Wilbur, head and shoulders, high collar, cap, facing right.
PEPHO facing 106

Cartoon of Wilbur and Orville in Wright airplane flying over ocean on return to the United States, Uncle Sam at right, cane in hand, hat thrown in air, extending welcome.
ADAMSF 107

Cartoon of Orville and Wilbur as birds of the air, by Homer Davenport, drawn in 1909. They are escorted by a giant-sized, smiling gentleman wearing striped trousers and with star-covered vest, who represents the United States.
KELMKH b. 238–239

Cartoon entitled "Howdy, Brother!" by Jay Norwood Darling. Wright brothers in two airplanes approach the United States on their return from Europe in May 1909, Wilbur, in the first, doffing his cap to two eagles perched near their nest, one exclaiming "Great Heavens! What Kind of a Bird Is That!"
Des Moines Register, May 9, 1909

Cartoon of Orville and Wilbur, shown with wings attached being welcomed back to nest by eagle portrayed as Uncle Sam. Caption: "Back to the Eagle's Nest."
Dayton Daily News, June 15, 1909 (from Columbus Dispatch)

Cartoon of Wright airplane flying overhead, top of a ladder shown below. Caption: "For him who ascended Fame's ladder so high, From the round at the top he has stepped to the sky."
ACAWMB; New York World, June 11, 1909

Cartoon of the Wright brothers in Wright airplane, smiled upon by sun, moon, and heavenly bodies, by Fred Morgan. Caption: "Monarchs of the Air."
ACAWMB; Philadelphia Inquirer, June 10, 1909

Orville and Wilbur, bedecked with medals and ribbons, standing before President William Howard Taft, to receive Aero Club of America gold medals at the White House, June 10, 1909. Caption: "Now, If I Can Only Find Room to Hang Them on These Two Birds."
Detroit Post, June 11, 1909. Similar: Washington Star, June 10, 1909

Wright brothers bedecked with medals and ribbons, standing before President William Howard Taft at the White House,
June 10, 1909. Young boy watching medal presentation at right
comments: "Gee! I'd Rather be Wright than be President."
ACAWMB; Cleveland Leader, 1909

Wright brothers astride a Wright airplane, Wilbur carrying
rolled up "Govt Contract," Uncle Sam below doffing his hat
saying "My Hat Off to the Wright Records," Washington
Capitol and Eiffel Tower pictured on either side of the Atlantic
Ocean.
Aeronautics, v. 5, Sept. 1909: facing 81

Cartoon of Orville and Wilbur as birds, atop the walls of Fort
Myer, about to fly down, soldier below extending welcome.
Ill Aero Mitteil, v. 13, Sept. 1909: 846

Cartoon with earth peering into mirror at Wright airplane
perched on top of her with caption "I Always Buy my Hats of
Wright Bros.," by Briggs, Chicago *Tribune.*
Literary Digest, v. 39, Sept. 11, 1909: 374

Cartoon of Wright airplane in flight being welcomed to Ger-
many by a German officer holding onto rope dangling from the
German airship *Zeppelin II.*
New York Herald, Paris, Aug. 31, 1909

Cartoon of Wilbur in airplane flight over Hudson River, crown
over him and the airplane, with caption "King of the Air!"
New York Evening Journal, Oct. 5, 1909

Cartoon of Wright brothers by W. A. Rogeit. Wall Street is in
the background as Wilbur and Orville fly an airplane bearing
legend "Million Dollar Aeroplane Company," and caption reads
"Going Some."
New York Herald, Nov. 29, 1909

Cartoon of Wilbur, with an elongated neck, wearing a business
suit and cap, his hands in his pockets, peering up at an airplane
overhead, 1910. Caption reads, "A Forecast of the Future: The
Areoplane Neck!"
ASHWB 58

Caricature of Wilbur by Mich. Pictured as an American with
Indian feathers and tomahawk, Wilbur is shown as the French
see him in connection with the Wright-Paulhan patents action.
Flight, v. 2, May 14, 1910: 378 (originally published in
L'Auto)

"Continental" caricatures showing tall figure of Wilbur facing
short Santos Dumont at the Paris International Air Show, 1910,
by Mich.
Flight, v. 2, Dec. 10, 1910: 104; LVTNA 284

Cartoon of Wright brothers by W. A. Rogeit. Wilbur and Orville are being presented with gold medals for their achievements by Uncle Sam, who wears a ball and chain with legend "Indifference of Congress." Wright airplane is shown tied to Washington Monument in background, American eagle at right, and caption reads: "Honored, if not Rewarded."
ACAWMB; New York Herald, 1910

Caricature of Wilbur, head and shoulders, by Fabius.
La Revue aérienne, v. 4, Aug. 10, 1911: 395

Caricature by Mich of Wilbur, three-quarter length, bareheaded, wearing buttoned coat and high collar, cap in left hand at his side, facing left.
Avia, v. 1, Mar. 15, 1912: 295

Cartoon of the Wright brothers, Uncle Sam pointing to Smithsonian Institution, its roof tilted open, as Wright airplane approaches.
Collier's, v. 82, Dec. 8, 1928: 28

Cartoon of Orville, enlarged head, hat surrounded by numerous airplanes, coat bedecked with medals. Caption: "What a Difference Twenty Five Years Make."
Washington Evening Star, Dec. 18, 1928

Caricature with caption "Dinner with Billions" drawn from life by Oscar Berger at National Pioneers Banquet sponsored by the National Association of Manufacturers in New York, February 27, 1940. Orville, with elongated head and smiling, is depicted as the tallest at the banquet table. Berger identifies the guests as "The Honoured Pioneers, as I Saw Them: George Eastman (photography), Orville Wright (aviation), Henry Ford (motor cars), Thomas A. Edison (invention), Harvey S. Firestone (rubber), Julius Rosenwald (merchandising), Charles M. Schwab (iron and steel)."
BERFF 66

Appendix:
Audiovisual Materials

Audio Tapes

The Wright brothers. 1⅞ IPS audio tape cassette. Produced and distributed by Educational Development Corporation, International Teaching Tapes, Lakeland, Fla. (From The United States history—an audio chronology. Group 4 series).

The Wright brothers. 1⅞ IPS audio tape cassette. Produced and distributed by Listening Library, Inc., Old Greenwich, Conn. (From The American inventors series).

The Wright brothers. 3¾ IPS 1 track audio tape. 30 min. Produced by University of Colorado and distributed by National Tape Depository, University of Colorado, Boulder, Colo. (The history of flight series).

The Wright brothers. 1⅞ IPS audio tape cassette. 15 min. Produced and distributed by Creative Visuals, Inc., Big Spring, Tex. (From The world's great inventors series).

The Wright brothers—biographical sketch. 3¾ IPS 1 track audio tape. 15 min. University of Minnesota Radio Station KUOM. Distributed by National Tape Depository, University of Colorado, Boulder, Colo. (Let science tell us series SC 35).

The Wright brothers—boys among the birds. 3¾ IPS 1 track audio tape. 15 min. Produced by University of Texas Visual Instruction Bureau and distributed by National Tape Depository, University of Colorado, Boulder, Colo. (The what's the big idea series).

Wright's flight around New York City—1909. 3¾ IPS 2 track audio tape. 15 min. University of Michigan Radio Station WUOM, University of Michigan Audio-Visual Education Center, Ann Arbor, Mich. (Sky trails series AV-1).
 Wilbur's flights over New York, September 29, October 4.

Microfiche

Photographs by the Wright brothers: prints from the glass negatives in the Library of Congress. A micropublication commemorating the seventy-fifth anniversary of the first flight by the Wright brothers, December 17, 1903. Washington: Library of Congress, 1978. 21 p. and 5 fiche.

> The 303 negative photographic plates received from the estate of Orville Wright, May 27, 1949, which are a part of the Wilbur-Orville Wright Collection in the Library of Congress, are of two different sizes (174 are 5 by 7 inches; 129, 4 by 5 inches), cover the period 1897-1911, and provide excellent pictorial records of the Wright brothers' early gliding experiments and original airplane flights.

Motion Pictures

First Army aeroplane flight, Ft. Myer, Virginia. National Archives, Motion Picture Branch, Washington. 230-H-1175. Reel 1. 270 ft., 16 mm or 35 mm.

> Includes close-up view of Wright airplane and pictures of Orville and a group of notables witnessing the Wright flights at Fort Myer, Va., 1908

Dare, birthplace of aviation. The people of Dare County, N.C. Made and released by Communication Center, University of North Carolina, 1952. 22 min., sd., color, 16 mm.

> Color film depicts first flights of the Wright brothers, Kitty Hawk, Dare County, N.C., 1903.

Wright brothers—wings over Kitty Hawk. Produced by Twentieth Century-Fox Film Corp. and distributed by Star Film Co., 1952-1953. 15 min., optical sound, 16 mm.

> Presents an account of the Wright brothers' first flight at Kitty Hawk, N.C., December 17, 1903, compiled from Fox Movietone News Library footage.

Wings over Kitty Hawk. Movietonenews, 1954. 13 min., sd., b&w, 16 mm. (Greatest drama).

> Pictures events in the lives of the Wright brothers with an authentic account of their first historic flight, Kitty Hawk, N.C., December 17, 1903.

The first flight of the Wright brothers. CBS Television. Released by Young America Films, 1955. 28 min., sd., b&w, 16 mm. (You Are There).

> Telecast, January 16, 1955, on the CBS program "You Are There." Reconstructs the events of December 17, 1903.

The Wright brothers. Jam Handy Organization, 1957. 42 fr., color, 35 mm. (Famous Americans, no. 2).

> Pictures in color the childhood and youth of Wilbur and Orville and shows how their early experiments led them to build an airplane and become American aviation pioneers.

The Wright brothers, pioneers of American aviation. David J. Goodman, Inc., 1957. 47 fr., color, 35 mm.

> Adapted from book of the same title by Quentin Reynolds (New York: Random House, 1950). Color film showing how the Wright brothers developed an interest in the principles of flight, worked toward controlled flight, and developed their first airplane.

Flight history at Kitty Hawk, December 17, 1903. Richard B. Morros, Inc., in Association with Hearst Metrotone News. Released by Official Films, 1960. 5 min., sd., b&w, 16 mm. (Almanac Newsreel).

> Newsreel account of the flights made by the Wrights at Kitty Hawk, N.C., December 17, 1903. Portrays some of the honors given to the Wright brothers, including the annual tribute made at the Wright Brothers National Memorial at Kitty Hawk.

The Boy—"Gee! I'd rather be Wright than be President."

From the Cleveland Leader

When President William Howard Taft pinned medals on the Wright brothers, this cartoon appeared in the *Cleveland Leader*.

Wright brothers fly. Filmrite Associates. Released by Official Films, 1960. 3 min., sd., b&w, 16 mm. (Greatest Headlines of the Century).

> Short film portraying events in the lives of the Wright brothers, showing them in their bicycle shop as they experiment with flying machines and endeavor to understand the science of aerodynamics. Shows Orville's first successful powered flight, Kitty Hawk, N.C., December 17, 1903.

Wright Brothers National Memorial, North Carolina. Eye Gate House, 1961. 47 fr., color, 35 mm (National Landmarks, Memorials, and Historic Shrines, n. 6).

> Pictures in color the first airplane flights made by Wilbur and Orville in December 1903 and shows how the historic event is commemorated at the Wright Brothers National Memorial at Kitty Hawk, N.C.

The day man flew. Go Pictures. Released by McGraw-Hill Book Co., 1962. 17 min., sd., b&w, 16 mm.

> Pictorial account of the Wright brothers, explains how they solved the problems of lift and balance, describes the building of their first engine, and depicts their early flights at Kitty Hawk, N.C., in 1903.

Wright brothers' first flight. Anargyros Film Library, 1966. 4 min., si., b&w, 8 mm.

> Short loop film depicting the first successful powered flight by the Wright brothers, Kitty Hawk, N.C., December 17, 1903.

Kitty Hawk to Paris, the early years of flight. John H. Secondari Productions. Released by Learning Corp. of America, 1970. 54 min., sd., color, 16 mm.

> Traces the formative years of American aviation beginning with the early experiments of the Wright brothers at Kitty Hawk, N.C.

Wright brothers. [Motion picture in five parts] Produced by U.S. Navy Department and released by National Audiovisual Center, Washington, 1970. 29 min., sd., b&w, 16 mm. (History of flight series).

> Well-documented and authoritative motion picture dealing with the history of the Wright brothers narrated by Paul E. Garber, Historian Emeritus of the National Air and Space Museum. Shows how Wrights became intrigued with the problems of flight and portrays their first attempts to fly with gliders, the construction of the first powered heavier-than-air flying machine, and its initial flights at Kitty Hawk, N.C., December 17, 1903. Reviews their experiments to increase flight time and distance. Pictures the first flights of the Wright brothers' airplane in Europe and America and illustrates many of the historical flights by the Wrights. Recounts Wilbur's death, Orville's ensuing activities, and the various honors and memorials to the Wright brothers for their contributions to aviation.

Wright brothers. Thorne Films, 1971. 3 min., si., b&w., super 8 mm. (The eight mm. documents project no. 330 series) Loop film in cartridge.

    Short motion picture depicting the achievements of the Wright brothers. Includes some of the 1908 flights of Wilbur in France, his demonstration flights before King Victor Emmanuel III of Italy at Centocelle Field, Rome, on April 24, 1909, and Orville's flight on July 26, 1909, at Fort Myer, Va., witnessed by President William Howard Taft.

Orville and Wilbur. Film produced, directed, and written by Arthur and Evelyn Barron and Amanda C. Pope. National Educational Television, 1971. 90 min., sd., color (NET Playhouse Biography).

    Explores the dramatic months preceding and including the first successful flight on December 17, 1903. A flying replica of the Wright brothers' first airplane and of the glider they flew before the first motor flight were used in the film. Stacy Keach plays the part of Wilbur, James Keach the part of Orville.

The winds of Kitty Hawk; 75th anniversary of first powered flight/Wright brothers. An ITT television report on NBC, December 17. Produced by Charles M. Fries Productions, Inc., in association with New Ingot Co., Inc., 1978. 120 min., sd., color.

    Dramatization of early flying experiments of the Wright brothers, culminating in the successful flight of December 17, 1903. Replicas of the original Wright airplanes were constructed by Tom and Nancy Valentine for the film's flying sequences. The aircraft were flown by Odell Burton. Michael Moriarty plays the part of Wilbur, David Huffman the part of Orville. The script was written by William Kelley and Jes Rosebrook. The television drama was produced by Lawrence Schiller and directed by E.W. Swackhamer. Marvin McFarland was technical director.

Phonorecords

Tooley, Howard. **The Wright brothers, pioneers of American aviation.** [Phonodisk] Enrichment Records ERL 104. 1964. 1 s. 12 in. in. 33 1/2 rpm. microgroove. (American landmark series).

    A dramatization with music and sound effects, adapted from the Landmark book of the same title by Quentin Reynolds (New York: Random House, 1950).

Slides

Wright Brothers National Memorial. Produced by Meston's Travels. 8 slides.

    Includes four original Wright photographs, 1902-3, from the Library of Congress collections and four photographs from the Wright Brothers National Memorial, Kitty Hawk, N.C.

Index

A

AAF Fair, 36
Adelbert, prince of Germany, 106
Adams, Porter, 27, 29
Adlershof, Germany, 25
Aéro-Club de France, 15
Aéro-Club de Sarthe, 72, 168
Aero Club of America, 7, 43, 77, 138, 166, 167, 183
Aero Club of the United Kingdom, 5, 7
Aeronautical Society of Great Britain, 5, 69, 165
Akimoto, George, 179
Albemarle Sound, N.C., 57
Albert Medal, 25, 45
Alexandria, Va., 9, 103, 104
Alfonso XIII, king of Spain, 4, 18, 22, 43, 87, 88, 89
American News Service, 117
Armington, Caroline, 170, 177
Arnold, Gen. Henry H., 36, 121, 123, 127, 160, 172, 178
Arsyll (warship), 111
Associated Press, 117
Astra, Société de constructions aéronautiques, 150
Atwood, Harry N., 121, 132
Au Petit Bonheur (balloon), 12
August Wilhelm, prince of Germany, 106
Augusta, Ga., 121, 124, 133

B

Baden-Powell, Maj. B. F. S., 66, 69
Balfour, Lord Arthur J., 16, 83

Baltimore, Md., 33
Barber, Charles E., 166
Bariquand et Marre, 140
Barnaby, Capt. Ralph S., 179
Barron, Arthur, 190
Barron, Evelyn, 190
Barthou, Louis, 18, 67, 89
Battersea, England, 5
Battery Park, N.Y., 110
Bayside, N.J., 19
Beck, James M., 113
Becker, Frederick H., 45
Bedloe's Island, N.Y., 110, 178
Bell, Alexander Graham, 9
Bellville, Mrs. Frank, 96
Belmont Park, N.Y., 9, 10, 19, 24, 44, 120, 124, 125, 138, 141
Berg, Hart O., 4, 5, 12, 14, 15, 18, 22, 23, 24, 25, 63, 65, 68, 69, 78, 88, 94, 106, 159, 181
Berg, Mrs. Hart O., 13, 16, 41, 68, 82, 94
Berges, of American News Service, 117
Berlin, Germany, 23, 24, 25, 104
Bernstorff, Ambassador Johann H. A. von, 97
Bianchi, A., 177
Big Kill Devil Hill, Kitty Hawk, N.C., 52, 53, 56
Bigot, Paul, 169
Bingham, Sen. Hiram, 31, 172
Bishop, Courtlandt F., 3
Black, Fred, 33
Blériot, Louis, 16, 41, 82
Bollée, Léon, 12, 61, 63, 67, 140, 159, 181, 182

Bornstedt Field, Potsdam, Germany, 104, 107
Brenet, Albert E. V., 174
Brenner, Victor D., 166
Brereton, Lt. Lewis H., 126
Breton, J. L., 183
Brewer, Griffith, 5, 6, 14, 35, 66, 159
Briggs (cartoonist), 184
Brindle, Melbourne, 174
Brindley, Oscar, 131, 132
Brookins, Walter R., 9, 10, 125, 159
Buck Island, Dayton, Ohio, 24
Burkhart, Mayor Edward E., 166
Burton, Odell, 190
Burton, Sen. Theodore E., 31
Butler, Frank H., 5, 14, 43, 66, 68, 69
Byrd, Comdr. Richard E., 27

C

C-69 (Constellation airplane), 36
Cabot, Godfrey L., 27
Calderara, Comdr. Mario, 45, 93, 94
Calderara, Mrs. Mario, 45
Camden Airport, N.J., 124
Camp d'Auvours, LeMans, France, 12, 14, 15, 65-72, 169, 176, 180
Carillon Park Museum, Dayton, Ohio, 139, 146, 147, 148
Centocelle Field, Rome, 5, 91-96, 177
College Park, Md., 113, 121, 123, 126, 127, 178
Collier, Robert J., 122, 123
Collier Trophy, 167
Collier's Weekly, 61, 164
Columbia Broadcasting System (CBS), 187
Columbia University, 34
Columbus, Ohio, 32, 120
Commerce Building, Washington, D.C., 31
Congressional Medal, 166
Cooper, Ray, 29
Coronado Beach, Fla., 132, 133
Corsair (warship), 111

Cover, Maj. Carl A., 35
Cox, Allyn, 176
Cox, Gov. James M., 33, 35, 36
Craigie, Maj. Gen. Lawrence C., 36
Crane, Spencer, 73
Cresson Medal, 29
Cruke, Enyart, 159
Cunraven, Lord Thomas W., 90
Curry, Maj. John F., 27, 28
Curtiss, Glenn H., 76
Curtiss Marine Trophy, 29
Cutter, Edward, 33

D

DC-4 (airplane), 35
Daniels, John T., 34, 160
Darling, Jay N., 183
Davenport, Homer, 183
Davis, Secretary of War Dwight F., 31
Davis, James, 24
Davis, Col. Milton F., 26
Davison, Assistant Secretary of War F. Trubee, 29, 31
Dayton Central High School, 21
Dayton Convention and Exhibition Center, 176
Dayton Homecoming Celebration, 7, 9, 29, 43, 162-64
Dayton, Medal, 167
Dayton, Ohio, 3, 24, 25, 27, 169
Dayton Union Station, 164
Dayton-Wright Company, 14, 24
Dearborn, Mich., 33, 34, 35, 135, 136, 140, 147, 154, 160
Deeds, Col. Edward A., 26, 33, 36, 37, 160, 172
Deeds, Mrs. Edward A., 37
Dennis, Mrs. Emma, 153
Detroit, Mich., 27
Deutsch de la Meurthe, Henri, 14, 61, 66
Dick, Robert, 182
Distinguished Flying Cross, 31
Dominguez Field, Calif., 121
Doolittle, Lt. James H., 26
Dorcy, Capt., 113
Douglas Aircraft Co., 35

Doumer, Paul, 70
Driving Park, Columbus, Ohio, 120
Dunbar, Paul L., 21
Durand, Dr. William F., 30, 31

E

Earhart, Amelia, 32, 172
Early Birds, 119, 141
Eastman, George, 185
Edge, Ambassador Walter, 170
Edison, Thomas A., 25, 185
Edward VII, king of England, 4, 5, 23, 90
Eiffel Tower, Paris, 184
Emmons, Lt. Harold H., 26
Engelhard, Capt. Paul, 23, 107
Estournelles de Constant, Baron Paul d', 169
Etheridge, A. D., 34, 160

F

Fabius (caricaturist), 185
Farman, Henri, 181
Fechet, Gen. James E., 27
Fess, Sen. Simeon D., 31
Findley, Earl N., 27, 29, 41, 160
Firestone, Harvey S., 185
Fjelde, Paul, 167, 179
Fleury (chauffeur), 12, 64
Flight Safety Foundation, 178
Flugmaschine Wright company, 25, 104, 140, 144, 151
Flyer (dog), 14, 66
Forbes, A. Holland, 7, 43
Ford, Henry, 32, 33, 34, 135, 154, 160, 185
Ford, Edsel, 33
Ford, Henry, Museum, Greenfield Village, Dearborn Mich., 33, 34, 35, 136, 140, 146, 147, 154, 160
Fort Myer, Va., Wright test flights, 184
    1908, 78–91, 187
    1909, 9, 39, 43, 44, 97–104, 118, 177
Ft. Sam Houston, Texas, 121, 122

Fort Thomas, Ohio, 163
Foulois, Brig. Gen. Benjamin D., 29, 31, 34, 97, 102, 103, 122, 123
Fowler, Robert, 126
Fox (artist), 181, 182
France
    Chamber of Deputies, 90
    36th Aviation Group, 170
Frankfurt am Main, Germany, 24
Franklin Institute, Philadelphia, 29, 32, 121, 148, 149
    Hall of Aviation, 147
    Wright Brothers' Aeronautical Engineering Collection, 142
French Institute, 69
Friedrich Wilhelm, crown prince of Germany, 105, 106, 107
Fries, Charles M., Productions, 190
Fürstenberg, Prince von, 23
Fullam, Adm. William F., 27
Furnas, Charles W., 75

G

Gabard, Ernest, 170
Garber, Paul E., 189
Gasnier, Pierre, 43
General Motors Corporation, 160
Georgian Bay, Canada, 32
Germany, 23, 103–7
Gibbs-Smith, Charles H., 95, 111
Giris, C., 180
Glinsky, Vincent, 167, 178
Go Pictures, 189
Goff, Harper, 178
Gordon Bennett International Balloon Trophy, 29
Gordon Bennett races, 142
Governors Island, N.Y., 19, 107–13, 168, 171, 178, 186
Grand Beach, Fla., 124
Grant's Tomb, N.Y., 19, 111, 112, 113
Great Britain, War Office, 5
Granville, Ohio, 37
Gray, George A., 124
Green, Richard, 177

Greenfield Village, Dearborn, Mich., 33, 34, 35, 136, 140, 146, 147, 154, 160
Greer, Arlo, 174
Griscom, Ambassador Lloyd C., 96
Grumbach, Mrs. Carrie Kaylor, 158
Grumbach, Charles, 158
Guggenheim, Daniel, 30
Guggenheim, Daniel, Fund for the Promotion of Aeronautics, Inc., 29
Guggenheim, Daniel, Medal, 31
Guggenheim, Harry F., 29

H

Haldane, Richard B., 5
Hall of Fame for Great Americans, 167, 179
Hammer, William J., 113
Hansen, Oskar J. W., 178, 179
Harding, Pres. Warren G., 26
Hare, James H., 61, 97, 123, 164
Harmon, Gov. Judson, 7, 164, 166
Harmon Trophy, 30, 166
Harmsworth, Lord Alfred, 83
Harter, Harold M., 31
Harwood, Van Ness, 117
Haskell, Henry J., 45
Hawley, Alan R., 3
Hawthorn Hill, Dayton, Ohio, 25, 27, 29, 31, 33, 37, 39, 45, 155, 159, 168
Hazelhurst, Lt. Leighton W., 124
Hearst Metrotone News, 188
Heaslip, William, 174
Hegenberger, Lt. Albert, 29
Henderson, Daniel, 159
Henry County Memorial Park, New Castle, Ind., 170
Hergesell, Prof. Hugo, 23, 106
Herring, Augustus M., 52
Hervé-Mathé, Jules A., 177
Hildebrandt, Capt. Alfred, 93, 105
Hildebrandt, Mrs. Alfred, 105
Hill of the Wreck, Kitty Hawk, N.C., 48

Hollinger & Company, 178
Honorary Pilot's Certificate, 36
Hoster, William, 61
Howard, Benny, 35
Hoxsey, Arch, 120, 125
Hubble, Charles H., 174
Hudson-Fulton Celebration, 19, 107
Hudson-Fulton Celebration Committee, 113
Hudson River, 27, 109, 110, 111, 123
Huffaker, Edward C., 48, 49
Huffman, Daniel, 190
Huffman Prairie, Dayton, Ohio, 57, 59-60, 159, 172
Humphreys, Col. Frederick E., 34, 113
Hunaudières, France, 159
Hunaudières Race Course, Le Mans, France, 12, 61-65, 169, 170, 180
Huntingdon, Prof. A. K., 6

I

Icare (ballon), 23, 41, 59
Idzack, Sgt. Stephen L., 120
Indianapolis, Ind., 9
Institute of the Aeronautical Sciences, 34, 178
Institution of Civil Engineers, London, 5
Instruction publique, 45
International Aviation Tournament, 9, 19, 24, 124, 141
International Civil Aeronautics Conference, 29
International Good Will Flag, 173
International Telephone and Telegraph Corporation (ITT), 190

J

Jersey City, N.J., 110
John Hancock Mutual Life Insurance collection, 176
Johnstone, Ralph, 10, 19, 24, 25, 123
Juvisy, France, 10

K

Kansas City *Star,* 45
Keach, James, 190
Keach, Stacy, 190
Kelley, William, 190
Kenney, Lt. Gen. George C., 36
Kergariou, Marquis Edgard de, 89
Kessel, Gen. von, 105
Kettering, Charles F., 33, 34, 160
Kidder, Harvey, 176
Kill Devil Hill, Kitty Hawk, N.C., 46, 48, 55, 56, 61, 113–17, 161
Kill Devil Hill Life Saving Station, N.C., 46, 47, 51, 52
Kitty Hawk, N.C., 27, 46, 54, 169, 172–73, 179, 187, 188, 189
Kitty Hawk, N.C., Post Office, 46
Kitty Hawk, N.C., Weather Bureau Station, 46, 47, 52
Knabenshue, Roy, 10
Koerner, John G., 156
Kronprinzessin Cecilie (steamship) 19, 43
Kruchman, Arnold, 117

L

La Chapelle, Duval, 24, 123
Lahm, Col. Frank P., 34, 35, 62, 76, 77, 78, 101, 102, 177
Lambert, Maj. Albert B., 24
Lambert, Count Charles de, 4, 16, 18, 22, 24, 41, 66, 71, 82, 83, 182
Lambert, Countess Charles de, 3, 18, 22, 24
Lambert Island, Canada, 32
Landowski, Paul, 169
Langley Field, Va., 31, 35
Langley Medal, 9, 166
Laroche, Jean, 66
Latham, Hubert, 25, 43
Lawrance, Charles L., 29
Lawyers' Club, New York, 7
Le Mans, France, 12, 37, 61–72, 95, 168, 169, 177
Leandré, Charles L., 180

Lewis, George W., 27
Library of Congress, 176, 187
Lidov, Arthur, 178
Lindbergh, Col. Charles A., 27, 28, 30
Lindemuth, Mr., 158
Lindemuth, Mrs. 158
Little Hill, Kitty Hawk, N.C., 52
Liv, Clarence, 159
Llewellyn Park, N.J., 25
Loening, Grover C., 130, 131, 132, 160
Lokal-Anzeiger, Berlin, 104
London Aero Show, 125
London *Daily Mail,* 61
London, England, 5, 7, 43, 125
Losques, Daniel T., 180
Lourdoy, M., 182
Lucas-Girardville, Capt. Paul N., 4, 16, 41, 66, 82, 83, 87
Ludlow, Israel, 10
Lupin, Charles, 181
Lutz, Maj. Charles A., 29
LZ. 6 (airship), 24

M

Macchiati, Serafino, 176
McCoy, James C., 3
McCoy, John T., Jr., 176, 177, 178
McCracken, William P., 33
McFarland, Marvin, 190
McGowan, P. H., 61
MacKaye, Percy, 27, 45
McMahon, John R., 39
Macready, Capt. John A., 29
Maix, Leo, 180, 181
Manca, Albino, 169
Manchester, William, duke of, 83
Manila Bay, Philippine Islands, 127
Mannheim, Germany, 24
Marconi, Guglielmo, 19
Maresco (caricaturist), 182
Marevery, Yves, 181
Margherita, dowager queen of Italy, 69
Marshall, Fred A., 141
Martin, Col. Frederick W., 33
Martin, Glenn L., 33

Martin, Glenn L., Company, 33
Martin, James V., 125
Melik, Efrem, 179
Mentzer, William F., 35
Miami River, 24, 60, 127, 128, 129, 131, 132
Mich (caricaturist), 181, 182, 183, 184, 185
Michelin Cup, 72, 166
Miller, Harold S., 157
Milling, Lt. Thomas DeW., 121, 123, 127, 178
Mineola, N.Y., 133
Mirabello, Adm. Giovanni, 96
Mitchell, John, 117
Mitchell, Gen. William E., 27
Mitchell, of New York *Herald*, 117
Moltke, Gen. Helmuth J. L. von, 23, 105
Moltke, Mrs. Helmuth J. L. von, 105
Montgomery, Ala., 120
Moore-Brabazon, J. T. C., 6
Morgan, Fred, 133
Morgan, George T., 166
Moriarty, Michael, 190
Moris, Col. Mario, 93, 94, 96
Movietone News, 187
Mueller, H. M., 178
Muller, J., 31
Muse of Aviation, 165
Musée de l'air, 140
Mutchler, Dwight, 179

N

Narco, P., 180
National Advisory Committee for Aeronautics, 31
Executive Committee, 26, 33
National Aeronautic Association, 168, 169, 171
Contest Committee, 27, 29
National Aeronautic Association Medal, 27, 167
National Air and Space Museum, 126, 144, 146, 174, 189
National Air Museum, 119, 179
National Association of Manufacturers, 185
National Audiovisual Center, 189

National Cash Register Company, 26, 160, 172
National Commemorative Society, 167
National Educational Television (NET), 190
National Museum, 118
National Pioneers Banquet, 185
Naval Air Station, Anacostia, Md., 29
Neue Automobil-Gesellschaft, 140
New Castle, Ind., 169, 170
New Ingot Co., Inc., 190
New York, N.Y., 7, 20
New York Aero Show, 126
New York *American*, 61, 117
New York *Herald*, 61, 117
New York University, 167
New York *World*, 117
Newslat, A., 166
Newton, Byron R., 61
Nichols, Ruth, 172
Northcliffe, Lord Alfred C. W. R., 16, 18, 25, 45, 83, 89

O

Oberlin College, 40
Oberlin, Ohio, 40, 45
Oberschöneweide, Germany, 140
O'Donnel, Tom, 177
Ogilvie, Alexander, 113, 114, 115, 116, 117, 125
Ohio Medal, 7, 16, 164, 166
Ohio National Guard, 163
Ohio State Capitol Building, 178
Ohio State University, 32
Orange, N.J., 25
Osborn, Agnes, 40
Overman, Sen. Lee S., 31

P

Painlevé, Prof. Paul, 69
Paris, France, 15, 24, 180
Paris Automobile Show, 181
Paris International Air Show, 184
Parmalee, Philip O., 122, 123

Pasay, Philippine Islands, 127
Patrick, Maj. Gen. Mason M.,
45
Patterson, Frederick B., 27
Pau, France, 2, 4, 12, 16, 17,
22, 44, 82–91, 169 170, 177,
183
Pennsylvania Railroad, 110
Phi Delta Kappa Fraternity,
170
Philadelphia, Pa., 25, 32, 121,
148, 149
Philadelphia Chamber of Com-
merce, 29
Philadelphia Mint, 166
Philippine Islands, 123, 127
Piessen, Gen. von, 23
Pitcairn autogiro, 31
Pitcairn, Harold F., 31
Plymouth, England., 43
Pont-Long, Pau, France, 12,
82–91
Pope, Amanda C., 190
Port Aviation, Juvisy, France,
16
Port Washington, Long Island,
N.Y., 29
Post, Augustus, 77
Potsdam, Germany, 104, 107
Prentiss, Billy, 159
Prentiss, Eleanor, 159
Pulitzer air races, 27
Pupin, Dr. Michael I., 27
Putnam, Mrs. Amelia Earhart,
32, 172
Pyrénées Mountains, 82, 90,
91

R

Reece, Jan, 39
Reed, S. Albert, 27
Reeder, George, 158
Reichel, Frantz, 68
Reid, Marshall E., 124
Reinickendorf, Germany, 144,
151
Reynolds, Quentin, 190
Rickenbacker, Capt. Eddie, 26
Rightmire, Dr. George W., 32
Rinehart, Howard M., 26
Ritz Hotel, London, 7
Robins, Gen. Augustine W.,
33
Rogeit, W. A., 184, 185

Rolls, Charles S., 6, 7, 14, 66,
69, 84
Rolls-Royce Limited, 6, 66, 84
Rome, Italy, 5, 91–96, 177
Roosevelt, Franklin
Delano, 35, 36
Rosebrook, Jeb, 190
Rosenwald, Julius, 185
Roussel, Paul, 166
Royal Aeronautical Society,
177
Royal Society of Arts, 25, 45
Ruhl, Arthur, 61
Russell, Frank H., 125
Ryan, Allan, 19
Ryan, John D., 30

S

St. Julien Cathedral, Le Mans,
169, 170
Saint-Lazare railway station,
Paris, 3
Salon de humoristes, Paris,
180
San Antonio, Texas, 122, 123
Santos-Dumont, Alberto, 180
Savoia, Lt. Umberto, 91, 92,
93
Schiller, Lawrence, 190
Schneider, Dean Herman, 25
Schroeder, Maj. Rudolph, 26
Schwab, Charles M., 185
Science Museum, London,
139, 140
Scipio (St. Bernard dog), 26
Scott, Georges, 177
Secondari, John H.,
Productions, 189
Selfridge, Lt. Thomas E., 22,
77, 79–81
Sheepshead Bay, N.Y., 134
Shellbeach, England, 5, 6, 7
Sherry's, New York, 20
Shooter's Hill, Alexandria,
Va., 104
Short Brothers, 5
Short, Horace, 6
Short, Oswald, 6
Shoup's Mill, Dayton, Ohio,
158
Sidney, Ohio, 168
Silliman, Harriet, 40, 41

Simmons, Sen. Furnifold M.,
31
Simms Station, Dayton, Ohio,
24, 120, 121, 125, 127, 130,
132, 133
Sines, Edwin H., 135, 160, 161
Smithsonian Institution, 9,
119, 166, 177, 178, 179, 185
Society of Automotive En-
gineers, 26, 168
Sonnino, Sidney, 96
Sperry, Elmer, 27
Spratt, Dr. George A., 48, 52
Squier, Maj. George O., 77,
89, 97
Statue of Liberty, New York,
109, 110, 178
Steeper, Bertha Ellwyn, 156
Steeper, Harold W., 156
Stefansson, Vilhjalmur, 27, 45
Swackhammer, E. W., 190

T

Taft, Charles P., 97
Taft, William Howard, 7,
43, 101, 183, 184, 190
Tate, Daniel, 47, 49, 51, 52,
53, 54
Tate, Tom, 47
Tate, Capt. William J., 34, 46,
47, 160, 161
Taylor, Charles E., 7, 10, 32,
34, 58, 59, 79, 97, 98, 109,
113, 140, 141, 153, 161, 171
Tegel Field, Germany, 23
Tempelhof Field, Berlin, 23,
104-7
Texas City, Texas, 120
Thompson Products, Inc., 174
Tissandier, Paul, 4, 16, 22, 41,
82, 83, 85, 86, 177, 182
Toledo Beach, Toledo, Ohio,
132
Tucker, Alonzo, 159
Turpin, J. Clifford, 10
Twentieth Century-Fox Film
Corp., 187

U

Union Station, Washington,
D.C., 7
United Nations, 173

U.S. Air Force, 119
U.S. Air Force Collection, 177
U.S. Air Force Technical Data
Museum, 124, 176, 178
U.S. Army, 73, 97, 104, 177
U.S. Army Aero Squadron,
120
U.S. Army Aeronautic Board,
122
U.S. Army Aeronautical Mu-
seum, 178
U.S. Army Air Corps, 29
U.S. Capitol, 176, 184
U.S. Chamber of Commerce,
30, 31
U.S. Congress, 31
U.S. Mint, 166
U.S. National Archives, 187
U.S. Navy, 89
U.S. President's Aircraft
Board, 27
U.S. Senate, 31, 172
U.S. Signal Corps, 77, 118-19
U.S. War Department, 31
University of Cincinnati, 25
University of North Carolina,
187
University of Strassburg, 106

V

Valentine, Nancy, 190
Valentine, Tony, 190
Vanderbilt, Cornelius, 120
Velsey, Seth M., 178
Victor Emmanuel III, king of
Italy, 5, 95, 96
Vidal, Eugene L., 33
Viet, Sidney B., 169
Viktoria Luise, princess of
Germany, 106, 107
Villasana, Juan G., 26
Voisin brothers, 181

W

Walcott, Dr. Charles D., 9
Wallace, Don, 39
Warner, Edward P., 33
Washington, D.C., 7, 26, 27,
29, 30, 31, 43, 166, 176,
183, 184
Washington Monument, 185

Weiller, Lazare, 14, 66, 68,
181
Weiller, Mrs. Lazare, 14, 66,
69
Weiller, Lazare, Syndicate, 14
Weismann, Jacques, 176
Welsh, Arthur L., 24, 123,
126, 127
Wetmore, Alexander, 179
White House, 7, 26, 43, 121,
166, 183, 184
Whiting, Capt. Kenneth, 36,
160, 172
Whiting, William F., 29
Wieboldt, Elmer P., 128
Wieboldt, Mrs. Elmer P., 178
Wilbur and Orville Wright
Memorial, 36, 171–72
Wilbur Wright (flying boat),
27, 45
Wilbur Wright Junior High
School, Dayton, Ohio, 32,
45
Wilbur Wright Monument, Le
Mans, 37
Wilhelm II, emperor of
Germany, 23, 107
Wilkins, Sir Capt. Hubert, 32
Williamson, Pliny W., 39
Woolf, Samuel J., 178
Wright, Bertha, 156
Wright, Helen, 156
Wright, Herbert, 156, 157
Wright, Horace, 39, 41, 113,
117, 157, 158
Wright, Ivonette, 157, 158
Wright, Katherine, 3, 5, 6, 7,
9, 16, 22, 23, 25, 27, 39,
40–41, 42, 43, 45, 82, 84,
89, 94, 97, 105, 107, 156,
157, 162
Wright, Leontine, 158
Wright, Lorin, 7, 33, 38, 43,
113, 116, 117, 156, 157, 164
Wright, Mrs. Lorin (Lou), 158
Wright, Bishop Milton, 7, 8, 9,
32, 38–39, 41, 43, 156, 157,
163, 164, 170
Wright, Milton, 157
Wright, Orville
accident, 80–81
awards and honors, 25, 29,
31, 32, 36
experimental devices,
142–43

flights, 9, 22, 24, 26, 39, 44,
57–60, 73–80, 97–107,
174, 176
incidence indicator, 137
medals, 25, 27, 31
memorials, 170
portraits and busts, 178, 179
Wright, Reuchlin, 39, 43, 156,
157, 164
Wright, Susan Koerner, 43,
156, 157
Wright, Wilbur
awards and honors, 15
flights, 61–72, 82–90,
93–96, 107–13
memorials and monuments,
37, 170–73, 177
portraits and busts, 176,
177, 178
Wright airplanes
1903: 55–57
1904: 57–58
1905: 59–60
1907–1909: 68–96, 107–11
1909 (Signal Corps
machine): 118–19
model B, 119–24, 178
model C, 126–27
model CH (single pontoon),
129
model CH (twin pontoon),
127–29
model D, 127
model E, 128, 129, 130
model EX, 126
model F, 130
model G, 130–32
model H, 132
model HS, 44, 132–33
model K, 133
model L, 133–34
model R, 10, 124–26, 138,
141
Wright brothers
anniversaries, 27, 135
bicycle shop, 135–36, 147,
160-61, 179, 189
caricatures and cartoons,
180-85
family, friends, and
associates, 158–61
flights
Bornstedt Field, Germany,
104, 107

Camp d'Auvours, France, 12, 14, 15, 65-72, 169, 176, 180
Centocelle Field, Italy, 5, 91-96, 177
College Park Md., 113, 121, 123, 126, 127, 178
Fort Myer, Va., 73-81, 97-104, 160
Governors Island, N.Y., 19, 107-13, 168, 171, 178, 186
Huffman Prairie, Dayton, Ohio, 57, 59-60, 159, 172
Hunaudières, France, 12, 61-65, 169, 170, 180
Kitty Hawk, N.C., 56, 57, 61
Pont-Long, France, 12, 82-91
Simms Station, Dayton, Ohio, 24, 120, 121, 125, 127, 130, 132, 133
Tempelhof Field, Germany, 23, 104-7
gliding experiments, 46-55, 56
home, 152-55
medals and trophies, 7, 8, 165-68
memorials and monuments, 169-73
motion pictures, 187-90
motor, 138-41, 161
paintings, portraits, and busts, 176-79
propellers, 144-45
wind tunnel experiments, 146-49

Wright Brothers' Hill, Dayton, Ohio, 172
Wright Brothers' Medal (SAE), 168
Wright Brothers Memorial Trophy, 168
Wright Brothers National Memorial, Kitty Hawk, N.C., 140, 174-75, 179, 188, 189, 190
museum, 146, 147, 173
visitors center, 146, 147, 173
Wright Company, 9, 119, 124, 126, 133, 137, 142, 143, 150-51, 160
Wright Cycle Company, 11, 33, 134, 135
Wright Exhibition Company, 10, 19, 130, 159
Wright Field, 27, 28, 33, 35, 36
Wright Flying School, 10, 24, 123, 172
Wright-Paulhan patent suit, 184

Y

"You Are There" (television program), 187
Young, Clarence M., 31
Young America Films, 187

Z

Zens, Ernest, 13, 41, 67, 89
Zepplelin, Count Ferdinand, 23
Zeppelin II (airship), 184
Zuloaga, Maj. Angel M., 26